MUSLIM MYTHBUSTING

WHAT ONE-FOURTH OF THE WORLD REALLY BELIEVES

SAM MAK

AUTHORS PLACE
—PRESS—

Published by Authors Place Press
9885 Wyecliff Drive, Suite 200
Highlands Ranch, CO 80126
Authorsplace.com

ISBN: 978-1-62865-749-4

CONTENTS

CHAPTER 1

MAY PEACE BE UPON YOU

"MAY PEACE BE UPON YOU."

My parents were greeting Uncle K, who was really just a family friend, as he walked in the door. A college professor, he was a kind man with eyes that smiled. At this time, his three beautiful daughters were teenagers with amazing South Asian eyes and flawless, caramel-brown skin. Uncle K and his family had come to the United States from Pakistan many years before we had, and one of the things they loved was going out to eat at a famous American restaurant: McDonald's.

I was five years old, we had only been in the United States for about two months, and they wanted to treat us to a genuine American experience and a taste of all-American food. We piled into our 1972 Ford station wagon and made the trek behind Uncle K's woody wagon, a huge cream-colored station wagon with wooden side paneling. We drove through the streets of Fort Collins; I was at the very back of the station wagon, no seat belts needed. I was looking at the contrast of the empty parking lots and the beautiful mountains. I had never heard of McDonald's, but the first thing I noticed was the big yellow arches as we approached the restaurant. The parking lot was packed, and I thought, This place must be good! I was excited.

We went in for the McDonald's apple pie. I was given a small green cardboard carton. The carton was warm, with both sides folded. I opened it to find a crisp, light-brown pastry. My first true taste of an American icon! I took a big bite of the pie. Gross! The restaurant people had cooked the apples. In all my four long years of life in Pakistan, I had never eaten hot, cooked fruit. Apples are supposed to be cold and crunchy, but these apples were coated in some sweet sauce and so soft. I had jam before, but this was nothing like a jam. I wanted to spit it out. So, I looked at my sister, who was making a face. I didn't want to be rude, so I gulped the bite down. The pie was disgusting.

Fast-forward to now, I've happily lived in apple-pie culture for decades, and I have become an apple pie fan. I even have preferences: I like my pie heated, with whipped cream. I like it with toasted pecans or almonds to give my pie some extra crunch. I have also developed favorite restaurants for great apple pie. I even learned to make it myself, and I must admit, I am a good baker.

The first time we experience something different it might look disgusting or strange. But I learned to be open to new experiences and new people and, well, just like apple pie with whipped cream on top, my life is richer for it!

"GOD WILL EXAMINE NEITHER YOUR PHYSICAL APPEARANCE NOR YOUR POSSESSIONS. GOD WILL ONLY EXAMINE YOUR HEARTS AND YOUR ACTIONS."

PROPHET MUHAMMAD

My religion, the religion of my heart and billions of hearts around the world, is a religion of peace. From the deserts of Morocco to the foothills of the Himalayas, one phrase is heard in every shop, every school, and every street corner: *Us Salaam Alikum*. This universal Muslim greeting means, "May peace be upon you." Breaking it down, *Salam* is the word for peace,

Alikum means "on you," and *Us* is the formal term, meaning "the peace." *Us* refers to the ultimate level of peace—the peace that radiates from a source greater than us all, that equally embraces each of us. Learning this one phrase gives us the gift to say hello, goodbye, and nice to meet you. When visiting a Muslim country or simply walking past a woman with a scarf on her head in the mall, this simple, beautiful phrase unlocks the door to a connection of the heart.

The reply to *Us Salaam Alikum* is *Wa Alikum Us salaam,* or, "And may peace also be upon you." *Islam* means "submission" in Arabic. The correct way to say "Islam" is with the *s* sound in the pronunciation, not "Izlam" with a *z* sound. Phonetically the word is pronounced *is' lam*. Similarly, a follower of Islam is called a Muslim. Wishing peace upon those whom we meet is a way to show that we care. Muslims use the universal greeting of "May peace be upon you" throughout our waking hours.

Our intentions need to be sincere, even when we address a stranger. Greeting someone with kindness and a smile is considered an act of charity in Islam. Spreading peace between all people is part of our religious duty. For example, our sacred book, the Holy Quran, says: And when you are greeted with a greeting, greet in return with one better or at least an equal greeting (Quran 4:86). Since Muslims know the value of responding with a kinder greeting, many relatives of mine reply with "And may the peace and blessing of God be upon you." We can also enhance our response by adding a smile of kindness for the individual we are speaking to.

The Muslim greeting carries the intention of filling our world with harmony. Intentions are critical to being a good Muslim. My intentions are to be of service: caring, doing good deeds, and connecting with those whom I meet. My personal goal is to always fill each day with as many good actions and thoughts as I can. Even if I cannot actually *do* a kind action, I can always think a kind thought of peace toward myself or another. The simplest yet most powerful thing I can do (in my thoughts or out loud) is to say to my fellow human beings, "May peace be upon you."

Our traditions follow the life of our leader, Prophet Muhammad (🕌[1]; may peace be upon him, or pbuh[2]). His stance on peace was so strong that he had a Hadith saying: "That you will not enter paradise until you believe, and in order to believe, love each other. Spread the greet of peace in your community." In Islam, *Hadith* is the word used for the collected sayings of Prophet Muhammad (pbuh).

Because of the Prophet's teaching, my life's purpose has evolved to spreading peace among the many different people that I know and honor. Tolerance and acceptance are considered paths to good behavior in every society. In Islam, the road to good behavior starts with education. Whether resolving an issue between my kids, my colleagues, or between two world views that have been erroneously pitted against each other, my goal is always the same: to find a way to educate and sow another seed of understanding. As both an American and a Muslim, I am dedicated to sharing my experiences with the kind sources on both sides of the oceans. I hope to build bridges of understanding so we can easily cross over and enjoy the benefits of new friends. When we can honor our different perspective, we can all live in peace.

My bicultural perspective began at the age of four, when I took my first transatlantic flight. I was born in Pakistan and blessed with an amazing family that loved to travel. We travelled all over the country since our extended family lived in each of the four provinces that comprise Pakistan. My first big adventure was a trip across the Atlantic Ocean from Asia to North America. After my vague memories of a very long flight and fidgeting in airplane seats, we landed at Stapleton Airport in Denver, Colorado.

---

1   The may peace be upon you written in Arabic calligraphy form.

2   Muslims say *pbuh*, which stands for "peace be upon him," after a prophet's name as a form of sending blessings to him.

My dad had traveled to the United States a few months earlier in 1970. My mom, little sister Saima, and I arrived to join him in August 1971. Our dad met us at Stapleton Airport in Denver and drove for what seemed like hours and hours to Fort Collins. I was amazed by the beautiful Rocky Mountains with their blue-gray tinge tipped with white snow, set against a perfect, blue, sunny sky. The landscape rolled by, adorned with little houses and farms. My family moved into married student housing at Colorado State University in a complex known as Aggie Village. The apartment was small but comfortable. We entered into a modest living room with a kitchen off to the side. Down a short hallway were two bedrooms and a tiny bathroom. I had no idea where I was or how far I had traveled. But this was my new home.

In Pakistan, my father, Rashid, had worked as a civil engineer for a private company and was an expert in designing bridges, dams, and irrigation systems. He rode a motorcycle to his office in the Water and Power Development Authority (WAPDA) building. The offices are a known for their white marble and beautiful architecture. Seeing the half domed structure with its many balconies lets us know that we are approaching the city center of Lahore. He worked with several of his school friends on water distribution along the Indus and Ravi rivers. He made an impact on Pakistan's energy system by using dam design to provide electricity. He was pursued by many companies for his excellent design work, and his skills brought him to the attention of the US government. The US was interested in highly technical skills, especially individuals with education and expertise in medicine and engineering. At that time, the US government actively recruited people from around the world to come develop a better America.

When we moved, we left behind all of my extended family. We had a blessed and prosperous life of eating at restaurants, traveling around the country to visit family, and having fun with our cousins. In Pakistan, like many families, we lived in a multigenerational household. I always had playmates, and at least once a day, the ice cream man arrived on a bike with a giant cooler on front to sell ice cream at our gate. His bell on the handlebar jingled, signaling all of us children as he approached our homes. My goal was to persuade my grandmother and aunts for enough spare change to buy ice cream, undetected by my parents. Living together provided ready and strong community and communication. Everyone participated in chores, and we were an active part of each other's daily worlds. We celebrated birthdays, holidays, and things big and small together as one big family.

I had the pleasure of visiting our house in Lahore again when I attended my uncle's wedding at eight years old and then again when my paternal grandmother passed after my twelfth birthday in 1978. My parents spoke about this house often as their first home together. I, too, as a baby had spent many years in that home, sharing a room with my parents. My favorite place was the backyard of my paternal grandmother Biji's house, full of sweet-smelling honeysuckle bushes in which woodpeckers, sparrows and crows sang and danced. Outside the house gate, pigeons searched for food on the uneven asphalt roads and often pecked through the trash piles on the sides of the wall surrounding the house. Once a month, we would set the trash pile on fire, and then the pile was ready for more garbage.

My grandmother loved plants and insisted on cultivating flowering bushes along the inside of the tall concrete wall. The bushes provided both beauty and privacy. Once a week, our gardener arrived early on his bicycle, with a large cutting blade hanging off the rear rack to cut the lawn. He squatted in the yard for hours, meticulously cutting the grass by hand, flinging his metal blade back and forth, back and forth in a hypnotic, steady motion. The blade made a quiet swish as it glided over the grass; little bits of green turf flew up in the air and disappeared in the ground. After effortlessly cutting the vast lawn, our gardener returned to his bike, put the blade away, and took a buffalo hide the size of his slim body from the bike. He came to the faucet in the middle of the yard, filled the hide with water, and used the spout on the hide to water the plants and bushes in the perimeter of our yard. As soon as he left, my cousins and I were back playing tag or jumping rope on the plush, carpet-like lawn.

During the summer, my cousins and I played with water hoses in the back of the home. My paternal grandma Biji has a huge patio and stairs made of smooth concrete. Biji threw large buckets of water on the patio, and the patio transformed into a slide. My paternal grandmother sat on a twined rope and wooden bed, watching her grandchildren glide and laugh. In some moments, she served as our referee. Each time I returned, the surrounding home and yard enveloped me in its beauty and peace. I did not realize how much I would miss by relocating to the other end of the world.

Many of our new neighbors were also offered visas to immigrate to the United States, not just to study or to visit but to make a home and contribute to the American economy. My father joined this wave of educated immigrants. In the 1950s, President Dwight Eisenhower began to construct a national infrastructure of highways, bridges, and dams, and the US needed more engineers. The common belief in developed nations is that all immigrants come due to dire circumstances, looking for freedom or a chance at a better life. During many decades of US history, this was true. The brutal Irish Potato Famine of 1845 and bloody wars and pogroms in 1881 drove desperate people to seek peace and shelter in the States. However, when we immigrated, families like mine came to develop the US with their much-needed scientific background and specialized skills.

My father completed his master's degree at Colorado State University and worked odd jobs to earn money. He was a student in his early thirties, fit, with jet-black hair, a mustache, and olive skin. His blue-gray eyes contrasted his dark appearance. With his light eyes and dark hair, Dad was a study in contrasts, like the snow-covered mountaintops on a sunny day. He left our home in the early morning to attend classes, work, and then return for dinner. Every evening, all four of us dined together. Then Dad relaxed and read the newspaper. After his reading, I perched in his lap and told him of the adventures of my day.

On weekends, my parents' close circle of friends, comprised of a large number of South Asian professionals with high levels of education and financial resources, looked for adventures in their new home. Sometimes they played volleyball in the apartment courtyard, and in the evening they invited each other to dinner. Talib, one of my father's friends from his student days in Lahore, lived across from us in the courtyard. Another engineer invited from Pakistan to the US lived four doors down from us. These professionals—doctors, engineers, and other technically proficient individuals—were actively recruited from developing nations such as Pakistan, India, Bangladesh, Iran, and Afghanistan. The British Royal Society termed this recruitment of skilled individuals the Brain Drain. After declining the invitation to move to the US several times, my father eventually relented, and that is how I came to live in the shadows of the magnificent Rocky Mountains.

After moving halfway across the world in 1971, daily communication with family in Lahore was no longer possible. Our journey was before the era of mobile phones, Skype, and text messaging. The only practical way to communicate over long distances was through letters. International phone calls were difficult and expensive. We had to book calls with an international operator over a wireline dial-up phone. And in a mere two weeks, our family in Pakistan would receive a letter sent from the US for the price of a postage stamp. I'd often see my parents receiving and writing letters, a funny contrast to life now where we can text internationally in under two seconds.

Five short days after our arrival in August 1971, I started kindergarten. I had not attended any preschool before. I had no idea what I was getting into. My father had asked me to come see the new school. We drove to a pretty brick building with yellow buses in the front. School buses in

Pakistan were regular city buses and were gray. By contrast, these yellow buses burst with color. I noticed that the school had a playground on the side with an eagle's nest climbing set. The eagle's nest was a semi-spherical dome made of metal bars connected in a triangular pattern. I did not know that I would soon be getting several bloody noses falling from this contraption.

The school and the playground seemed perfect. My dad and I entered the office. The office counter was very high for a four-year-old child. I couldn't see over it and had no idea what my dad was doing. He asked me if I wanted to start going to school that day. I said no, I was only four! I was certain that I would be much better prepared to start school three days later when I turned five. I felt relieved that I could go home with my father. I wanted to make sure I was old enough to handle formal education, so waiting for my official birthday was my decision. My dad agreed and brought me back after my birthday.

School sounded like a fun adventure, but I did not realize that I was now entering a place where I could not communicate. At home everyone understood me, but on the first day of school I realized that I couldn't talk to anyone! No one spoke Urdu and I spoke no English. I was lost and felt alone. I remember feeling frustrated and needing to turn inward and create a protective shell around myself. The hours and days dragged on and on with nothing to do and no one to talk to. I moved with a stream of kids from desks to the floor for reading time and then wandered the hallways aimlessly. I couldn't wait for the day to end. I just wanted to go back to our apartment and play outside on the swing. There was no way to connect with these children, and I missed my cousins back home.

Being a former British colony, Pakistan's official language is English. My parents had learned both Urdu and English in school, but I had not yet gone to school when we lived in Lahore, so I didn't know any other languages. Without knowing English, how was I going to make any friends and have the wonderful American adventure I had planned on?

Making friends wasn't the only challenge. Since I couldn't read or speak English, ordinary activities became an exercise in survival. I was not able to read simple signs such as which bathroom was for girls and whether to push or pull a door.

The elementary school was just under a mile from Colorado State University student housing. According to the school system, no school bus was provided for children within a mile of the school. So all of the kids in student housing walked the nine tenths of a mile to the school. Like my neighbors, I was supposed to walk to a place, yet I could not even read a road sign. I memorized landmarks to get to school. We lived in a simple time where kids made it through life walking alone and riding in cars without seat belts. Special programs for non-English speakers didn't exist. In life, we are all given the opportunity to sink or swim. I was born ready for a challenge. So even though I was the kid in class who spoke no English, I was expected to keep up with my schoolmates on my own

Communication with the teachers, kids, administrators, everyone . . . it was all very hard. I can still remember the frustration I felt at not being able to tell people what I needed. I began to get into trouble regularly. I couldn't understand the directions, and therefore I was not following directions. I couldn't understand the teacher's instructions; in my mind she was constantly babbling. I never knew if I was supposed to line up or sit down or turn in my work. I became a problem child, and the kids called me stupid. I was in culture shock.

My parents had planned to stay in the States for only a couple of years, and according to them, going to school in the United States was going to be a great educational experience. They kept telling me what a wonderful adventure it was going to be and to think about all the new friends I would make. But all I could think of was being frustrated at school. The teacher rambled for hours on end, I couldn't understand anyone, and the lunch food tasted awful. I was immersed in new sounds, new people, and a new cuisine. I had no idea that in a short ninety days, I would conquer the language, the kids, the culture, and the food. The United States is known as the melting pot, and I melted at lightning-fast speed. As the winter holidays approached, I made new friends and the teacher quit speaking gibberish and started speaking in real, understandable words. My parents assumed that in any challenge, I would land on my feet. Their belief that things would work out and that kids are resilient allowed me to flourish. I wish I had known at five that I was so smart, strong, and adaptable.

Once I was able to speak English fluently and connect with others, I made friends, and I loved learning. School became much easier, and I wasn't getting into trouble in gym class for not knowing which team I was on. Looking back, I am grateful for the experience of having to learn how to communicate based on body language and facial expressions alone. These skills that I acquired in kindergarten have served me well ever since. My five-year-old brain had kicked into overdrive and helped me succeed. I began to enjoy exploring my new home and surroundings.

The sorrow of leaving my extended family was fading. My cousins were still in my heart, but so were my new friends. We were taking weekend vacations to explore the mountains. I discovered new lakes, new restaurants, and experienced the Colorado outdoor life. Our favorite spot was Loveland, Colorado, a quiet city in the mountains with great views and great food. My dad just had to say "Loveland" and my sister and I were dressed, with our shoes on, sitting in the car. In Loveland, we would always go to the same restaurant with a wall of windows. Overlooking the expansive vista, we would eat at the buffet of fried chicken, salad, breads, and pasta. The restaurant menu was the All-American All-You-Can-Eat, and the price for kids was ten cents times our age. After dinner, we raced around in the cool mountain air on the lawn surrounding the restaurant. Saturday nights in Loveland were the best.

By Christmastime, I was speaking and reading fluent English, but living in a new country still had challenges. I needed to master the language, food, and many new ideas. My name, Samarina, challenged my friends. They kept mispronouncing the name as either Sabrina or Samantha. I noticed that not only did I have darker hair and skin than my friends but the other children consistently mispronounced certain sounds in my name. One day on the playground, one of the little boys said, "Can we just call you Sam?" I had no idea what to say so I just stood there. By the end of the week, the entire class of kids, including the teacher, referred to me as Sam. The name made me uncomfortable, because I thought it was a boy's name. I thought, What a strange school; they don't even know I am a girl.

All of the learning and understanding that came with a new home took more practice and time. I focused on getting through the school day and learning the social rules of interacting with my classmates. I did not know that all my moves were scrutinized by the principal and teachers. In the eyes of school administrators, the questions about my contrasting behaviors continued. The approaching holidays highlighted the separate paths. I had never tasted turkey and had no idea what a pilgrim was. And when we were making headbands for Indians, well, I never saw an Indian that wore one of these feathered headgear.

By the Christmas holidays, the stark differences between my classmates and me gave me more unwanted attention. Holiday lunches often included pork or pork products, and even the bread was made with lard or fat from pork. I couldn't always eat what the other kids were eating, and so the questions began. The kids would ask me why I didn't eat pepperoni or have a Christmas tree, and why Santa didn't come to my home to give me presents. Frankly, I did not know. I had no idea I was Muslim and that Christmas was for Christians. My parents told me not to eat pork, so I just thought that's what I am supposed to do. I asked my parents about a Christmas tree, and they said that we don't do that. I just accepted the answers that I was given. But I remember my friends singing Christmas melodies in school and I would always wonder how they knew the words to all those songs. I didn't know the religious significance of Christmas carols, but I did know that I enjoyed singing with my friends.

I learned that the most important part of Christmas was Santa and presents. At school, I heard fabulous tales of a jolly man with a large belly and red suit. This man came to our homes bringing awesome toys. All I needed to do was write a letter to "Santa" with a list of requests of what I wanted. After hearing this news, I thought my new country was fabulous. There was no Santa in Pakistan. I remember running home that day to write my letter. I burst into the door of our small apartment, asking my mom for paper and crayons. My mom asked what I was doing, and I explained this fantastic guy named Santa to her. My mom took me in her lap and said that Santa was just a story, not actually a real person. She also explained that reindeer did not fly and it would be hard for eight deer to pull a sleigh all over the world in one night. Bummer, I thought, I was not getting any new toys from Santa. Very concerned, I had to warn my friends.

I told the kids in my kindergarten class the next day that Santa was not real. I still remember the bewildered expressions on their little faces and the disbelief in the teacher's eyes. They hated me. Some of them even came back the next day and told me that their parents said I was a liar. I had undermined their entire holiday without realizing it. I couldn't understand how telling someone the truth was not acceptable. My parents told me to drop the Santa issue and respect the traditions of my friends. I obeyed my parents. I let my friends enjoy the illusion of Santa. I was taught to respect their beliefs even if I was the only kindergarten student in the school that knew Santa didn't exist. After surviving my first Christmas at school, my holiday of Ramadan and Eid rolled around. Ramadan is the month that Muslims around the world fast from dawn to sunset. All I knew was that, all of a sudden, we were having really great food for dinner at home.

The kids in class asked why I was fasting when I should have been eating lunch. The administrators and school kids did not know that it was the month of Ramadan, during which Muslims did not eat at typical mealtimes. Frankly, I did not know it either, but my family was fasting, and I just wanted to be a part of the fun. I thought it was cool to wake up at four a.m. and have my dad make me eggs and toast and then go back to bed for a few hours before leaving for school. I wanted to be like my mom and dad. Since my dad would not take lunch, I would tell the kids at school that I was not taking lunch. It was fun and a different routine. I felt like I belonged to something bigger than me. My pretend fasting was a game to me, and I just wanted to play. The last day of Ramadan is celebrated as Eid ul Fitr.

Eid is celebrated with festive clothing, yummy desserts, and decorating our hands with henna. The night before the Eid holiday, my mom had mixed some water with henna powder in a small glass bowl. She is a talented artist, and with a toothpick, she fabricated a pattern of paisleys and flowers on my left hand. I still needed one hand to get ready for bed, so my right hand did not get a design. Before going to bed, my mom gave me a lump of the leftover henna for my right hand and wrapped both hands in plastic wrap to keep the henna from staining the bedsheets. The scent of henna evokes memories of celebrations, family, and love. We woke the next morning excited that we were going to prayers and visiting our friends. Best of all, no school on a weekday! I had a great day playing with friends and showing off my mom's intricate designs on my hand.

The day after Eid, I returned to school wearing henna tattoos. The henna color takes about three weeks to fade from our skin. My hands smelled fantastic and had that rich, red-brown henna color. Unknown to me, a storm was brewing. My teacher asked me what happened to my hand. I proudly said, "Don't you love it?" I informed her that I was wearing henna that my mom decorated on my hand. My teacher reported that my right hand had been burnt by my mother. I was called into the office where administrators questioned me if my parents had burned me.

I said, "No, this is henna," and I had them smell the scent I enjoyed so much. They asked how it had gotten under my nail. I explained that henna was sometimes used as a nail color and some people used it as a hair color. I thought I did a good job, but they kept asking if my hands hurt. I explained in my innocence of youth, "It's like nail polish—how can it hurt?" With that, I went to lunch to show my decorated hands to the other girls.

In the afternoon, the teacher told me to step into the hallway and meet a lady. Apparently, no one took my word for the henna, and the incident had been elevated to the school social worker. The social worker stood in the hallway, glaring down her nose and through her spectacles. For the third time that day, I explained henna, how my mom did this amazing design with a toothpick, and the yummy smell I liked. She immediately said, "Are you SURE your hand is not burnt?"

"No," I said, and I told her how I held the henna all night to get this rich brown color.

She said, "So your mom did not put your hand on the stove?" I was getting upset. Why did no one understand me?

"No," I answered, "I was in my bedroom, and we do not have a stove there. Why would she need a stove?" I asked, totally frustrated and confused. The social worker then poked my hands, asking me if the pressure hurt. I angrily said "NO!" Then I poked my hands and clapped them five times, I am fine—can't you see?

My parents were called after this incident not only by the principal but also the school system. I think they wanted to hear another version of what happened to my hands and see if I was covering for child abuse. Later in life, I understand and appreciate that the school and social workers thought that they were protecting me. There was no social media to explain the beauty of henna adornments and that these were a sign of festivities and honor. The traditions of henna seemed so natural to me. I began to learn at five years old that what I knew of life made me stick out.

My classmates were more curious, especially about why I was absent on a regular school day. I really did not know why I did things the way I did. But the questions were always coming, and the questions always highlighted our differences. In retrospect, I know that they just wanted to understand why I didn't do things like them at that time. They wanted to know where I came from, what I believed, and what made me unique. Just like I wanted to fit in, they, too, were trying to understand why I didn't. We were too young to understand that these were differences between two cultures and two religions. At the age of five, I did understand that people were cautiously curious about me, and I wanted to give all these loving, curious beings in my life the answers they were looking for. There were many ways I was different, but most of the time I was just like my friends. We shared common values like honesty and love. We had common interests like recess and softball. We had similar goals like earning good grades and making our parents proud. Although on the outside we looked different, on the inside our hearts longed for the same connection and acceptance.

Enjoying the US Experience

While I was at school, my dad was at school too. After finishing his master's degree in civil engineering at Colorado State University, he went on to earn an MBA from the University of Colorado in Boulder. Our stay in the United States was meant to be two short years—a temporary but fun sabbatical from Pakistan. So during the summer holidays, we would get in our station wagon and drive. My parents had a used blue station wagon with genuine vinyl seats where the middle seat could fold forward for more room in the trunk. The car was huge. It was both a vehicle and a camper. We drove the interstates during the day and searched for KOA (Kampgrounds of America) campgrounds at night. Sometimes we camped by a river and other times in a national park. Our family enjoyed exploring, and we spent our two year stay discovering attractions across the country.

In the era before car seats, seat belts, and air bags, my sister, Saima, and I would hop over the rear seat to the very back of the car and watch the world pass by. On my father's student budget we could afford the low gas prices and the campground fees. My parents would take turns driving while Saima and I played in the back. I was mesmerized by the landscapes. We flew by big trucks and cars with real campers. My sister and I talked about being so rich one day that we would own a real Winnebago camper and drive in style. We decided that we wanted to see as much of the United States, Canada, and Mexico as we could before returning to Pakistan. And I was blessed with parents who wanted us to appreciate people and places, who were teaching us that diversity was a good thing and to be grateful for new perspectives.

We went to that twenty-eight cents a gallon gas station, filled up the car, bought a road atlas, and took off. We drove the entire continent for two summers. The summer before first grade, we visited Disney Land, Yosemite, the Grand Canyon, and Yellowstone National Park. We only had three months to experience a whole new part of the world. Because of these long road trips spent bonding with my family through the entire North American continent, I still love long drives. I find peace on interstate highways with green road signs, watching the world go by. The roads in the United States are amazing, and the facilities such as the state rest areas make travelling with small kids convenient. In the same spirit of making the most of our time here, we also drove through Canada and all the way down through Mexico City to the beaches of Acapulco. I remember negotiating at the markets of Mexico and climbing the Pyramid of the Sun. We were grateful for our time to experience all of North America, the American, Canadian, and Mexican cultures, the great people, delicious foods, and the amazing sights.

There were so many treasures to see and experience. The second summer, my father's friend Talib and his family decided to go with us. They had a blue station wagon similar to ours. We headed to the east coast for the summer break. After visiting the beaches in Florida, we headed north through Washington, DC, to New York. For my seventh birthday, I celebrated in New York City at the top of the Empire State Building. I remember having cake in Central Park. I loved spending time with my family or lying in the back of the station wagon, staring at the skyscrapers. That summer we travelled all the way to Maine and back to Colorado. Summer vacation flew by while we enjoyed the simple things like the open road. Since we were driving, I was able to see many other sites, from gazing at Death Valley in California to visiting Boston Harbor and the ships of the Boston Tea Party. I saw people of different shapes, sizes, and colors spending time with their families. I realized that even though we all may look different, many of our values were the same.

We wanted to make the most of our short stay here. When the time came to go back to Pakistan, we wanted to return knowing that we really had really appreciated all that the United States has to offer. By the age of seven, I had been to forty-four states, along with Mexico and Canada. America the Beautiful does not even begin to describe what I felt in my heart. I traveled to the Native American reservations in Utah, I met French Creoles in New Orleans, and I played with all the kids I could find. We were different, but we could play freeze tag no matter what our race or religion. Playing nice in the sandbox is what kids do naturally. I was so grateful to play in the sandbox of the USA, but it was time to go back. All our family in Pakistan were ready for our return. We had a house waiting for us and many, many relatives who loved us.

The US government, however, still needed engineers and persuaded my family to stay by offering my father a job for a minimum of five years. My father was still needed to work on the irrigation systems of Indian reservations in the US. Our government convinced him that this additional experience would elevate his stature, give him credibility, and allow him to share the newest engineering techniques when he returned to Pakistan. When my paternal grandmother heard the news, she was distraught. Her son was not coming home. We had just lost my maternal grandfather and missed his funeral. My maternal grandmother heard the news that we were not coming back, so she missed us and decided to come and visit us. We had not seen her for two years.

With my father's new job, our family moved to the state capital, Denver, about seventy miles south of Fort Collins. In Denver, we purchased our first home, and I completed elementary school. My English became better than my spoken Urdu. My mother, Bano, started a job at a local preschool, and my grandmother, Sajeela, was our summer entertainer. I now wore shorts and tank tops, shopped at Kmart, and spoke with the same American accent as my classmates. I had Pakistani insides with an American exterior. I had morphed into a better version of me in which I leveraged the influence of two cultural philosophies.

My dad commuted by bus to work in downtown Denver. He travelled to Arizona, New Mexico, and Nevada and to Indian reservations farther up north in the Dakotas. Sometimes he was on business for a week, but many times it was longer. Quite often, he would come back with pictures of his travels and experiences on the reservations. My father loved photography, and he was authorized to photograph the sacred indigenous ceremonies that he attended as a guest of the chief. We heard many great stories of life on the reservations and the traditions of the original American peoples. From my father, a Muslim born in India, I developed a huge respect for Native American customs and the way they honored the Earth.

As our stay in the United States changed from temporary to permanent, those early days and experiences shaped my life. I was American, but as an immigrant and as a Muslim, I was still viewed sometimes as an outsider. With kindness and curiosity, my friends and peers in school continued to ask questions. Questions and curiosity are my confirmation that Americans are not simply tolerant but are rather accepting and accommodating of new ideas and people. Recently, both Islam, the religion, and its Muslims followers were forced into the spotlight for several reasons—some good, more bad—and so the questions from friends have become more complicated, more detailed, and more nuanced.

A MUSLIM VIEW ON CHRISTIANS

The people of my childhood all had different faiths and different backgrounds yet seemed to enjoy supporting each other. We shared our beliefs and also our celebrations. In Colorado, we were assigned host families; we had one host family in Fort Collins and one in Denver. A host family was a local family that would teach new neighbors some of the customs of the new country and become their friends. At one of the Thanksgiving dinners at their home, I met a man who was Agnostic. I had never heard the word, so I asked him what it meant. He explained his beliefs, and I remember thinking, But I will still believe in God.

Forty years later, we are still friends with the generous-hearted people who accepted us and shared their traditions. They welcomed us into their homes, shared their food, shopped with us at thrift stores, and loved us for who we are. Although we do not see them much, I will always cherish how they opened their hearts to an immigrant family. We still receive Christmas cards from our two host families in Colorado. My journey in America has given me many friends of every faith. To understand what I truly believe about the Christian faith, I want to dedicate to my current and future Christian friends the letter Prophet Muhammad (pbuh) wrote as a testament to Christians over fourteen centuries ago. This is a brief summary of how Muslims view our Christian brothers and sisters:

"This is a message from Muhammad ibn (son of) Abdullah, as a covenant to those who adopt Christianity, near and far, we are with them. Verily I, the servants, the helpers, and my followers defend them, because Christians are my citizens; and by Allah! I hold out against anything that displeases them

No compulsion is to be on them. Neither are their judges to be removed from their jobs nor their monks from their monasteries.

No one is to destroy a house of their religion, to damage it, or to carry anything from it to the Muslims' houses. Should anyone take any of these, he would spoil God's covenant and disobey God's Prophet. Verily, they are my allies and have my secure charter against all that they hate.

No one is to force them to travel or to oblige them to fight. The Muslims are to fight for them. If a female Christian is married to a Muslim, it is not to take place without her approval. She is not to be prevented from visiting her church to pray.

Their churches are to be respected. They are neither to be prevented from repairing them nor the sacredness of their covenants. No one of the nation (Muslims) is to disobey the covenant till the Last Day (end of the world)."[3]

I have been blessed with a bicultural, bicontinental life. I have had the pleasure of having friends of different faiths with unique cultures, and the life I get to live is not only rich in new traditions and adventures but also in line with the basic teachings of Islam. I have chosen to adopt a belief system that celebrates and protects all people by honoring them for who they are.

---

3   http://www.ptwf.org/index.php?option=com_content&view=article&id=209:muslims-are-
    commanded-by-muhammad-to-protect-christians-and-their-churches-until-the-end-of-
    days&catid=86&Itemid=526

CHAPTER 2

DIVERSITY

"MAKE THINGS EASIER, DO NOT MAKE THINGS MORE
DIFFICULT, SPREAD THE GLAD TIDINGS, DO NOT HATE."
PROPHET MUHAMMAD

What happens when you take a Buddhist child, a Hindu child, a Muslim child, a Jewish child, and a Christian child and put them in a gym? You have a basketball team. Not only does my son's team look like a mini United Nations but so does the opposing team at the recreation basketball game. The gymnasium is packed with parents of different races and religions, cheering for their kids. This Saturday afternoon I am reminded of our humanity and that, no matter where we come from or what we look like, all of us want to see our kids succeed. I notice that everyone is so different—different clothes, different accents—yet they're all getting along. Some of the moms come over and compliment my son. All the kids play hard but fairly, and I feel it is because of parents who have taught them great values—basic human values that are shared regardless of race or religion. Mutual respect is priceless.

For real connections, we need to understand the basic values we all share. Let's start with some similarities to build understanding of the Muslim point of view and build on our mutual respect for each other. I have heard many questions of whether Muslims consider the Prophet

Muhammad divine. Some of my Christian friends believe that Prophet Muhammad is to Islam as Christ is to Christianity, and there seems to be some confusion as to who Muslims worship. The easiest response is that Muslims worship the God of Prophet Abraham (pbuh) and Prophet Moses (pbuh). We also share in our knowledge of the Prophet Jesus (pbuh), or for my Christian friends, I would say Jesus, son of Mary.

WHO IS ALLAH?

The Arabic word for God is Allah. Muslims believe in one God who created the heavens and the Earth. The Islamic concept of Allah is that Allah is unique; Allah has no gender and Allah has no plural. According to Islam, all things belong to Allah. For example, I have eyes, ears, hands, and a tongue. These items, however, are not mine at all but belong to God. In the Holy Quran, and in the example set by Prophet Muhammad (pbuh), I am taught how to treat these items. I can use my hands to eat and hold my children or commit crimes. In Islam we believe that at all times we must act as if God is watching and use the intellect and physical body we have been blessed with to serve God and humanity. Being from two cultures simultaneously, I tend to use both Allah and God interchangeably.

Our main goal as Muslims during our time on Earth is to remember and praise God. In return, we are promised a great life after death. Not only does praising God help in the afterlife but also in obtaining happiness and peace in this life. In Islam, God is defined as kind and loving, full of forgiveness, and wanting to protect all of creation. Following the simple lessons of the Quran, anyone can earn God's love and blessings. Every chapter and recitation of the Quran starts with the phrase, "In the name of Allah, the most beneficent, the most merciful." Muslims use this phrase to begin every meal, to start their day, or at the start of a journey—all daily acts start with the remembering of God.

The concept of Allah in Islam is that God is not our father nor is God the son. There are no masculine terms associated with the one, true, universal God. Also, God is kind, and if you are in a state of challenge, it is because God wants to bring you back on the straight path to heaven or to grow you spiritually. In Islam, we are taught the concept of Jihad, or struggle. We are taught that we need to exert effort to promote good and stand up to injustice. Islam stresses good deeds for ourselves and our community. Whether we are struggling or celebrating, God is guiding our lives.

I know that I am never alone and always have God as that loving entity looking out for me. When faced with a challenge or bad day, I just ask myself what lesson God wants me to learn, so I can take the lesson and throw away the experience. In Islam, we have assurances throughout the Quran that Allah is a bountiful provider and that there are always provisions and space on the Earth for all of God's creations. Not only does God create life but also provides for the sustenance of life and room on the Earth for each creation.

I want to share the terminology used in Islam as compared to the other Abrahamic faiths, because I have had experiences where the terms are not used correctly. I've also had many conversations where I realized the other person believed that Muslims worship Prophet Muhammad (pbuh), which is not true—we believe in only one God, Allah, and in Islam, Prophet Muhammad (pbuh) is a messenger of God.

Religion:	Islam	Judaism	Christianity
Follower:	Muslim	Jew	Christian
Place of Worship:	Mosque	Synagogue or temple	Church or cathedral
Holy Day:	Friday	Saturday	Sunday
Revelation:	Quran	Torah	Bible

Prophet/ Founder:	Muhammad (pbuh)	Moses (pbuh)	Jesus (pbuh)
Worships:	One God	One God	One God

All three of these faiths trace their roots to the patriarch Prophet Abraham (pbuh). All my religious classes stressed the importance of honoring the guidance given to both Moses (pbuh) and Jesus (pbuh). The story of Moses (pbuh) and the Pharaoh is the most repeated story in the Quran, with each version stressing the qualities of Moses (pbuh) and his faithfulness to God. I participated in many discussions with my Christian colleagues on their belief of Jesus (pbuh) as the son of God or as a prophet. Although years of religious classes and attending mass in Catholic schools did not sway my belief in Islam, I respect the values of love and justice that Jesus (pbuh) brought to our world.

QURAN

The Holy Book in Islam is the Holy Quran. Loose translations of the term *Quran* could be "to recite" or "to collect." The Quran is a collection of chapters, or *surahs*, with one hundred and fourteen total surahs arranged according to the specification of Prophet Muhammad (pbuh). The Holy Quran is the most recited book in the world. Muslims recite sections of the book daily in their five prayers. The verses of the Quran are also used to bless weddings, pray for the sick, and be the religious part of the funeral ceremonies. Furthermore, memorizing the Quran is encouraged at all grade levels of schooling in Muslim countries. I spent part of seventh and eighth grade memorizing the surahs in the Quran along with my friends. I even used the translation to read to my kids for bedtime stories.

The Quran is not a linear book, as some may expect, but rather is a matrix that moves through subjects and stories the way the human mind thinks. This structure takes a little bit of getting used to. One summer, I read the entire Quran over and over again six times. I started to notice a rhythm and changes in perspective throughout its stories. The more I studied the Quran, the more fascinating the book became to me. With each reading I saw something different. I remember during my sixth pass of the book wondering, Was this section in here all along? Whenever I need to relax, an online video reciting the Quran is my solution.

It is no surprise that the Quran is not only preserved on paper but also in the many human minds of the Muslims who have taken time to memorize the entire book (about the size of the New Testament). There are competitions for memorizing and reciting the Quran. In Muslim nations, many kids will spend a year or two of school memorizing the Quran at special religious schools. One of the memorization techniques uses slate tablets. Students write a verse on the tablet in chalk and carry the tablet around with them in their daily activities. Since the verse is frequently viewed and always with the student, the student easily memorizes the verse. Once the student is confident that they know the verse, the memorized verse is erased and a new verse is put on the tablet. Instead of repeatedly listening to songs and memorizing lyrics, these Muslim kids repeat individual verses of the Quran and learn the entire book. The way the book is organized makes it easy for the human brain to memorize. If all paper and software copies of the Quran were to be destroyed, the message would still live on and could be reproduced and checked by all the "protectors" of the Quran that took time to memorize the entire book.

The Quran is believed to be good for our human eyes, ears, and heart. The melodic recitation of many *qaris,* or scholars, of Islam sounds like a composition of a perfect harmony. An imam is considered a religious leader, and a qari is considered a religious teacher. The Quran will often soothe our hearts while the different tones in the verses resonate in other parts of the body. For the eyes, there is the blessing of looking at the words of the Quran while reading. But Muslims have taken this to a whole new level where calligraphy of the Quran has become an art form. From the wooden carvings of the verses in Indonesia to the woven rugs of surah in Turkey, the creativity of Muslim artisans is showcased in many forms. Who knew a book with such humble beginnings would impact the world?

Islam began in a small cave outside of Mecca, known as the cave of Hirah. Prophet Muhammad (pbuh) used to get away from the hectic city and go to the cave of Hirah to think. He would wonder why some people were corrupt and why others in Mecca at that time were putting their faith in stone idols. He went to the cave to contemplate the meaning of life and wondered if there was more to this life than the hedonist activities of the Meccan Arabs.

In the last few days of the Islamic month of Ramadan around the year 610 AD, Muslims believe Angel Gabriel appeared before Prophet Muhammad (pbuh) and commanded him to read. There was nothing in the cave but dirt and rocks. Prophet Muhammad (pbuh) was scared, and to top it off, there was nothing to read. He did not know what kind of spirit could just appear while he was all alone in the cave. He had never had an experience like this before. Gabriel commanded again, "Read." And Prophet Muhammad (pbuh) stammered, "But I cannot read!" Gabriel then said, "Read in the name of your Lord whom created you." Interestingly enough, the first word ever recited about the Quran was the word *read,* or *Iqraa*. According to the Muslims, Angel Gabriel would make Prophet Muhammad (pbuh) repeat the verses until he had memorized them and could repeat the verses exactly as taught. Muhammad (pbuh) would then return to Mecca, where some of his followers would write down the verses since Muhammad (pbuh) himself did not read or write.

Muslims believe that the Holy Quran is written by God. My non-Muslims friends, however, sometimes attribute the Quran as a book written by Prophet Muhammad (pbuh). Prophet Muhammad (pbuh) is known as "the unlettered prophet" to the Muslims because he could neither read nor write. So what my non-Muslim friends believe is that an illiterate man produced a book that empowered women, gave rights to the poor and slaves, gave honor to all the religions that preceded it, is full of mathematical and scientific miracles, and still influences the world over fourteen centuries later. If we go with the belief of some non-Muslim scholars that Muhammad (pbuh) wrote this book without any help from God, then we have to admit, Prophet Muhammad (pbuh) was a pretty incredible man. I still believe the Quran is a divine revelation, taken in from Gabriel and memorized by Muhammad (pbuh), then written by the local scribes. Either way, we can all agree, whether one chooses to believe that the Quran was created by God or the Prophet (pbuh), the impact of the Quran is still being felt fourteen centuries since its introduction to our world.

My experience with the Quran is that it is a calming, peaceful book. The phonetic arrangements of the sounds usually just melt my stress away. Along with worshipping only one God, the Quran stresses great character, emphasizes self-control, and is progressive. The Quran is always there for us. I have an app on my phone that I use on airplanes. The sounds of the verses provide a beautiful symphony of voices in harmony that help me fall asleep on a flight. Other days, I focus on the messages in the stories. There are stories and lessons for whatever path we are on in life. The morals and messages embedded in the Quran not only teach us something but also teach us how to improve our surroundings.

I had memorized several surahs, or sections, of the Quran when I was five but did not learn to read Arabic until I was twelve years old. I loved the perspective of learning both English and Arabic simultaneously. English is written from left to right whereas Arabic is written from right to left. English has vowels as part of the alphabet, but in Arabic many of the vowels are dashes and symbols both above and below the letters. Arabic has only a cursive, or connected, letter format where the letters have different shapes depending on the locations within the word; however, English words can be either printed or put in cursive. Learning how to read and write two different languages gave me unique perspectives on how to view every event from two different sides. For this ability, I will always be grateful and cherish the blessings of seeing each event in my life from many different angles.

WORSHIP

Muslims worship in a mosque. I am often asked if I go to the temple. The term *temple* is usually associated with the Jewish, Hindu, Buddhist, Mormon, and Sikh faiths. I have visited many temples that are ornately decorated with sculptures and paintings. Mosques are quite simple. A little trivia about mosques is that they usually do not have doors that lock because everyone is welcome in a mosque. Also, mosques do not have altars because we do not want to give the impression that we are worshiping an object or person other than God during prayers. Muslims only worship the one true God, Allah. In most mosques, the floor tiles or carpet squares are laid out in the direction of Mecca, a city in Saudi Arabia that is home to the largest mosque in the world, also known as the House of God. No matter where we are in the world, all Muslims pray with their faces toward Mecca.

Growing up in the States, I saw my friends go to church on Sunday mornings and spend the rest of the day with family. In Islam, our holy day is Friday. Muslims usually pray at home or at work during the week, but on Fridays we congregate for the midday prayer at a mosque. I remember my parents taking us to the mosque when we were kids. My sister, Saima, and I came up with every excuse we could to get out of all religious worship except celebrations. Now my husband goes to the mosque on most Fridays, and my kids are finding ways to avoid joining him. Because of the large crowds that pray on Friday, many local Islamic centers rent hotel ballrooms and have five to six prayer sessions back-to-back to fit different work schedules. Some of the companies I have worked for also had a prayer room for their employees. After the prayer there is a short sermon about various religious topics such as kindness, helping the poor, or respecting our parents. Fridays are usually religious holidays in most Muslim countries, or sometimes, Muslims will work in the morning and then take the rest of the day off to pray and spend time with their families. It is also a good idea to give charity during this prayer.

My parents invited me to the local community center for a lecture. The community center was in a warehouse complex with one office and a moveable wood wall partitioning the space. My parents and their friends brought donations to the center where poor individuals could take jackets, clothes, and shoes as needed. When I walked in on this sunny Saturday morning, the main area had chairs and looked like a meeting hall. Along with a podium, two men stood at the front greeting people in the room.

The group had sponsored an event with a religious speaker, who was dissecting different sections of the prayer in Islam. He was talking about inclusion and how we, as Muslims, are taught to support other faiths. He began to discuss the final part of the prayers and explain the frequency of the Muslims' prayer of five times a day. The closing verses of each prayer are based on a conversation between Prophet Muhammad (pbuh) and God. These famous verses are known as the *Darood Ibrahim* and are the prayer of the Prophet Muhammad (pbuh) to God. There are two verses in this prayer that say, God, please send prayers and blessings continuously to the family of Abraham and the followers of Abraham. And the next section is similar, by saying, God, please send prayers and blessings to the family of Muhammad and the followers of Muhammad as you did for the people of Abraham. The prayer ends with the verse, "Indeed, God, you are the Majesty."

Imagine that almost two billion people worldwide read this prayer at least five times a day. This prayer is read in all time zones around the world. This part of the prayer asks for blessings and peace for the followers of Prophet Abraham (pbuh). What hit me was that for the last fourteen hundred years, most Muslims have prayed at least five times a day that peace and blessings come to our fellow Jews and Christians since we are all together as followers of Prophet Abraham (pbuh). As a Muslim, I feel honored to have a set prayer where I can pray for and respect the religious beliefs of others who are not just like me. We Muslims are praying right now for all the followers of Prophet Abraham (pbuh), so may peace and blessings from God be given to you.

My hope is that our global community, like my son's basketball team, can accept and celebrate what makes each of us unique. The diversity of the team made it strong—each child in the game played a part in the team's success. I feel blessed to live in a country where my children will grow up, as I was able to do, with a wide assortment of people. My kids have attended holiday parties, Quinceañeras, Bar Mitzvahs, and Hindu Diwali celebrations. We can all celebrate our differences by not only supporting each other but also celebrating with each other, so everyone is uplifted and honored.

Diversity and respecting our differences are basic manners. However, sometimes I have noticed that these concepts are preached and not always practiced. I feel like we need to highlight the times in life when things went right, instead of each time things went wrong. In traditional Muslim cultures, society valued character and education over being rich and famous. I make sure I pay attention when excellent character is exhibited. I got the treat of good character the day I met a man named Shah Saab.

In September 1998, the phone rang on a hot Friday morning. It was my aunt in Ohio telling me about a Pakistani man from the town of Rawal Pindi who ran an orphanage. "You really should go see him," she encouraged. The man from the orphanage, Shah Saab, would be visiting Virginia, close to where I lived. She wanted me to meet him and see if I could give a small donation for the orphanage that he had started. Earlier in the year, my aunt had visited this orphanage and felt that the kids were well taken care of and were happy.

Taking my sister Saima along with me, I agreed to meet him and got up early on Sunday to drive out to the meeting. I was driving through the lush, green foliage surrounding the George Washington Parkway headed to Alexandria, Virginia. I was still waking up, a little tired from the early morning start. I kept glancing at the old brick houses, looking for numbers to see if I was close. I was headed to the Best Western hotel off the parkway. I was still second-guessing myself, but an orphanage was a good cause. I parked, and we walked into the hotel lobby. I saw a familiar face. I guess my aunt had also called our youngest sister, Amina. We walked to the meeting room and hugged our little sister.

I was hesitating and had no idea what to expect. I didn't even know if this was a lecture or if I needed to talk. I was pretty sure Shah Saab and I had no subjects in common. There on the sofa sat an old man appearing to be in his late seventies. His white hair and white beard were a contrast to his mocha-brown skin. His eyes had smile lines and looked peaceful. I went and said, "May peace be upon you," to Shah Saab. Without skipping a beat, he returned the greeting with a smile. He motioned me to a chair to sit down.

Shah Saab (Saab meaning "sir" as a sign of respect) was there along with three assistants. He was dressed in traditional Pakistani dress with a loose trouser, *shilwar,* and a long shirt, or *cameese,* that came to his knees. He had round spectacles on his eyes, a shawl with tassels, and the traditional flat, circular, wool hat. There was a kindness in his manners, and when I spoke to him I felt a sense of peace. I got to spend twenty minutes talking to Shah Saab about his work and the plans for the orphanage.

Shah Saab was a noble man and had studied the principles of Islam and the Quran extensively. In Islam, we are instructed to take advice based on knowledge and study of the faith. It is better to actually practice what we learn instead of using the term *Muslim* as just a title. If we ask for religious advice, it is on us to make sure the person we are asking is a good scholar and has extensive, valid knowledge of the faith in the given subject area. Our leaders need to earn our respect through their actions. I got a sense of serenity and could see this man was a caring leader. Saima wanted some support with her relationships, and I wanted to move up in my career. Shah Saab gave us his insights from a religious perspective, often quoting the Quran or the example set by Prophet Muhammad (pbuh). I donated some money to the orphanage, as did my sisters. Shah Saab also gave his blessings to our family. It was an ordinary visit and did not leave a huge impression on me. I did, however, get his orphanage business card, and whenever life got tough, I'd call him in Pakistan and ask him what actions I could perform, such as prayers or charity, to get me to a better state.

Ten years later, Saima visited Shah Saab at his orphanage with her fiancé. Being an Italian American man, her fiancé could have passed for someone from Pakistan, but his height gave him away as an outsider. Both my sister and her fiancé had been working at the same company, and as two lawyers, they had worked on several projects together. On top of the cultural differences, my sister's fiancé was a Christian man going to visit a Muslim scholar in the Pakistani town of Rawal Pindi. Islamabad, the capital of Pakistan, is known for its diversity with embassies from all ends of the globe. However, Rawal Pindi is more of a small town that does not have the resources and sophistication of neighboring Islamabad.

When Saima later told me about her visit, I held my breath. How would Shah Saab, a Muslim scholar, react to a marriage that not only had two different religions but also two different cultures? I braced myself as my sister continued with the story. I had seen differences in religion cause prejudices on both sides of the globe. I had no idea how a man who spoke no English and spent most of his life in Rawal Pindi would react to someone who was so different. I certainly did not expect Rawal Pindi to be a hub for diversity and inclusion. Saima continued with her story of her trip to the orphanage. My sister and her future husband had gone to get Shah Saab's blessing for their marriage. My sister said, "And do you know the first words Shah Saab said to my fiancé when I introduced him?" I was in the kitchen listening to her story and just shrugged my shoulders, implying that I didn't know. My sister explained that Shah Saab said in broken English, "I love you." That was the greeting he gave an Italian American Christian man visiting Rawal Pindi, Pakistan.

That was the day I realized that Shah Saab was truly a man of God. He practiced what I had read about the Prophet Muhammad (pbuh) genuinely caring for people. I was expecting judgment of all the things that would be challenges for the marriage and the differing belief systems. Like Prophet Muhammad (pbuh), Shah Saab just treated everyone as human beings created by God. Having character, honor, and respect were more important than judgment and fear. What I learned that day was that I need to look past all the religious, cultural, political, and national labels we wear, and just start with love. All religions teach unconditional love, but I had never before seen a Muslim demonstrate unconditional love the way Shah Saab did to my brother-in-law.

CHAPTER 3

FIVE PILLARS OF ISLAM

"YOU CANNOT ENTER HEAVEN UNTIL YOU BELIEVE, AND YOU
WILL NOT TRULY BELIEVE UNTIL YOU (TRULY) LOVE ONE
ANOTHER."

PROPHET MUHAMMAD

The basic theology of Islam is based on a system of five pillars, which are the foundation of the faith. In Sunday school, I was taught that Islam is like a table with legs holding up the table. If the table of our faith has five legs, or pillars, supporting us, then we have a strong and unshakeable belief. The five pillars of Islam are: faith, prayers, fasting, charity, and pilgrimage to Mecca. Prophet Muhammad (pbuh) summarizes the pillars: *"Islam is that you testify that there is none worthy of worship (in truth) but God and that Muhammad is the messenger of God, you establish the prayer, you pay the charity, you fast in Ramadan, and you perform pilgrimage to the House (of God) if you have the capability."*

FAITH

It's funny how moving to a different continent changed my outlook completely and I morphed into a new person. Had I stayed in Pakistan, my faith would have probably never been challenged. Life was easy. The majority of the people had the same brown eyes, the same olive skin, the same black hair, and the same religious faith. We would get together for a social event such as high tea, but often these events were combined with religious worship. For example, a tea party may be preceded by a ceremony of saying poems, called *Naats,* that praised Prophet Muhammad (pbuh). Religion and culture are mixed in most Muslim countries. But coming to the United States, every act of culture and faith was challenged for me. I was questioned constantly. As an adult, I realize that we can receive the most incredible clarity in our spiritual beliefs when they are tested each day by another belief system. Coming to the United States made my parents and me much stronger Muslims and pushed us to become liaisons between Islam and the American culture.

We never know what we have inside us until we are tested. My tests of faith began early. After my culture shock in Fort Collins kindergarten, I experienced a shock to my faith in Denver when my formal Islamic education started, and as an adult I see what a huge blessing it was to learn what you stand for at such an early stage in life. We had moved from Fort Collins to Denver, where we met some other Muslim immigrants. The group had formed an organization called The Colorado Muslim Society. Naturally my dad was the president and a founding member. The Colorado Muslim Society had bought an old house on Ash Street and used it as a mosque. The living room and dining room were a prayer hall. We prayed toward Mecca, which happened to be the front of the house. Behind the living and dining room was the old family room that became a small, shag-carpeted community hall. The family room led into the kitchen with lime green Formica counters and linoleum flooring. The kitchen door led to the backyard, and that's where we all entered.

The basement was used for the kids. Colorado winters meant half a year of snow in the backyard, so we often played in the basement. But on Sundays, the basement became our Sunday school. This is my first memory of actually learning about Islam. The teacher, Ms. Syed, was from Egypt. Ms. Syed was a robust woman with a scarf on her head. There are different types of head covering in Islam, and the one she wore was like the bandanas that were in fashion at that time. This type of head covering is called a *hijab* in Arabic. She always came to Sunday school with a button-down shirt, a long skirt that went to her ankles, and a scarf that matched the skirt. Even with her hijab, Ms. Syed was making her own fashion statement.

She had two daughters that were Saima's and my ages. Ms. Syed had volunteered to help teach the kids. She had a great Arabic accent over her English. In fact, all the adults had accents, but when we children spoke English, it was like we were native speakers. I had no idea that teaching Sunday school was from the heart. It never occurred to me that the teacher was not being paid. I just thought Ms. Syed wanted to be there every Sunday to hang out with us kids and tell stories.

I loved the backyard at Ash Street because it had rhubarb plants growing along the back wall of the house and surrounding a decaying shed in the back corner. This home was where we prayed, its yard was where we played, and it's where I made friends for a lifetime. I'm not sure why the previous owner had planted rhubarb—I had never heard of rhubarb before—but these plants were a blessing and a source of fun for all the kids at Sunday school. The rhubarb was too sour to eat so we would use it as a bat for our bouncy balls and play baseball in the back yard. When a new kid came to school, we had an initiation. We would tell them how delicious the rhubarb plants were, and we would all eat them, acting like they were delicious. Then we would watch in anticipation when the new kid took a bite! After the initiation we would invite the new kids to play baseball or freeze tag. That was the procedure for making friends at Ash Street.

Ms. Syed taught us that faith is like a table with multiple legs. There are five pillars in the Islamic faith: four of them mandatory to support your religious "table top" and one optional leg, or pillar. The table with five pillars is how most Muslims view their faith. Continuing with the analogy, if one's religion only had one flimsy leg to stand on, one's faith could easily topple with any event in life. A table with two legs is still unstable and can fall easily. Three legs are better and a table with four legs will hold up to many forces. Our goal as Muslims is to make sure all our pillars of Islam are very strong. Therefore, even when life hands us a hurricane, our religion will endure and we will come closer to loving God, because our faith has multiple pillars supporting it. She drilled the concept of a strong table into all thirteen of us in her class.

The first pillar that you must have to be a Muslim is faith. Ms. Syed wrote the declaration of faith on the blackboard. Loosely translated, "I declare there is no god but God, and Prophet Muhammad is the messenger of God." In the Islamic faith, Muslims negate any other gods or idols beside the one true universal God and declare that there are no other gods, recognizing the oneness of God. Faith in Islam means that God is unique and there is no entity in existence that is similar to God.

Ms. Syed said I needed to love God. I wasn't sure. I had never seen God or met God, so how I was supposed to love God? She explained that God was watching us every minute of every day. After learning that I was being watched in Sunday school, I became very conscious of my actions. It bothered me that I was being observed so much. I asked Ms. Syed if it was a bad thing to be watched all the time. She explained that God was always with me, loving and protecting me. The explanation gave me comfort, and I started being okay with having God around and watching me.

In Islam, faith starts with the basic belief in God, but faith also requires believing in two other aspects: the seen and the unseen. Muslims believe in seen creations of God such as the Prophets and the books, but Muslims must also believe in unseen creation of God such as heaven, hell, and angels. If a Muslim chooses not to believe in these elements of faith, then they are considered to be "outside" of Islam. For example, if I did not believe in Prophet Jesus (pbuh) and the virgin birth, I would no longer be considered a Muslim. So in order to be considered a Muslim, we must believe in Jesus Christ (pbuh). Ms. Syed taught us about having faith in God and also insisted that all prophets and messengers of God must be treated with respect.

In between lessons on faith, Ms. Syed wove in lessons from Islamic history. I particularly remember the one about an Arab sheep herder. The sheep herder noticed that the sheep on one side of the pasture had much more energy and moved quicker than the sheep on grazing on the other side of the pasture. The sheep herder wanted to learn why the two groups of animals behaved so different. What he noticed were little brown bean that were being eaten by the energetic sheep. The sheep herder had discovered coffee, a drink that spread around the world for its zestful qualities. Ms. Syed continued her lesson with the use of coffee houses as meeting places that encouraged spirited debates. A combination of coffee and diverse ideas were a cornerstone in Islamic culture.

I hoped her lesson was over so I could go on break. I doodled in the workbooks, an old habit I developed in kindergarten. When breaktime came, I headed to the little kitchenette and there was a large red tin can of coffee. My mind raced. I could get energy and ideas from the magic potion of instant coffee. I invented a new drink composed of hot water, a teaspoon of instant coffee, a tea bag, white sugar, brown sugar, milk, and powdered milk. The ingredients consisted of everything at the drink station. I dubbed my new drink coffa-let-tea. It tasted great. I bragged about my creativity to all the other kids at Sunday School. From then on coffa-let-tea was our drink of choice. Each of our Sunday school lessons ended with Ms. Syed reminding us that all we have is a gift from God. I gave thanks to the Lord for giving me such a delicious break.

As a child, I not only invented coffa-let-tea but I saw Sunday school as a burden that put a damper on my weekend. I never understood the importance of the oneness of God until I began to study my faith as an adult. When learning Islam became my decision, I became fascinated by my religion and discernment I received.

I have noticed that when non-Muslims distance themselves from my beliefs, I hear them say that Muslims do not worship God, that Muslims worship *Allah* instead. One thing I want to clarify is that *Allah* is just Arabic for God—just like *Dios* is Spanish for God. Same God, different languages, so different names for God; all Abrahamic religions worship the same God. I prefer to use the term Allah for several reasons. *Allah* has no plural form in Arabic. There is only One God and a huge part of the Islamic faith is attributed to recognition that Allah is only One. Another reason I prefer using Allah as the name for God is that in the Arabic language, nouns have masculine or feminine genders, but *Allah* is gender neutral. There is no male reference to God in Islam such as calling God terms like "father," "heavenly father," "son," or "he."

I enjoy being a rebel and I believe in women power. Even at the age of eight my strong opinions emerged. Not only did I meet new friends, invent new drinks, but I also met God for the first time on Ash Street. Thanks to all my lessons of Sunday school, for Ms. Syed and her persistence of coming every Sunday, I am now really glad to be watched over by God. I now even ask God to watch over my kids.

PRAYER

The second pillar of Islam is prayer. One of the basic acts as a Muslim is a constant connection to God. The five daily prayers in Islam provide many benefits that may not be apparent to people outside the faith of Islam. About praying, the Holy Quran states: "Those who believe in the unseen, observe the prayers, and give charity out of what God has provided for them. And they believe in what was revealed to you, and in what was revealed before you, and with regard to the Hereafter, they are absolutely certain. These are guided by their Lord; these are the winners" (Quran, 2:3-5).

While there are benefits to praying alone, there are more benefits to praying as a group. Some of my favorite memories of group prayers are from the old white house of Ash Street. Ash Street attracted Muslims from all over the city, and Friday was prayer day. There's nothing like the power of a diverse group of people coming together as one. The Colorado Muslim Society was an amazing bunch of immigrants from all over the world. The room was filled with a rainbow of different races and outfits from all parts of the world. There were the Arabs with their long flowing gowns, *abayahs,* and tons of embroidery, showing up on Fridays with amazing baklava or walnut pastry and grape leaves. Then there were the South Asians in their traditional garb, *shilwar kameez,* with the flowing scarves and tons of jewelry. We also had Muslims from Africa with hand-woven material and turbans. All parts of the globe were represented, and we all prayed together and ate together. Because after a group session of prayers, who wouldn't want food?

The names for food were so different because of the multiple cultures represented. Each food item had a unique name in each country, and the same item could be called several names. We all had multiple vocabularies but were united when we read Arabic and recited the same Quran. My American accent was heavy, but I could also do a Pakistani accent. I needed the Pakistani accent or I would speak Urdu like a non-native speaker. I enjoyed the different accents in the group. The one I tried to mimic and learn was the Arabic accent because the pronunciation of the Quran by native Arabic speakers seemed so effortless and musical. I am still trying to get all the sounds right. But I am grateful for the diversity present at the Ash Street Mosque for making me realize the melody in the recitation of the Holy Quran with an Arabic accent. I had learned something new about myself. I not only enjoyed the sounds of the seventies pop music but now the sounds of the Quran being read. I added a new genre to my life.

Food and religion complemented each other at the mosque. Each of the dishes was unique with a different blend of spices and texture, plates of food as special as the people and cultures that created them. The smell of food was everywhere, but we kids were under the tables, eating in our secret hideouts. We would peek out from underneath the tablecloths and grab dessert without our parents noticing. Ms. Syed's girls liked baklava. I had never had baklava before or even heard of the dish. I thought making baklava was the most complicated process in the world. I wondered how they stuffed all the nuts between the layers of the flaky, crispy dough. I kept asking the Ms. Syed family how to make it. Ms. Syed kept saying in her heavy voice, "It is very easy, very easy."

Another regular attendee at the mosque was Hoda. Originally from Palestine, her family owned a butcher shop selling halal meats and Middle Eastern groceries. Hoda and her husband had two young boys. I loved having her at the gatherings, Hoda was outspoken and opinionated. She showed me that a woman could speak her own mind and also fulfill the traditional roles of mom and caretaker. In our tradition, I called her Hoda Aunty. Since she was a fantastic cook, Hoda showed up with a new dessert concoction every week. She had some rolls with pistachio and others with nuts, honey, and filo dough. I spent most of the meals thinking Hoda Aunty was a magician, that is, until I learned to make the food myself. Hoda was right; it was simple—simple to make and simply delicious. Within minutes, her foil pan emptied and I scraped the sides to get a little more of her treats. The mosque was a place for new experiences, new friends, and new food. We would eat and share the dishes we loved until it was time to pray. The call to prayer would be our preparation to line up and get ready to remember God.

In the middle of dinner, we would go to the living room designated for praying and line up in the direction of Mecca. The old carpet was full of stains and had masking tape to show everyone the direction to stand in the rows. I would stand in the middle row and look at the mustard-yellow, semi-gloss paint on the walls. The ceilings were plastered with swirls. I needed to focus on praying, but my mind was wandering. I couldn't stop my thoughts. I'd look out of the windows and then listen to the recitations in Arabic. Remembering God and listening to the *Imam*, prayer leader, made me feel like a part of something bigger than me. I started listening to each word and learning the sequence of the prayer. We all moved to the bowing position at the same time. I was part of the group. I belonged. I loved the prayers and how everyone flowed in motion like one body of humanity. I was now centered and able to concentrate on my connection to God.

I had prayed for years in our makeshift home-turned-mosque, but I had not been in a full-fledged mosque in a while. On my first trip back to Pakistan after living in the United States for two years, I couldn't believe how nice it was to hear the call to prayer, or *Azaan*. Since I was familiar with the sounds and reverberations of the call to prayer, I could hear it a mile away. I think the *Azaan* has the most unique feeling of peace and connection. On one trip back during my teenage years, I could actually hear the call to prayer from the local mosques while taxing on the runway after I had just landed. This was the song of welcome to a Muslim land.

A typical Muslim day revolves around prayer. The prayer schedule is set according to the position of the sun, so the prayers spread out in the summer and get close together in the winter because the days become shorter. It takes anywhere between five to twenty minutes for completing the requirements of each prayer. Muslims pray facing toward the city of Mecca in Saudi Arabia. Depending on where we are in the world, the direction of prayer changes. When I travelled before, I used a compass to estimate where to pray. Now, I am now grateful for my new smartphone that has an app to find the direction to Mecca based on my location. On Muslim airlines, the direction for prayer is shown on the map display screens of the aircraft.

Not only must we face the correct direction toward Mecca, but we also must be clean before we pray. When standing before God, one must be clean and properly dressed, similar to dressing up for temple or church. The cleansing *wadu* is a spiritual cleansing in addition to a physical cleansing and must be completed prior to each prayer. Also, it is important to pray in a clean area, so Muslims often use a prayer rug on top of the carpet or floor to make a clean section for praying. Therefore, with the cleaning five times a day, Islam has a built in personal hygiene system. Keeping ourselves physically purified reduces the carrying of germs and diseases. Physical purification and spiritual purification work together in Muslim life. The Morning Prayer can be as late as six a.m. during the winter months and as early as three and four a.m. in the summers. Some Muslims start the day after *Fajr*, yet others (including myself) go back to bed afterward.

I find the morning prayer, *Fajr*, to be meditative and to help set the tone for the day. If I am worried about anything, it's great to leave it with God at the crack of dawn. Muslims believe that just like our bodies need food at certain times of the day, our souls need to reconnect with God at certain times to feel completely fulfilled, and so the second prayer is usually around lunchtime. This afternoon prayer, known as *Duhr*, also breaks our focus from business back to our faith. We are reminded that one day we will be gone and actually have to stand before God. In the late afternoon, it is time for the third prayer of the day, *Asr*. By now the kids may have arrived home from school. All prayers are important, and *Asr* being the middle prayer has a saying of Prophet Muhammad (pbuh) that emphasizes its significance. The Prophet (pbuh) said, missing the *Asr* prayer is like robbing your family of all their wealth.

The evening prayer, *Maghrib*, is valid from the time the sun sets to when the last slivers of the sunlight remain in the sky, a very short window of time. I do my best not to miss the window for this prayer. I really don't want to pray late. This prayer often coincides with dinnertime. So I keep reminding myself, God before food. Some days I just feel like I am constantly struggling to do the right thing. When Muslims fast, *Maghrib* is the time that we can break the fast and finally eat. In Muslim countries, we often see everyone running around to finish up the day before the sun sets and it's time to pray. Late prayers in Islam do not get the full credit; only praying on time gets full credit. Prayers are for punctuality.

And when we go to bed, we have the honor of standing before God for the final time with the fifth prayer. The night prayer, *Isha,* is the longest prayer of the day and has the largest time window of any prayer, as it can be said between the time night begins and dawn the next day. It is also a time for great reflection, and it gives me a chance to thank God for the blessings of health, food, kids, and home. If there is anything that is weighing on my mind, I can give the worry to God for the night. The next day begins at dawn, and I will start again, having the honor of repeating this practice for the rest of my life.

Part of the *Azaan,* call to prayer, says "hurry for prayers, hurry for success." In Islam, prayers are our connection to God, and a strong relationship with the Lord is true success. Personally, I'd like to tell you that I have prayed five times a day for my whole life. Not true. I did go to a Muslim summer camp when I was eight where, for the first time ever, I prayed five times a day. To me, it felt like a lot of work and that I was praying all the time, maybe because I was eight. But the camp changed me, and ever since, I have prayed the first and last prayer each day. That seemed possible, and those five days at camp started a new habit for me. If I forgot to pray and went to bed, I'd somehow wake up in the middle of the night to say my last prayer of that day. I remember praying every day and every night my entire childhood, vacations, high school, and college. I was always aware of the times of only these two daily prayers.

During the day, I would see my mother and grandmother pray the other three prayers, but it didn't bother me that I was not participating. My grandmother even invited me, but I said I was busy. I have no idea why I thought I was too busy for a five-minute ritual. My awareness did not seem to be there for the middle three prayers. However, as an adult, I started noticing that I was calling myself a Muslim but only praying twice a day. I made goal posters of how I would eventually obtain this full five prayer goal, I wrote it in my journal, and I even prayed to God to help me pray correctly. After college, I got a job as an electrical engineer. I felt like I just didn't have enough time in the day to add three more prayers.

I would have to be dressed to pray, get cleaned up, and find a clean spot in the building where I could be undisturbed for a few minutes each day. This felt impossible to me in a corporation where I was running propagation models and having lunch meetings. I was so busy achieving material success, looking for the next promotion and trying to put my mark on the world, that I did not know the spiritual price I was paying. I guess I was young, but I had never developed the good habit of spiritual growth. The days flew by, and I never remembered the midday prayers. Next thing I knew, I was approaching forty, had four kids, and still only prayed two times a day. I feel like those thirty years were a big blur for my faith.

But Islam stresses education, so I was regularly listening to a program about Islam on CDs in my car, and it hit me. I was finally ready for the lesson, so this time I heard my calling. *Prayers equal success.* I had that feeling of being struck by lightning—praying five times became clear and seemed so simple. I was at a point in life when I was frustrated and confused, feeling like I was working really hard but not going anywhere. I realized what I was missing was really those three prayers a day and a stronger connection to God. So I decided to give it a try; I would participate in all five prayers every day. The plan was to quit after trying it for a month—so much for a strong faith, right? At first, it seemed excessive and like a lot of work. But by the second week, I was used to the extra prayers, and by the fourth week, I was actually looking forward to praying.

I think my favorite prayer experience was at the great mosque in Mecca. We had just ended our pilgrimage to Mecca and were getting ready to leave the next day. This was the final prayer before our flight back home. There were over a million men and women in the mosque praying as one, moving through this ritual as a single body. The imam (prayer leader) read one of my favorite sets of verses from the Quran, titled, "*Surah Tin.*" I had been memorizing the verses earlier that week, and the imam's Arabic recitation was amazing. The sun had set, all the lights of the mosque were on full power, and I remember feeling a cool breeze as the night came on, even with the heat of the lights. I was with my husband and son. My husband had even run into a cousin he hadn't seen in years at the mosque that very night—four family members praying in the grand mosque together. I knew I would be flying home the next day and taking with me the awesome sense of peace. I had never felt so much ease and complete control of my entire life.

Ever since that fateful month when I was listening to my compact discs, I make all five prayers. If I miss one prayer or am getting late for a prayer, I get fixated on the fact that I need to pray, so now I have an internal reminder instead of relying on external ones. Through the daily act of prayers, we receive protection from straying from our faith through the constant connection with God. Since I began praying five times a day, my experience of the world has changed. Everything seems to come more easily to me. I notice what is great about this world, and I notice how many blessings I really have. I remember before I began praying five times a day, some people would drive me crazy, so I avoided them. Now, I don't get triggered as quickly—I have more patience and love for the amazing people I share this planet with. My prayers have given me peace and compassion. I discovered that I was able to recover from setbacks in life more quickly. Having peace in the knowledge that God has a plan for me and is doing things in my favor, in this life and the next, has been the keystone for my ability to find peace during a crisis.

FASTING

The third pillar of Islam is fasting. Islam is a religion of self-control, and fasting is one of the best ways to master this. Once a Muslim has established their faith and mastered their daily prayers, the next step is creating self-control. An important thing to note is that fasting is compulsory only for healthy people. Muslims who take regular medication, are pregnant, or have certain illnesses are excused from fasting. The Islamic calendar is based on a twelve-month lunar calendar in which the ninth month is

Ramadan—the month that Muslims fast. The fast begins at dawn and ends at sunset, starting with *Fajr* and ending with *Maghrib*.

Before and after the fasting period, Muslims are allowed to eat and drink. Most Muslims get up an hour before dawn during Ramadan and have a light meal to start their fast. I am lucky to have a husband that wakes up before the crack of dawn and makes food for the kids and himself. My kids love the time with their dad, eating all the foods my husband ate before fasting when he was young. I, on the other hand, wake up, have a protein shake by my bed, clean up for prayers, pray my morning prayer, and go back to sleep. I am still working on being a morning person. At dawn, it is time to make the intention to fast the entire day. Ramadan is a holy month, a time for reflection on the next life and to repent for any regrets of the year that has just passed. It is said that during Ramadan, all the seven different gates to heaven are open and prayers are answered. For this reason, several Muslims may spend the entire month in the mosque worshiping God and reflecting on the spiritual paths of their lives.

This is a month to ask for forgiveness and atone for wrong actions by giving charity or feeding the poor. The last ten days of the month are extra special. Muslims believe that prayers are answered during these ten days. The Quran came to Earth at this time. In addition, one of the final ten nights of Ramadan, there is call *lailat-ul-qadr*, or night of power. Muslims believe that praying on *lailat-ul-qadr* is equal to praying for one thousand months. As a kid I was told that the night of power occurs on the eve of the twenty-seventh day of Ramadan. On that eve, many Muslims will pray all night until the break of dawn. We believe angels come down on that night and take prayers straight to heaven.

The typical comment that I get in the United States regarding fasting in Ramadan is, "What, no water *all day*?" Many people find it difficult to believe that it is healthy for a person to go without food and water for so long. Finally our culture of overindulgence is beginning to see the benefits of fasting. Contrary to popular belief, a little self-control is not that unhealthy. I have been fasting since I was eight years old and am in great health. Fasting has not caused stress on my body, but rather cleansed my body and made it more efficient. Once, I was with a group of friends who practiced Hinduism. I mentioned how I was fasting all day without water, and the response was totally amazing. They told me about their much longer fasts. They said you get to eat and drink at the end of the day and began to comment on how easy it is to fast in Ramadan. To most eastern cultures, fasting is a part of life. My Hindu friends told me that they fast for ten days straight without food, just water. What's difficult, healthy, or unhealthy really is a matter of perspective. In fact, I feel that not eating and drinking is pretty easy compared to the less tangible fast Muslims partake in during this month. In Ramadan, not only do Muslims refrain from food and drink but we also work on controlling our thoughts and emotions.

Controlling emotions like anger, jealousy, impatience, and irritability are much harder than controlling hunger and thirst. Imagine driving in the car with four kids fighting in the back seat, while I am fasting, feeling both hungry and thirsty, and trying not to lose my temper. How strong is our faith when we are cranky? Sometimes we are kind or loving when it is easy, but under stress or pain a different person emerges. Fasting teaches us patience in times of hunger pains and also allows us to empathize with individuals who do not have enough food or access to clean water.

Even though Ramadan is a challenging month, it is a very exciting month. In Muslim households, there is a high level of elation, joy, and expectation in the air, in anticipation of spending time with family and connecting with our faith. Muslims invite family and friends over during this month for the evening meals to share the gift of food—a gift some of us take for granted. At night, we are together with extended family, with rooms full of uncles, aunts, and cousins all praying together. One of my memories of Ramadan was being fourteen and visiting aunts, uncles and cousins in Pakistan for the summer. I loved it because Pakistan does not participate in daylight saving time, so although the fast started earlier, it also ended earlier. My three best friends from junior high lived nearby, so they would come over right before the opening of the fast and we would watch a movie together or just hang out. After opening the fast, we would stay up till three a.m. to eat the pre-dawn meal and then go to bed again. I had time to relax and unplug so I could have a summer of connecting to people. We spent the time talking about our dreams, but we were so hungry that the conversation often turned to what we would eat the next day.

My aunt lived in a cottage behind her mom's home. The compound was beautiful with a large lawn, gardens, and the main house of my Great-Aunt Zubaida in front. As the gravel driveway swung to the back of the main house, there was parking for my aunt and mom's cousin Samina. One night, my aunt Samina and I snuck out at 2:30 in the morning and went to the local bazaar to eat the *sahoor* meal before the beginning of the fast. We did not want to wake up her mom. If my Great-Aunt Zubaida had heard us, she would have said we were crazy and told us to stay home. Since my great-aunt was an elder, we would have had to respect her decision. Therefore the exit had to be so quiet that the sound of the motor or the wheels moving on gravel would not be noticed.

My aunt Samina, a local psychiatrist, had the car in neutral, and I was pushing it out of the driveway onto the street. We kept the engine off until I had pushed the car out of the gate and slowly closed the green metal gate to avoid any squeaking. Once safely on the road, we started the car and took off to the main bazaar. The roads were empty, and we made it to the city center, *Sadr,* shopping area in record time. But as we turned into the narrow alleys leading to our favorite food stalls, the scene completely changed. The bazaar was packed with people buying fresh food for the early morning meal. We were sitting in the narrow alley with crowds of people on either side and in front of the car. We couldn't even move! There was no way to get out of the car, no place to park; I couldn't even open my door. We hadn't thought out our entire adventure to this point.

My heart raced as I felt the buzz of energy in the air, the entire city preparing for the next day of fasting. Everyone was looking forward to great food and time with family. We saw a kind-looking man approaching our car, and he stopped the pedestrian traffic so we could move near his store. My aunt rolled down her window and motioned and told him we were looking to eat our *sahoor* meal. Samina told him our order. She asked if he would go to the food stall and place the order and bring us our food. The kind man agreed. It is typical in many Muslim cultures for a man, even a total stranger, to run an errand for a woman so that she is treated like a lady and served with kindness. He went to call a food stall waiter for us so we didn't even have to leave our car.

A few minutes later, the food stall waiter came to our car with the order. Common practice in Pakistan is to go to local restaurants and have waiters come to the car. This is the Pakistani version of the drive-thru. We sat in the comfort of our car and enjoyed the food and could take the leftovers home. We decided to go against all common sense and eat in the overcrowded bazaar. That meant eating on dishes that were washed in questionable water, food made with love but no safety standards, and never knowing if the utensils were sanitized or just wiped. This is what I call third world living at its finest. Just go with it. Let the night give us an adventure, and either way we go home with a full stomach and an experience of a lifetime. I loved that Ramadan summer I spent with my aunt and will always cherish these memories. I got to brag to my friends about my great adventure the next morning, and, to the best of my knowledge, my Great-Aunt Zubaida never figured out that we snuck out that night.

There are many different traditional celebrations for the end of Ramadan, or Eid, and the greeting for this holiday is "Eid *Mubarik*" or "Happy Eid." One fairly typical way to spend an Eid celebration is to attend special prayers on Eid morning. Prior to praying, everyone must give charity to God. And, yes, the poor have the opportunity to give charity too. In Islam, regardless of our financial status we are reminded that there are people less fortunate than us, and everyone can make someone's life better, even if they are poor. We all have something to contribute to making life easier for each other. Again on Eid, a smile is really an act of charity.

I am blessed with great Eid celebrations in the States, but they are so different from those I spent in Muslim lands. On all holidays, my grandmother's home in Pakistan was transformed. The home would turn into Grand Central Station. Every twenty minutes or so a new visitor would stop by for an hour or more just to see how our day was going. They would bring us some food and wish the family Eid Mubarik. Everyone, including the kids, was dressed up and complimenting each other on their beautiful outfits. We would then serve our guests tea and sweets while we chatted about the current politics, activities of the family, or future travel plans. I think we must have had fifteen cups of tea each. By the end of the day, we had seen everyone and been to all their houses. Like other holidays, Eid requires lots of cooking and cleaning for guests. The celebration is a day of connection with loved ones, a day of charity for those in need, and a day of gratitude for all our blessings.

Food is a blessing and a source of celebrating. When I was younger, I remember my parents cooking dinner for the entire community. We needed containers large enough to serve five hundred people, and laundry baskets lined with aluminum foil to cover the holes did the trick. The day before Eid, I would be the manual carrot shredder for a carrot desert named *halwa*. This was way before modern kitchen appliances existed, so at eight years old, I acted as a human food processor, using a grater to grate the carrots before my mom could cook them into a thick consistency similar to mashed sweet potatoes. The carrot dessert was seasoned with cardamom pods and ricotta cheese. It was my favorite dessert because it was like I was having vegetables. I was never happy to do chores, but cooking my favorite dessert felt like my love of playing with food and not work. This was our special celebration dish. My friends had other dishes they enjoyed like baklava or Turkish bread pudding. Eid is a multiday food and friends celebration, but it also marks the end of Ramadan. Similar to New Year's Day, it means the festive season is gone.

For me, Eid is nostalgic because it means the Ramadan holidays are over and we have to wait to enjoy the blessings of fasting as a community again. I was asked if I minded fasting when everyone else was eating. I don't mind at all. Fasting is a blessing. To me it means that I am growing my faith, I am enjoying the benefits of health, and I get to be a part of a community movement much larger than me. Even when I am celebrating the end of one Ramadan with Eid, I am anticipating the gift of having another Ramadan to fast in this lifetime.

CHARITY

Charity, or *zakat* in Arabic, is the fourth pillar of Islam. It is incumbent on every Muslim of enough means to give charity from the blessings that God has provided for them. Because of the strict requirements for every Muslim to give charity, Muslims are one of the most charitable groups. Giving charity is considered a way of purifying your wealth, a concept that is critical in Islam. All wealth is a blessing from God, and the manner in which one obtains wealth is also important. If your wealth is not obtained in a pure manner, for example, through selling illegal drugs, then anything that you do with that wealth will not be a blessing for you.

Muslims must make a conscious decision on the ethical nature of the companies that we work for. Islam encourages being aware of how money is made so that no one is harmed in the earning of money. For example, if you receive a paycheck from a company, are you sure that the company obtains their profits in a totally ethical and honest manner? The concept of *zakat* is honored in both the Quran and the traditions of the Prophet Muhammad (pbuh). In the Quran the word *zakat* appears over a thousand times with verses such as: "Who give to charity during the good times, as well as the bad times. They are suppressors of anger, and pardoners of the people. God loves the charitable." (Quran 3:134).

Zakat protects our wealth by purifying it, and making it safe from social vices. For example, I have own a smart phone, and that. During the manufacturing of the smart phone is manufactured in China, the worker who made it (yes the tracking information stated it shipped from Shanghai) one of the workers working on my smart phone may have been mistreated. If In that is true, then case, I am enjoying the benefits of a smart phone at the expense of someone else's misery. Product whose creation involved a violation of a human being right to dignity and decent treatment. I want to protect my wealth using the concept of charity. Zakat will purify my wealth by giving assets and give me the honor a way of atoning any way I may receive money or wealth. It also helps to clear me mistreatment in the way I acquired my assets. Even if I am not aware of exactly how my smart phone is manufactured, God is aware of the conduct of the manufacturers, distributors, and sellers. In the case of social injustice, I am cleared of the responsibility of a social injustice that may have happened in making or acquiring the device. So, giving *zakat* will free me from my parts of any misdeeds done by the company that created the smart phone. We do not only give charity because we think our process of earning a living is not ethical or our employer is not honest. We give charity to eliminate the possibility that something that is beneficial to us came at the expense or suffering of another soul. For potentially benefiting from someone else's misery.

I have a tender spot in my heart for the underdog. I felt relieved that my faith accounted for the treatment of the poor and weak in all aspects of life. I give charity because I think our process of earning a living is not entirely ethical or our employer is not honest. I also started my own business because I did not like the way some of my employers conducted business. I give charity to eliminate the possibility that something that is beneficial to me came at the expense or suffering of another soul. I want my values to be reflected in how I achieve my goals as how I make money.

Like soup kitchens in the United States, most Muslim countries also have regular distribution centers for giving charity, whether by money or by food. My grandmother had a tradition of giving food to the needy. In the main city of Lahore, Pakistan, in the inner town area, the landscape totally changes. The buildings become denser, and the streets become narrower. With the increased traffic, filled with rickshaws, bicycles, tons of motorcycles, and plenty of Japanese cars, there is no question that I am in the heart of the city. The traffic is jam-packed with beggars and sellers going from car to car. They offer balloons, coconut slices for a snack, or necklaces made out of roses. It's always dusty and muggy with the humidity soaring in the summer. In the middle of all this is a place where you can sit and watch cooks make huge pots of rice, or *daigs* as they are called.

The vats are almost as tall as the man who is stirring the rice in them so it won't stick and burn. By the time the rice has cooked, the poor are already lined up with containers asking for food. Large silver plates are used to dish out the rice to the many hands holding up any shape or size of container for food. Every holiday or celebration, my grandmother would order one of these large *daigs* of rice and we would distribute food to the poor. For most Muslims, giving charity is a family tradition. In Islam, all religious holidays emphasize the importance of charity. We give charity after all holiday prayers and most joyous occasions. In Islam, a new baby, new job, passing a major certification, or a wedding are also great times for charity. What better way to honor a new milestone than to acknowledge the blessings from God?

Charity is the best way to show gratitude for our blessings even if it is just a tiny act. Giving a meal to a neighbor is an act of faith. So is volunteering to dig a well or feed hungry animals. In Islam, there are different types of charity to give for different occasions. During the month of Ramadan, feeding the poor and needy people is considered a great charity. But so is having a bird house and giving the birds water. In Pakistan, many wealthy people provide a year's worth of education by sponsoring school children as charity or building infrastructure such as water wells for a local village. I like to serve my community on different levels such as planting a tree.

In Islam, when we plant a tree, we get good deed benefits of all the years the tree provides shade and food for both people and animals. When my grandmother saw a "tree hugger," she would say, "*Mashallah*," the saying for a deed that is accentuating the will of God.

There are also different levels of charity. Even if a person is not in a position to give financial assistance, saying a kind word or helping someone cross the street is considered an act of charity in Islam. Even giving someone a smile is considered a form of charity. Visiting someone who is sick is a form of charity and gives a person many good deeds in the next life. One may also teach someone to read or give them protection so that they may peacefully practice their faith. We are taught that living was meant for giving.

PILGRIMAGE TO MECCA: *HAJJ*

The fifth and final pillar of Islam is a pilgrimage, called *Hajj*, to Mecca. This is a huge desire for every Muslim. Family members talk about going to Mecca like a dream come true. Since this pilgrimage is a big undertaking, not many Muslims have the honor of completing this pillar. This is why the pilgrimage to Mecca is the fifth and final pillar. The pilgrimage is asked of each Muslim once in their lifetime, if they can afford the journey and have the health to complete the trip. Hajj is the pillar that is optional (of the five pillars of the faith, the other four being the ones that keep the table of faith sturdy). Hajj gives the extra support to our table of faith.

The ritual follows the footsteps of Prophet Muhammad (pbuh) who performed the pilgrimage following the footsteps of Prophet Abraham (pbuh). Prophet Muhammad (pbuh) performed his last Hajj at the age of sixty-three, right before he died. Hajj is now the largest religious gathering in the world. Hajj is a special time to connect with God and helps us remember that our time on earth is temporary. One of the days in Hajj is the day of *Arafat*—a reminder that we will ultimately be making the journey back to our creator. During the day of *Arafat*, Muslims rehearse for the final judgment of their life when God will flatten the Earth to a level field. All of humanity will stand before their Lord and be judged on how they lived their lives and what they did with the many blessings God gave them.

Hajj also reminds us of our humanity—how we are all human beings and creations of One God, how no one is better than anyone else except in their ability to honor God. Everyone dresses in simple, humble clothing without jewelry or marks of wealth. All humans are the same in front of God. Our humanity is based on our internal values, not our external appearances. People from every corner of the Earth, using every type of transportation, show up for this amazing event. Some even walk for a year across the Saharan Desert just to be a part of this event.

The five pillars of faith have been the five pillars of strength in my life. I learned to appreciate my faith, and I learned the power of discipline. I won't tell you that I am a master yet, but I know that when I pray on time or exhibit self-control with fasting, my day goes well. Also I discovered my anxiety-fixer: charity. For some reason, giving charity always seems to make my problems go away. I just returned from a weeklong trip to Florida. I came home to a huge stack of mail, and I counted thirty-six pieces of mail from charitable organizations. I guess even the local charities know who I am! Like all other faiths, Islam is built on rituals and disciplines that enhance our inner well-being while making our world a better place. Each faith is built on a system to help us live a fuller, more peaceful life.

Chapter 4

LESSONS FROM MY FATHER AND GRANDMOTHER

"O People! Do your tasks with energy. Because when you become weary of prayers and worshipping, God will be weary in recording blessings. The most pleasant effort to God is that which is little, but constant."

Prophet Muhammad

My father, Rashid, and maternal grandmother, Sajeela, have been the strongest guiding forces in my life; they both embody the most important Muslim values and virtues. From schooling to entrepreneurial prowess, both of them were my cheerleaders and stalwart supporters. The Muslim value of service to others is a beautiful lesson my grandmother lived in her daily life, which I saw firsthand after living with her for several years. Education is a strong focus for all Muslim families, and my own upbringing was no different. I was taught the value of greeting people with kindness, treating everyone with respect, and honoring a different point of view. We knew that we lived in two cultural traditions and both of these traditions contributed to a richer life. All of these are lessons from my childhood I'm now sharing today with my own children.

BEGINNINGS

Like America, Australia, and Canada, Pakistan is a former British colony, and my father was born in a village called Pind Dadan Khan, then in British-occupied India. Pind Dadan Khan is centrally located between the Jhelum River and the Kerwa Salt mines and about a two-hour drive from Islamabad, the capital of Pakistan. Ironically, about ten miles from Pind Dadan Khan is where my husband was born—and it would take both of us a trip across the ocean to meet each other.

My dad was forced to grow up early in life. At the age of sixteen, he lost his father, a local judge. My father had to step up to take care of his mom, his younger brother, Javed, and his five sisters. My father's older brother, Akram, was away at college at this time. As a Muslim, my father knew how to honor and empower women. He understood that it was now on his shoulders to help his sisters become educated and successful. His father had supported education for his oldest sister, Arjaman, but now it was time for the other four girls to go to school. He encouraged his sisters to attend a good college and finish their degrees, even if it meant leaving home. In the era when women in the United States couldn't even get a loan without a man's signature, this Pakistani Muslim man was encouraging his sisters to get educated.

My Aunt Arjaman was five years older than my father and felt she could not pursue an education due to the family finances. This would mean Rashid having to barter and work odd jobs to make sure that the family was financially set. It would also mean that as a teenager, my father would go to court and get the legal rights for the transfer of property and assets. In this struggle, my father, Rashid, gained strength. We don't fully realize that decisions we make in the moment can come back and serve us. And encouraging Arjaman to go to college ended up being a good idea. At school, Arjaman made a new friend who ended up becoming my maternal grandmother, Sajeela. All kindness is reciprocated, so when it was time for my father to get married, Arjaman called her college friend Sajeela. She knew Sajeela had a daughter named Bano who had just finished her degree. A meeting was arranged, and that's how my dad ended up marrying my mom, Bano.

Arranged marriages are common in many cultures, including Islam. In an arranged marriage, the couple's parents determine what type of partner is the best match for their son or daughter. My aunt and grandmother were good friends so they knew what type of family values and character that this marriage would cultivate. Even though they did not meet each other before their wedding day, my parents have been happily married for over fifty years with three great daughters. Imagine, all of this from a decision to inspire a sister to go to college.

MUSLIM WOMEN

My maternal grandmother, Sajeela, grew up and got married just as the British were leaving India, and she eventually started a family of her own as Pakistan was being formed. As a Muslim woman, she had the right to choose and approve of her husband, she could decide if she wanted to work or be a mother, and all the money she entered the marriage with was hers. Her husband must provide for her and her children but he had no rights to her wealth. Islamic marriages follow shariah, and in shariah, a woman has full control of her financial assets and wealth. My grandmother knew her rights and she passed on this tradition that she was raised in to her children, grandchildren, and great-grandchildren. She lived her life being the example of a strong Muslim woman with both a family and career. Even after my grandfather's death thirty years later, she was an independent woman with her own financial investments, a president of a charity, and a traveler of the world.

At the age of ninety-three when she passed away, Granny (as I called her) was still independent, alert, and working for her charities. I've always admired her dedication to her health—she walked a mile every day, and even into her nineties she drank at least eight glasses of water a day. Sajeela was an encyclopedia of how to heal the body naturally. Throughout my life, I learned the value of controlling what I ate and how to rest. My grandmother's good health meant that our family was not burdened with her basic care. At ninety-two years old, my grandmother published her own book, the memoirs of her life. I discovered so much about the amazing life she led, and I decided that I, too, could finish my own book.

While grieving for my grandfather, my grandmother needed a change of scenery. Her sons recommended that she visit her daughter, Bano, in Denver. My grandma came to Denver to stay with us for the summer of 1973. Two young granddaughters were the perfect diversion. My sister Saima and I, then almost five and seven years old, kept Granny on her toes so she didn't have time to think about losing both her husband and her father in the same year. My mom needed some help with the two of us, so my grandmother chose to stay with us for a couple of years, to help raise my sister and me as well as to go back to school.

At the age of fifty she went back to college for another degree. Sajeela had been advised by a friend that helping others would help her with a grief. In light of her friend's advice, my grandmother started a master's degree program in abnormal psychology. She enrolled in the University of Denver and went to class with other students half her age. New country, new school, and new life—the same transition I had made just two years earlier. We were on parallel paths, both learning new systems and exploring our environment. In Islam, the recommended path out of any type of despair is charity and service. Granny went on to combine charity and service in multiple ways. After finishing her degree, she worked with disabled children at a home for teenage boys. With this new experience, my grandmother decided to return home to Pakistan and implement a similar system there.

In Pakistan, she started several centers for disabled kids. Not only do the kids make handicrafts to sell for money but they also participate in the Special Olympic ceremonies in Japan and Nigeria. My grandmother received honorary doctorates from these nations for her work. This is the striking example of a Muslim woman I saw modeled: women writing books, running organizations, and working on issues concerning education or the poor. I feel lucky to have a religion that stresses education for women, gives us financial independence, and supports service. Granny set that standard for our family.

EMPOWERING DAUGHTERS

My dad is a regular Muslim father and, like most of our close family friends, insisted on higher education for his daughters. He also encouraged my mom to have her own career. My father wanted the best for us. He taught my two sisters and me to have high standards for ourselves, work hard to be successful, have integrity, and do the right thing. He also wanted us to pursue post-secondary education and degrees. I loved math and science, so I decided to take the easiest subject in college for me. I went for a master's degree in engineering, just like my dad. My two sisters and I greatly benefited from a loving father. One of my sisters is an attorney and the other is a business consultant. We learned powerful work ethics and a love of education from my dad. If there was an opportunity for service, for learning something new, or traveling to another land, my dad always had our backs. My dad has always been a gentle man. I can't ever remember him getting upset or yelling at us. But I do remember him giving us long explanations with explicit details—explanations that only an engineer could give—on every aspect of life.

My father has dark black hair, a Pakistani's olive skin, coupled with light blue-green eyes. He wears glasses and has a slight limp—a motorcycle accident at the age of seventeen left him with an injured ankle that never quite healed. The bone was not set properly, so the doctors offered to re-break the bone and set it correctly. My father refused. Even now, at the age of eighty, he walks with a limp.

My earliest memories of my father are of him coming home from work. Usually, he would walk in the house with the mail or a newspaper. He would then sit down in his favorite chair in front of the living room window. The chair gave a perfect view of the entire house along with the television set. When my sisters or I showed up, he would want to know what was going on in our lives. I still remember his interest in my day-to-day life from my childhood. On report card day, I would bring home my grades and the first person I would show them to would be my dad. I was excited to share my news with him. He would go over each item and grade, telling me when he was proud of me and showing me the subjects in which I needed improvement. Having his daughters educated and financially self-sufficient was important to my dad and important in Islam. He did the same with my younger sisters. After I was done with my turn, my sister Saima would plop on my father's lap and go over her report card, and years later our baby sister, Amina, would do the same. My dad would encourage my sisters and me to keep up learning at school. I knew school was important to my dad—he wanted us to be smart and make our own decisions.

My dad also holds a degree in business, and he was always trying to implement what he had learned. As a child, I remember my parents talking about starting a business. By the time I was in seventh grade, my father had been offered a position in the Middle East as a civil engineer working on oil pipelines. Not knowing what the international schools were like there, my parents decided to send Saima and me to live with my grandmother Sajeela in Pakistan, while our sister, Amina, stayed with them because she was only a toddler. They felt Pakistan had a strong educational system and that Saima and I would flourish there with family, so I spent seventh and eighth grade in Peshawar, Pakistan. Even though my father's job in the Middle East fell through, Saima and I still went to Pakistan to live for two years with our grandmother while my parents stayed in Colorado.

While in Pakistan, I ended up running a business. I never actually thought about having a business, especially in junior high school, but as with many great ideas, this one just fell in my lap. We were required to purchase all of our textbooks for school and to cover them in ugly brown paper to protect the book's exterior. All the girls used stickers and art to personalize their book covers. I had stickers that I had brought from the United States, and I used them on my books. The other girls loved the stickers and complimented my taste in decoration choices. The pieces of the puzzle were beginning to fall in place.

In school, I was learning about Prophet Muhammad's (pbuh) wife, Khadijah, and how she was a businesswoman. She sold goods on caravans not only in her hometown of Mecca but all the way to Syria. I was being empowered with stories of Muslim female business owners. I was only twelve, but a dream was born. I decided my stateside parents could be my suppliers. My mother had started a business of importing Pakistani shirts and selling them to shops in Denver when I was in elementary school. So, I started my own importing business in junior high school and began providing stickers to my classmates.

My main competition was the school canteen. The canteen was a small concrete shed-like building in the middle of the courtyard. The canteen had a slanted tin roof without gutters so when it rained, we would get wet just standing in line. Also, the canteen only offered local products. During recess, the canteen would open briefly for the girls to walk up and buy snacks. The inside was poorly lit and filled with shelves full of gums, candies, chips, and peanut pouches, but it also sold some school pens, erasers, and stickers. The stickers that the canteen had were similar to the ones that were available outside in the bazaar. And from the looks of the stickers, I imagine they were designed in either of the neighboring countries of China or Japan.

My stickers had better paper quality and did not rip as easily as the local stickers. I also decided to price them below the canteen stickers to make mine more appealing. The stickers I had brought from the United States were unique. So I wrote a letter to my dad in Denver and I requested he send me stickers—lots of stickers. When I received the stickers by mail about two months later, I cut up each sheet into individual pieces. I then sold the pieces at twenty-five *paisas,* or Pakistani cents, each. In the dollar standard that was about $.10 of stickers, roughly three times the price my dad was paying for them. I did not factor the postage due to my limited entrepreneurial skills but I very quickly had a booming business.

As soon as the teacher would walk out of class, I went to work and my classmates—or sticker clients—would start selecting their favorites. Some girls had the money right away. Others would tell me to hold on to a sticker and they would ask their parents for money the next day. My two best friends, Nafisa and Naheed, encouraged my new-found business and spread the word about my unique and high-quality stickers. I learned to get higher sales by not having change available. I encouraged the girls to buy extra stickers to make up the difference of what change I owed them. We usually had about eight minutes between classes and some time at recess when I could run my business. When my sticker supplies were running low, I would write to my dad and ask him to use my allowance to purchase extra stickers. My dad was my supplier, my supporter, my encourager, and my cheerleader. Because of his reinforcement, I was able to succeed.

At home, I was known for having cash. If my grandmother or uncle ever needed change or some cash for shopping or dining out, they came to my room. I always had lots of cash from my daily sales, and at the tender age of twelve, I was loaded. I had a small paper notebook in which I kept my accounts of the most popular stickers and how much money I had made. Over the period of seventh and eighth grade, I earned over eight hundred dollars in sticker money.

After two years away, my parents called us back. I had gotten to know so many relatives like Uncle Yusaf, his kids, and his siblings. Saying goodbye to family is not easy. And leaving my friends in Peshawar broke my heart. I had no idea if, with half a globe between us, I would ever see them again. When I returned for high school in the United States, my father asked me what I wanted to do with my money. I really wanted a trampoline because in my old neighborhood in Denver, all of the kids hung out at the house with the trampoline. I knew that my parents did not have the funds to buy one so I wanted to buy it myself.

At fourteen, the trampoline was my first major purchase in life. My dad helped me look through the papers to find a trampoline because I wanted a round trampoline and most of the ones available were rectangular. My dad also helped me bring the trampoline home and put it together. I was so proud of my trampoline because I had worked so hard to get it.

Our faith has strong values protecting women. The women's revolution was happening in the United States, and my mom's American friends were talking about the importance of women having a voice. I find it ironic that my American teachers and coaches were fighting for the rights Islam had given to women fourteen hundred years earlier. Prophet Mohammed (pbuh) taught Muslim men an example of honesty, kindness, and honoring women. The Prophet's (pbuh) first wife was a businesswoman, and women were ministers in Arabia as early as 635 AD. Between my faith, the Sunday school teacher, my parents, and the women's revolution, I learned to be proud to be a girl!

SCHOOLING IN PAKISTAN

When my parents sent me to Pakistan to live with my grandmother, it was the first time I had memories of living in an all-Muslim society, and it was a stark contrast to my experience as a minority all through American grade school. I finally looked like everyone else: black hair, olive skin, brown eyes, and I was no longer the shortest person in the class! I was enrolled in Presentation Convent Peshawar, a school affiliated with the Roman Catholic Dioceses of Islamabad and Rawalpindi, Pakistan.

I had traveled from my familiar Colorado to a different city, country, and continent. I was speaking a different language, learning a new alphabet, living in a different culture, and was amazed at the diversity of peoples and ideas. I had found two homes on two continents. It was nice to belong wherever I was. School in Denver had American teachers with their characteristics, but having nuns as teachers was another experience. I had not had so much structure, so many rules, and such mean "looks" as from the nuns at school. The nuns were a remnant of the British rule of India and Pakistan. The Pakistanis valued the diversity these nuns brought to our society. The nuns had a unique perspective. Just about every major city in Pakistan has a convent and a school run by nuns, and some of the convents are associated with hospitals. The nuns had come to serve missions and had decided to stay and make Pakistan their home.

I was having several "firsts" in my life, and I wasn't sure where I belonged. This was the first time I was going to private school, the first time I was required to wear a uniform to school, and the first time I had nuns for teachers. There were so many rules. Sister Agnes was the enforcer, and she was tall and chubby with lots of red in her face when she was irritated, and her face was red a lot! First rule that I learned: Avoid Sister Agnes at all costs. I kept tabs on where she was, and if I was going to do something, I would look over my shoulder to make sure Agnes could not see me. We started each day in assembly, and then the entire school of all girls would line up in the courtyard by grade. The principal, Sister Kristine, would pray and then we would all sing the national anthem—a tradition the nuns had brought from their time in England. In the warmer months, we stood in line and sweated while praying, and in the colder months, all of us girls were shivering in our sweaters. After acknowledging God and our country, and maybe some announcements, we were dismissed to go to class.

Our convent uniforms consisted of light blue shirts, the *cameese* style of Pakistan. The *cameese* is similar in style to the shirts in the west, but the length is about the same as a dress. It was important that our uniforms were ironed and clean, as both the nuns and our parents stressed respecting anything associated with school. We got graded on how we presented ourselves at school. Under the *cameese* was a white *shilwar,* or loose-fitting pants. The uniform was topped with a white scarf that was part of the Muslim dress, which also allowed us to wear our badges and pins on our uniform. The white scarf was worn in a perfect V shape in the front, over both shoulders. The backs of the scarf below the right and the left shoulder had to always match up or we could be giving cleaning duty. On the left shoulder, we put our pins and badges representing what sports group we belonged to for competitions in cricket and softball. We also got pins for class rankings and good grades on our exams. The look was completed with white socks and black shoes. And yes, the shoes had to be shined. Compared to my school clothes in Denver — jeans and a T-shirt — keeping my uniform sharp was quite a bit of work for me. Furthermore, we couldn't even skip school because if we did, everyone would recognize the uniforms and tell the school guards that we were skipping out.

The convent was in a beautiful compound in the center of Peshawar, close to the shopping district. I always knew I was close to school because I could see the majestic, tall trees that lined the compound. There was a grade school building, an upper school building, a chapel, and the nuns' housing quarters. The compound also had a softball field, a cricket field, and the canteen. The buildings were lovely red brick with huge porches, or verandas, made of gray concrete. There were no carpets in the entire school so the floors could be cleaned with buckets of water. Even in the 1970s, preserving energy was important to the nuns and the parents, so the rooms of the school were constructed in the Muslim fashion in which you can follow the sun for heat. In the summer, they would throw water on the floor and turn on the fans or open the windows—that was our air conditioning. In the winter, we could study on the huge porch to be in the sun during the morning and then go into the classroom to be in the sun in the afternoon. We also had small space heaters in the winter.

The heaters were not always working, and regardless of their operational status, I remember freezing at school all day long. Our driver would drive us to school every morning. My grandmother would sit with us in the back seat and make sure we were prepared. Regardless of any weather, inconvenience, or mean nuns, on Granny's watch we were going to get the best education in town.

In this convent, Pakistani traditions mixed with Catholic nuns; both groups valued education, women, service, and exercising in fresh air. Convents are a tradition in my family. My mother went to a boarding school at a convent most of her elementary and middle school life at Presentation Convent in Muree, Pakistan. My younger cousin went to the Convent of Jesus and Mary in Lahore, Pakistan. Other Christian groups had hospitals, and several of the nuns served there. The Muslims would raise money for the Christian hospitals. Working with Christian nuns and sharing their traditions has been a part of Pakistani education since the British rule of India in the nineteenth century. We were all doing good deeds and serving the same God, regardless of our race or religion.

In my convent, most of the girls were Muslim from well-to-do families all over the city. The nuns knew our faith, and we respected the nuns' values. We got off from school for both Islamic and Christian holidays. We knew the nuns were celebrating Easter or Christmas, and we rejoiced in getting to miss school. In December, there were small Christmas trees in the main office. Many of the teachers were also celebrating Christmas. The girls would go to the chapel and say Merry Christmas, just like at the end of Ramadan, the nuns would wish us *Eid Mubarik*. I learned to just accept people for who they are and found that a little mutual respect can make me a bunch of new friends.

Just like at the other public schools in Peshawar, having a strong educational foundation for their daughters was important for the parents. My friends Nafisa and Naheed, both Muslim, also attended the convent and lived in my neighborhood. Parents would sometimes drive an hour each way in traffic to make sure their daughters got a great education. I lived about forty-five minutes from the school. So, each day my grandmother and our driver would make two long round trips. Every afternoon, they would come back to pick us up. My grandmother spent her day investing in getting my sister and me to school. A strong educational foundation was also important to the nuns, and they strived to serve and educate girls. We were drilled in math and science. We had to learn Pakistani history along with British history. We were taught in two languages and tested in religious as well as secular knowledge. Due to the commitment of the nuns and our parents, we excelled at learning how to study and expand our minds. Most of the girls from my class ended up becoming medical doctors.

For the first time in my life most of my friends were Muslims, and I enjoyed them just as much as my Christian friends in the United States. Girls are girls all over the world. We all loved the same things. Regardless of nationality or religion, all my friends enjoyed shopping, reading, softball, cricket, and listening to music. In our own ways we were diverse. With our parents' support we learned to push ourselves. Their values of excellence became our values of excellence. With the nuns expecting perfection, we learned good school habits. The nuns stressed punctuality and cleanliness. First impressions mattered, and we represented both our families and a great institution of learning. Our behavior, manners, and image were all part of our character. Not only did I grow up, but I got to play softball on two continents with friends that were competitive and loved the sport like me. What I know now is that girls all over the world strive to be smart in school, and when I needed help, all my friends — Muslim, Jewish, Hindu, Buddhist, Christian and non-religious — were always there for me.

I also learned how to start a business and work with potential clients at this school. I was known for my great stickers. Once business at school had concluded, I focused on playing with my friends. Most of the school grounds had grass surrounded by trees, and the hardscapes had brick pavers. However, near the canteen, a Cathedral stood half erected. Cement piles and stacks of red bricks surrounded the construction zone. At recess, our ball or Frisbee could land in the middle of the dirt piles, and then one of us had to go retrieve our toy. That meant getting covered in dust and maybe risking a scolding from a teacher. Most of the girls avoided the construction area. But I didn't mind being dirty, and the teachers would just give me "the look." I was the odd one with an American accent that dared talk back to adults. Therefore, most of my friends volunteered me to do the dirty jobs. So, I climbed the dirt piles near the emerging cathedral to keep the games going during recess.

The cathedral was under construction for the entire two years I attended the convent. At the end of my eighth grade year, most of the structure was completed, and we were given a tour by the nuns. The brick was a stark maroon red, perfectly arranged outside with several white dome structures. Inside, there were high ceilings, white walls, and neatly arranged pews. Upon opening, the new cathedral was a simple and yet striking new church placed in the heart of Peshawar.

Some years later, I discovered that the architect of the cathedral is my mom's cousin and beloved Uncle Yusaf. He wrote about his experience as an architect designing the church. He wrote:

"A CHURCH FOR MY SCHOOL

The Presentation Convent School, located on Mall Road, in Peshawar, was the first school I attended until Class 3. From Class 4 on it became an all-girls' school, so my parents put me in another school exclusively for boys called "St. Mary's".

In 1977 after returning from Berkeley, having obtained my Master's degree in Architecture, was visiting my parents at Peshawar and happened to walk by the Convent School. Feeling nostalgic I stepped inside its compound and noted that the old British era Church made out of mud bricks standing there since 1851 . . . around which I had played as a child . . . had deteriorated and developed cracks. The Parish Priest came and we got to talking, and I introduced myself. He informed me the Church had become unsafe for occupants. When I told him I was an architect, and a former student of the school, he asked me to develop a new design to replace the old Church. Hence this project was granted to me, out of a chance encounter and a beckoning from childhood memories.

I designed the "new" St. Michael's Roman Catholic Church in 1977, including its liturgical furniture, i.e., the Altar or table the clergy use for Communion, the Apse or wall behind the altar, the Tabernacle which contains a fixed locked box where the Eucharist is stored, the Baptistery, the Speaker's or priest's lectern, and the pews or "chairs" upon which worshippers sit, kneel and pray. The Church was inaugurated on Christmas Day, 1979, by Lt. Gen. Fazl-e-Haq, the then Governor of KPK Province and the Archbishop of Pakistan.

The Church, so far, has served for 40 years and hopefully will continue for many more years to fulfill the religious needs and ceremonies of my Christian brothers and sisters, whom I deeply revere and cherish.

My only regret is that my beloved father Mohammad Said Khan, to whom I had shown its drawings, did not live long enough to see the completed building. Father was an outstanding civil engineer who obtained his degree from the University of Nottingham in 1932, and had designed many lovely and useful buildings in his working career starting in British India and culminating in Pakistan. He had passed away a year before in July 1978 leaving a deep void in my heart, which I suppose is felt by every son and daughter whose father "departs" upon his final journey."

I didn't even know that all the construction material I climbed over were for my Uncle's design.

LESSONS OF SERVICE

In Peshawar, strong female role models surrounded me not only at school but also at home. My mom's cousin Samina was a practicing psychologist at the local hospital. My Aunt Aysha ran a clothing boutique out of our house, catering to the fashions of the day. My grandma Sajeela was a powerhouse in serving the community for special needs children. For over fifty years, she raised money for mentally and physically handicapped children in Pakistan. And at the young age of ninety-three, she was still going strong with her love for her charities. I am proud of my grandma, and these acts gave me bragging rights on how a powerful woman lives.

Since salvation is not guaranteed for a Muslim, we must earn our fate in the next life through our deeds and God's grace.

My grandmother was always stressing character. She was proud of our family reputation and wanted us to understand our behavior was part of her legacy. Her specialty was giving the specific care that each child needed for a better life. I would often come home from school to a house full of my grandmother's friends and associates. My grandmother would be running a fundraiser or giving speeches on the importance of taking care of special needs children. She even raised enough money to rent an old city bus that would drive around the city to pick up children who did not have access to transportation. Her goal was to have the special needs children make handicrafts that would develop their gross motor skills, which her center then sold to raise money or donated to organizations for the poor. My grandmother's heart was attached to seeing these children as functional members of society.

Another strong Muslim woman in my circle of influence was Dr. Jinnah, a gynecologist who lived across the street from our house. She was a product of a culture that pushes women to succeed, and becoming a doctor shows dedication and intelligence. We could see a steady stream of cars pull up to her gate, as she ran her medical practice from her home. To me, Dr. Jinnah represented the strong educational foundation of Islam—a woman who was supporting her family and who valued her time with her family by being available in her home most of the day. Many times, Dr. Jinnah sent us leftover food from the celebrations of her patients who had just had babies. Giving to your neighbors is an important concept in Islam, and Dr. Jinnah was getting her good deeds from both healing the sick and contributing to her neighbors. Dr. Jinnah also valued my grandmother's charity work. She supported my grandmother with donations for her fundraisers. Furthermore, she told her friends of the work my grandmother was doing, and many of the doctors volunteered free medical care to the special needs kids.

While the nuns were making an impact by teaching young girls, my grandmother was making a difference with special needs children. Muslims are drilled to give. Charity is crucial to salvation since each act on Earth will be weighed on a divine scale, and having more good deeds means going to heaven while more bad deeds means we are closer to hell. Once we die, our book of deeds is closed, except for three special types of continuation. In Islam, we can earn good deeds after we die by leaving a legacy that continues to help our fellow human beings after we are gone. The first way to have good deeds after we die is by raising amazing children who follow God and do good deeds. Leaving the legacy of good children will add to the good deeds of the parents. The second reason we could have more good deeds is knowledge—for example, writing a book of knowledge that will benefit others while we are on Earth and also after we have passed. The third way is if we created a house of God or hospital where people still receive benefits from our services, then those good deeds will still be recorded in our individual book after we die. In raising good children and grandchildren, my grandmother's book of deeds will still grow after she is gone.

For example, if I donated money to a hospital and my donation were enough to create one room, then for every person that benefitted from that particular room in the hospital, I would receive credits in my book of deeds. And if that room was still around fifty years after I died, I would receive the deeds for fifty years after I died. These principles in Islam are global and universal. Therefore, according to the teachings of Islam, if a Christian builds a church, then that person will receive good deeds from that church in this life and the next life. If a Jew writes a book that helps people, then the Jewish author will receive good deeds every time that knowledge benefits another person. Regardless of our labels—Muslim, Christian, Jewish, Buddhist, Hindu, agnostic, tribal, or whatever label one prefers—it is the way we live our lives that counts.

* * *

When I returned to the United States after junior high school in Pakistan, my dad wanted continued excellence for my sisters and me. My parents had moved from Denver to Tulsa, Oklahoma. It was understood that private schools there offered a better education than the local public schools, so my parents started looking at private schools in the city. We found a private Catholic school, about forty minutes from our home. I did not like the school because the long ride resulted less sleep in the morning and less free time in the afternoon. In Pakistan, I had few distractions. We had only one television channel that came on at four in the evening. In the US, we had four television channels that were on all day and evening. I was a teenager and was sure I knew more than everyone. I wanted to eat junk food, sleep, and watch TV. My parents had other plans.

Tulsa was not embracing diversity at the level of the people in Peshawar. I was "different" from the other girls, and they made sure I knew that the school preferred girls from a Catholic faith. They were not flexible with my needs or willing to provide religious considerations. Because of the Catholic curriculum, I was required to attend mass twice a week, and learning Christian theology in religion class took up an elective every year. In this high school I only had seven class options each year. With the Catholic faith taking up my electives, I was not able to fit in many other classes such as advanced math. Furthermore, I had a strong academic background from my school in Pakistan so I ended up skipping ninth grade.

Two years later, I was a rising high school senior who had not taken trigonometry or calculus. The all girls' Catholic school did not stress math skills. In order to get the higher-level math classes, I would need to go to the all boys' school for math period. This school was about four blocks away and would require me walking to and from math class alone. Most people would see this as a problem, but not my dad. He decided to take me out of the private Catholic school and go back to our local public school where they offered many higher-level math courses.

After all, my dad was an engineer and math was easy for him. He told me that calculus was easy and that I could take calculus and trigonometry together. So he went to our public high school, Union High, and spoke with the administrators and math teachers. He convinced them that I was capable of taking both classes simultaneously. My dad even got the textbook for the trigonometry class. He decided he would tutor me.

Spending part of the summer learning math sounded awful. It was. But my dad told me that I needed to know some basic trigonometry so that I would understand calculus. So, for the entire month of August in 1982, my dad would come home from a long day of work and we would sit at the kitchen table for two or three hours while he taught me trigonometry. My dad didn't say much and would just sit there while I tried to solve the problems. I would look at the paper, then I would look at his face; it was totally expressionless. My dad showed no emotion. He never raised his voice or got angry. The only time his face changed was when he would laugh. There was not much laughter during trig lessons. But I knew all of his looks. And this one meant the answer is not right. If the answer were correct, we would have seamlessly moved on to the next problem. So I clicked my mechanical pencil for more lead and took another shot. Hopefully he would breathe a sigh of relief and we could move to another section.

My dad did not believe in calculators, he believed in using your head. He said that I could not get into a good engineering college if I depended on a machine. I learned to interpolate and see the math in my head. I began to trust myself. This time with my dad was priceless, not to mention learning that triangles, sines, cosines, tangents, and using trigonometry tables could be mastered in four weeks. Three days later, I started my senior year. I took trigonometry in the morning and calculus in afternoon. I was able to use all the stuff my dad taught me. I was better than most of the other students and was even selected to go to the gifted and talented program.

His confidence in my abilities—and dedication to my education—absolutely got me to where I am today. As a Muslim father, he knew that my education, and that of my sisters, was of utmost importance—and he unreservedly supported us in every way he could.

Chapter 5

ISLAM AND WOMEN

"There is no veil between the prayer of the oppressed
and God."
[God answers the prayers of those who are oppressed
therefore do not oppress another soul.]
"Beware of being cursed."
[Do not oppress someone or you may be harmed by
their prayers.]

Prophet Muhammad

While attending Catholic schools for most of junior high and high school, and living in the Bible belt in Oklahoma, I was given many opportunities to change religions. Well-meaning friends and even some strangers wanted to save me from a philosophy they thought oppressed women. Other believers felt that only they knew the path to salvation, and since I was not on their path, I was doomed. With all these opportunities to convert, I did not budge. I would tell my potential saviors what the Quran said, and they had no rebuttal. I have not seen a philosophy that is more respectful to women than the Quran and the example set by Prophet Muhammad (pbuh).

I had pondered these questions for myself in first grade when I compared the two different ways of living in Islam and Catholicism. I selected the best from both paths. I am not an overly emotional person. I am a master at math, science, or logic, and I can process large and varied amounts of data quickly and effectively. I continue to choose Islam because Muslim women have the most rights and are treated with respect. This religious message resonated with my values and family history. My grandmother, mom, and aunts were all examples of balancing financial independence while making an impact on the quality of their communities. They honored their marriages and their children. I grew up with the attitude that women are valuable. But somehow the TV shows, magazines, and even some of my teachers in the United States challenged these freedoms for women. The message I was getting was that women were not as important as men because a woman's impact was not as significant as a man's.

At Sunday school at Tulsa's Islamic Center, we were taught some Islamic history and religious practices such as praying. Since we had moved from Denver, Ms. Syed was replaced by my grandmother Sajeela as our teacher. We had lessons on the life of Prophet Muhammad (pbuh). I had heard the story before, but parts of the story troubled me. For example, Muhammad's (pbuh) father died before he was born, and his mother died when he was just six years old. It seemed so hard to be an orphan at such a young age. Each time I would hear this story, I felt so sad about all of his early tragedies. But this time, my maternal grandmother taught us the rights of women under shariah. I knew that she was strong and was a leader, but I did not know where she found that strength. In 1981, I only had one grandparent. My grandmother, Sajeela, still worked and travelled across the ocean like an energetic teenager. I felt like mentally and physically we were the same age. I lovingly called her Granny and so did most of my friends both in the States and in Pakistan. Her peers in their sixties enjoyed sitting at home, but Granny knew she still had dreams to live. Single and full of energy, she stayed with us for the summer months in both Denver and Tulsa and headed back to Pakistan to operate her charities for the remainder of the year. My grandmother taught me at our Sunday school class how my religion supported me, personally, as a woman.

I was half day-dreaming and half listening to my grandmother one fall morning in our little classroom. I was pro-women. And I got teased for it. There were so many subtle comments made in society that angered me. A key experience was when a stranger learned that a teenage girl like myself excelled in math. This scenario resulted in a puzzled look or a sarcastic comment. I grew up with the debate about the Equal Rights Amendment while I was in elementary school. I watched the struggle of women for equal pay and the fading of the hopeful glow when the ERA failed get state ratification in 1979. I didn't know what my "political" views were, but at least I knew where I stood as a woman in Islam, and I was certain God loved women. In junior high school I watched the nuns teach and pray. They were strongly committed to providing the girls studying in the convent with an education to support them. Then in high school, I watched my mom work and support our family when my dad lost his job. The pro-woman views I held came from the women I knew that wanted to make a social impact. I remembered my grandmother's loving and powerful voice again. Sunday school was still in session. Years later, these stories would define my worldviews and how I raised my own children.

We didn't have textbooks but flimsy paper manuals. My grandmother was teaching from the "Life of Muhammad," manual one. This was our Sunday school manual, printed pages of eight-by-eleven inch paper with a light blue cardstock cover. There were fifteen manuals total, each with a different color cover to tell them apart. We were assigned reading in this book the previous week, but I had been too busy jumping on the trampoline while listening to REO Speedwagon and playing with my friends to complete Sunday school homework. We were at the part that described the society at the time of the Birth of the Prophet (pbuh). Seventh century Arabia sounded horrible, and I felt the information was irrelevant during my days in high school. I had nothing in common with these people from centuries long ago. My parents forced me to attend

Sunday school, and it had no relevance to me. I did not like this story because I knew what would happen to his parents and how meanly the Prophet (pbuh) would be treated, but once again the story of Muhammad (pbuh) reentered my life. My grandmother asked each of us stand and read a paragraph or two. There were eight students in the class and we each had a manual. My grandmother began with the birth and early years of the story of Prophet Muhammad (pbuh). Although the story was somewhat fascinating, I felt I had heard it so often that I knew it well, and I tuned out.

Before the birth of Prophet Muhammad (pbuh), Arabia was a highly male-dominated, patriarchal, and unjust society built on male bravado, where men were considered better than women. Women had few rights. Many men were ashamed when they had a baby girl. Girls were considered a burden because they could not fight and usually did not earn income, whereas having a son would be helpful financially since the economy was based on herding animals and agriculture. In this society, when a girl was born, they were disappointed. However, one man, Mohammad (pbuh), took a stand for women and came up with a religion that restructured the entire belief system toward women. It occurred to me for the first time that I, too, could take a stand like Muhammad (pbuh): Girls are good at math. My new mission was born. Prophet Muhammad (pbuh) challenged his peers on the belief that women did not have value. I would set the example that women were technical giants. My mind drifted again. I had physics homework about projectile motion and all the tasks, such as lots of reading awaiting me when I got home. I would start by showing the power of a high school girl at rocking physics.

My sister Saima was next to my grandmother, and it was time for her to read from the book, and the next section described how Prophet Muhammad (pbuh) implemented the changes. Human rights in Islam started with infant girls. In order for women to have power, the society needed to be taught that even a baby girl has rights. Prophet Muhammad (pbuh) began his fight for women by opposing the practice of female infanticide. He narrated the following: "If anyone has a female child and does not bury her alive, or slight her, or prefer his male children to her, God will grant them paradise." While these acts sound normal or mundane in the twenty-first century, in a patriarchal desert society in the seventh century, these ideas were shocking.

Even though the Prophet was an orphan, grew up in a male-dominated society, and had no other example to follow, he championed the rights of women, equating treating girls well to receiving God's love. Across the Mediterranean Sea, our Catholic friends in this era were determining whether women even had a soul, but the Quran clearly stated that women, even tiny infant girls, did in fact have souls. My grandmother interjected while my sister was reading. She summed up the paragraph by saying all women have the right to being treated as a gift from our Creator.

My sister continued reading the next paragraph. In a few short years, the Prophet (pbuh) changed the status of women in his city by successfully challenging the practices and customs that mistreated women. This example of a man supporting rights for all women spread throughout Arabia and then around the globe. In the twenty-three short years that the Quran was revealed, Islam shifted the perception of women from being a "burden," who were considered worthless as property or livestock, to possessing not only the same rights as men but in some cases more rights than men. Such a standard for the high treatment of women had not been seen anywhere in the world until this time. Furthermore, financial rights for women had been changed to having the same respect and rights of men. The Quran made it clear that being a girl is not a crime and no one can punish a daughter based on gender. These messages that I learned in Sunday school captivated my heart. I quit making funny faces at my sister and began to pay attention.

Granny explained that the lesson of the story shows that great change can be brought in a short amount of time. In two short decades, Muhammad (pbuh) changed social views on both slaves and women. The technique was not to focus on changing minds but changing hearts. For example, every bad deed could be repented by freeing a slave. So the Arabs of the seventh century started associating good acts with freeing slaves. Furthermore, the best way to get to heaven was to obey our mothers and honor our wives. I was thinking that like those Arabs, I, too, needed a change of heart.

We were in a transition as a family. My father's amazing job as an engineer had disappeared overnight. At the beginning of the school year, my mom had come into my room early one morning and said, "I don't want you to worry, but Dad lost his job." My heart sank. I was supposed to go to the amusement park with my friends but could not even think of spending money or having fun. My mom put her hand on my head. She looked into my eyes and repeated, "Don't worry." She handed me a twenty dollar bill. That was enough for admission and some food. I told her that I did not really want to go. My mom said we already had plans and things would be okay.

I got dressed for the amusement park. I spoke to Saima, and we both decided to go but only pay for admission. I was shaken by the news of my father's job and did not enjoy the park at all. We were hungry but did not eat a funnel cake or have the sandwiches. There was no amusement this time at the park. I came home and gave my mom the change. She said, "Didn't you buy anything?" I said, "No, Mom, but we had a great time."

For the next year we cut back on all our expenses. My mom's fun side jobs of importing textiles from Pakistan and doing social work became our only income. She was the main breadwinner and paid all the bills. My grandmother was a powerhouse that raised a daughter who knew how to rise to a challenge. The examples from Sunday school of seventh century Arabia were influencing our lives. The trend that started in Mecca of honoring women was woven through all the generations that came before me, and I witnessed these women's convictions in my heart. My great-grandfather had insisted that all three of his daughters go to college, including my Granny Sajeela. My grandmother then sent my mom to the same schools she attended. Now the power of an educated mom with a job paid for our house, groceries, and living expenses. Mom acted as the glue keeping our family going.

Life at home was stressful. My father was often away taking odd engineering jobs with old colleagues in other states. We did not see him for months. He called every night, and we spoke on the phone. His voice was always upbeat. His favorite subject was my grades. "How is physics class?" he would ask. "What are you doing in math?" He was far away but still an active force in our lives. I never brought up the subject of college or college essays. Applying to schools meant admission fees and tuition, so I kept those worries to myself. My biggest doubt was whether I could even attend a university or if I needed to live at home and work my way through community college. Yes, education was a family tradition, but I knew that engineering school required resources. Our savings were dwindling. Everything my mom earned was spent as soon as it came in. My grandmother postponed her trip back to Pakistan to stay with my mom and the three of us. Now she also taught us at Sunday school as a volunteer.

Week after week we attended classes at the mosque. My grandmother had a solid faith. Our religion supported her through the hard times of her life. Back at the little boardroom that was our classroom, we returned to studying seventh century Arabia. I stood up; it was my turn to read the story of Prophet Muhammad's (pbuh) life. I started the section on the changes in the status of women and their impact on the society. The shift in the Arabian continent was quick and swift: In twenty-three years, the society totally changed. What was his secret weapon? Kindness. The Prophet had a gift for changing hearts. He preached to his followers that a wife had rights over her husband. Also, women became full members of society with the right to vote and hold office. Within this short period of time, women were allowed to own property, initiate divorce, have an inheritance, vote, and were given the respect and honor they deserve.

As the words were flowing out of my mouth, my soul stirred with these quick and deep changes. I could do that with my life! I was blessed with a mom that kept the roof over our heads, but now I, as an empowered sixteen-year-old, could contribute financially by earning money for college! I would not only excel at my physics homework, but I was determined to earn great test scores and apply for scholarships. I could also get the respect and honors I deserved, echoing the fates of those seventh century Muslim women.

Sunday school ended with snacks. My favorite were the chocolate-covered Little Debbie treats. My mom would let us bring cookies or brownies, but other moms would send in traditional samosa, pastry filled with potatoes and peas. I was snacking on orange juice and chocolate-covered cake. I wanted to implement the lessons and finance my college endeavors. The stories we read seemed ancient but they were also applying to my current situation. I was in control of my destiny and had the power to make choices that shaped my future. I didn't need my dad to pay for my college. Even at sixteen, I somehow knew I was going to be okay. We said our afternoon prayers and left Sunday school. I prayed for my dad to find a good job and for my mom to not be too stressed with the extra hours she was working. I also gave thanks to the Prophet (pbuh) for showing me a new way in the twentieth century.

As soon as I left Sunday school, I returned to my world of friends, school, homework, my trampoline, and sewing. I considered myself petite and needed to adjust most of my store-bought clothes. I learned to sew as a necessity to have basic fitting clothes. For school, I called my best friend, Cindy, and we completed our homework together over the phone. I was careful because using the phone would give all potential callers a busy signal. I did not want my mom to pick up the other line and tell me to get off the phone. I quickly told Cindy the problems I had solutions to and she told me about the ones she had solved. We both had big dreams of being engineers. I knew that Cindy was working hard to get into a good school. I realized that my math skills were great but my writing needed work. My mom found a tutor for English class. School all week, English tutor on Saturday, and I was back to the mosque on Sunday for religious school again.

Islam promotes community service and education. Just like the small beginning in Denver, my parents brought together the local Muslim immigrant families. Groups are efficient and began to organize celebrations for religious events. As word spread about the Muslim community, we would organize prayers at homes of the families or someone with a business would offer a conference room. Eventually our community grew and raised funds for a small building. The new Islamic center in Tulsa had started with a handful of families. Most of the families were from Pakistan and had school-aged kids. In our teen class there were girls from three families, and even with only seven people, we had two girls named Saima and two girls named Irum.

Our class was held in the small boardroom next to the prayer hall where they read the Quran. I was finishing the Quran in Arabic. My speed was slow because I had learned to read and write the Arabic alphabet at the age of eleven. While English is read from left to right, Arabic is written from the right side of the page to the left side of the page. My grandmother said that writing should be in the direction of the heart. My practice in the Arabic script was limited to my two years of junior high in Peshawar, Pakistan, and the current Sunday school classes. I needed practice to master the words and their meanings. In our culture it is customary to learn to read the Quran in Arabic and not focus on translations. The original language kept a beautiful rhyme and meter. My poor reading skills made this poetic book sound awful. Even with no Arabic talent, I would keep reading the Quran until I had finished all thirty chapters in Arabic.

When I read the entire book for the first time, both granny and my aunt helped me pronounce the words correctly. My grandmother read with me to watch for errors and explain the Arabic grammar system. Some of the other girls were just learning to read Arabic in high school. After the Quran we were back to the large blue manual on the life of Prophet Muhammad (pbuh), and in Pakistani education style, we stood up, read a paragraph, and then had a group discussion. The first Saima, my sister, would read, than the first Irum, then I read, then Nabeela, followed by the other Saima and the other Irum. The topic had shifted from the rights of infant girls to finances and voting. I still had all my Catholic religious training from the nuns fresh from my convent education. Irum, Nabeela, my sister, and I had attended private Catholic schools. I was constantly comparing the two religions to determine how my Christian friends' views were similar to mine.

These were my weekend friends. During the weekdays, I was at school and immersed in Tulsa teenage culture, and on the weekends, I was an immigrant learning about my faith. Monday through Friday consisted of jeans and a T-shirt while weekend parties were *shalwar kameese* and community dinners. The Irums, the Saimas, and I considered ourselves mutants. We looked like Pakistani immigrants, acted like US teenagers, and thought like neither. The Irums, Saimas and I considered ourselves as transcontinental mutants. I liked relaxing on weekends, where I could construct sentences using both Urdu and English and everyone still understood me. All of us complained about how our parents made us study another culture and our religion. The kids at school were going out, attending football games, and playing sports. By Sunday morning, we all were back in the mosques learning about our faith.

On this Sunday, my sister Saima went first and started reading a story of social justice at the beginning of Islam. The story was set in the town of Mecca again. I liked that in the story a woman challenged a Caliph, or local ruler. I was also a rebel. I liked this lady. In Islamic Law, the human rights of a woman are considered equal to men. Regardless if a man or a woman committed a crime, the punishment was the same. Men were just as responsible for their actions and were not allowed to side-step the law. The Caliph was setting limits on how much money a woman could receive from her husband. The woman challenged the Caliphate in the court and said, "How do you have rights to limit my finances when God did not limit my finances?" The ruling Caliph admitted that he was wrong and the woman was right. My grandmother taught us the lesson of the story. We are here to help give voices to the voiceless and no matter how important we think we are, if we are wrong, admit it. If our rights as women are being challenged, then we need to speak up to share our perspective. My grandma was sharing her gems of wisdom with her students. Theses nuggets equipped me to lead and mentor other women to stand up for their needs. God did not limit our financial rights, and no one else was allowed to suppress us financially.

The core of the lesson was all about using our voices as Muslim women. We began to research the Quran for support verses on women and their finances. Each of us agreed to find two verses that showed how the Quran financially liberated women. I located a verse that had nothing to do with the topic. I was reading the book in Arabic but not spending too much time on the English translation. I saw this verse and asked my grandma, "Is this true?" The Surah was about allegiance, and verse twelve said, "O Prophet! Whenever believing women come unto thee to pledge their allegiance to thee . . . then accept their pledge of allegiance." "Granny," I said, "accepting a pledge of allegiance to a leader is the same as a vote." Without a pause my grandmother began another revelation: Muslim women have enjoyed the right to vote since the year 620 AD.

American women suffragettes had gotten the vote fourteen centuries later. I read about the struggle of the movement and the discrimination the suffragettes faced. A vote is a pledge of allegiance to a leader. In many cultures, women had to fight for the right to speak in the political process. For me it was a relief to know that God knew I was capable in both religious matters and politics and had the right to share my thoughts. My grandmother had led me to the section in the Quran in which a woman pledges her allegiance, as in this case to the Prophet (pbuh), that the leader should accept the pledge. We believe that the verse is a command from God, the Lord of the Universe, an absolute ruling. I felt complete. I also realized that unlike the word of God, the nineteenth amendment to a constitution could be changed. The possibility existed that sometime in the future, an amendment to the United States constitution could remove the rights of women to vote.

The topic had started a spirited discussion in our group of seven. The two Irums were debating. Yes, there are religious rights that we are given in the Quran, but many of the Muslim countries were not practicing the religion as taught. The older Irum stated that this was because of some corruption in the civil government and social issues. The other Irum argued that all religions are ideal systems and not practiced as they are preached. I commented that for us as Muslim women, we had the example of society in Arabia at the time of the Prophet and that we needed to model that behavior. I continued that our cultural and religious boundaries had blended. Some of the actions that I felt were for religion were actually cultural biases from South Asia.

I was glad that I was learning what was and was not in the Quran. It was 1981, Ronald Reagan was our new President, and the Iran hostage crisis was wrapping up. My religion was being attacked in the news, by my teachers, and by my non-Muslim friends. So many times I had questioned the religious practices in Islam. It seemed that everyone around me hated me and my religion due to all the stories on the news. I needed real answers to why I was different and the answer given by most Muslim adults was that the Quran said so. My eyes opened. I had my own experience of what the Quran actually taught. I could respond to the questions and comments about Islam being violent or anti-women. I had the data I needed from Sunday school to back up my responses.

The following week, we continued our discussion of women and finances. The two Irums were still not satisfied with the manual or the discussion so far. They continued to debate on the merits of whether women should contribute financially to a household. After all if they can vote, then women can make all of their own financial decisions. One of the Irum's mom worked and the other Irum's mom stayed at home. We lived in the homogeneous society of Tulsa in a society of traditional Midwestern values. Some of our Sunday school discussions were challenging the status quo of the power of women in any community. We were trying to fit into the melting pot without melting our identity. Anyone different was vilified, and now with the tensions with Iran and the US, we noticed that we were not completely accepted. We understood our religious roles of education and participation in the political process, but implementing them in our daily lives was still unclear. The debates continued until our class ended. Another day of Sunday school ending with snacks of brownies, hot tea with milk, samosas, and the afternoon prayers.

The younger Irum's father attended a conference of Muslim leaders in Chicago. He had met a new scholar and invited Imam Khalid to come to our mosque. *Imam* means a religious leader or a scholar on Islam. On Friday night, we were told that we could not go to the school football game but instead had to go to a lecture at the mosque. Not my idea of a great Friday night, no friends and no watching TV, but more religious classes. We returned from school and dressed up with scarfs for a religious lecture. My grandmother had made my favorite dish, *haleem*, a combination of lentils and beef that has been slow cooked for over eight hours. I could smell the food when I entered my house. Along with the lecture from Imam Khalid, a potluck dinner was hosted at the mosque. As soon as my mom arrived from work, we piled in the car and went to mosque for a second time this week. I stared out the car window, thinking about all the fun my friends were having.

Our community was small but growing. The adults mingled and conversed while the kids raced around playing indoor tag. The potluck reminded me of the good ol' days of elementary school with potlucks in the mosque in Denver. We had food from all over the Muslim world, from Indonesian beef satay to the Moroccan chicken basilla. A small line of people waited to meet with Imam Khalid. Khalid was a short, stocky man with jet black hair and a neatly trimmed beard. He was dressed in the traditional long white robe or *thawb*. He also wore the traditional prayer cap and was pleasantly talking to the individuals about his work.

I finished dinner and went to sit on the side of the main mosque with my friends. We were all commiserating about all the other more interesting activities we could have done on a Friday night. However, we were in the Tulsa Islamic Center getting another class after spending six hours that day in school. Then I discovered his lecture was on motherhood in Islam. I was sixteen and had no interest in being a mother, but there was no escape. We drove one car here, and my mom had the keys. I looked at my watch and hoped this would be short. Imam Khalid slowly walked to the front of the room and took a seat. He lifted the microphone, and the feedback from the mike filled the room. Everyone stopped talking to see what had happened.

Khalid started with a recitation from the Quran followed by a short prayer of blessing in Arabic. He then thanked Irum's dad for inviting him to the gathering. Khalid took a sip of water and began the lecture about the verse of Quran he had recited. The Quran has a very high regard for parents. As with other traditions, the position of parent has a high degree of respect, and with age comes honor. Muslims are taught to honor the generations that have taken care of them. Khalid paused and took another sip of water. Out of the corner of my eye I saw my mom looking at me. I guess she thought we needed to add more respect for parents to our teenage manners. Khalid recited another verse in Arabic. The translation is, "The Lord has decreed that you worship none but God, and that you be kind to your parents. Whether one or both of them live to old age, say not a word of contempt nor repel them, but address them in terms of honor. And out of kindness, lower to them the wing of humility, and say: 'My Lord bestow on them Your Mercy even as they cherished me in childhood'" (Quran 17:23-24).

In Islam, it is not appropriate to talk back to your parents, even if they are wrong. This verse got me thinking. With all the financial stress in the house, I had not been patient with my mom. There were so many things I wanted to do including joining the basketball team. Since this activity required extra driving for her, she had to say no. I was still upset she had declined. I really wanted to be on the basketball team, but now I thought about it from my mom's viewpoint. Khalid had moved from examples from the Quran to the sayings of Prophet Muhammad (pbuh). A famous story was being told, famous because even I recognized the story immediately. A man came and asked the Prophet, "Oh Messenger of God, who is the person who has the greatest right on me with regard to kindness and attention?" The Prophet replied, "Your mother." The man persisted, "And then who?" The Prophet replied, "Your mother." The man asked for the third time, "And then who?" The Prophet replied, "Your mother." The man asked for the fourth time, "And then who?" The Prophet replied, "Your father." In another example, a young man wanted to join the fighting forces to serve Arabia and receive the reward of paradise. The Prophet advised him to serve his mother instead. "Paradise lies at the feet of your mother," the Prophet explained.

I loved this story. It aligned with my female power personality. After listening to Khalid, I decided to be more considerate about my mom's feelings. Maybe I could help a little more around the house, like mowing the lawn. I could be more supportive on what school activities I wanted. I knew that God wanted me to respect and honor my mom even when we did not see eye to eye. Next personal challenge: Go easy on mom.

Khalid spoke about the role of a woman as a wife. First, Islamic shariah, or Islamic way of living, uplifts women in marriage. In Islam, marriage is a contractual agreement, not a transfer of property. I was confused. What was the difference? I wanted to know my rights in marriage, but I had a long day at school and was getting tired. The lecture continued that in some cultures, a woman was a transfer of property and could be given to her father-in-law or brother-in-law. However, our faith taught that a woman was a full partner with all the rights that her husband had. Khalid began to list the rights of women in Islam such as the right to reject a marriage proposal, to own property, to keep her inheritance, and to initiate a divorce. He explained that this view of woman is different from some of the western customs where women were still fighting for basic rights. Some countries did not give women political rights until the nineteenth or twentieth century. He cited an example from Europe where the wife would be transferred as part of the estate in the case of a husband or father's death. He also cited the examples in the United States where women did not receive equal pay as their male counterparts.

His comments invoked memories of the Jane Austen books I had read in English class. Her characters were also striving for basic rights such as not being kicked out of their house when their husband died. The family home would legally and automatically be transferred to the deceased husband's brother or male heir. I was surprised at the amount of resistance women still faced. My mom came home frustrated because the bank would not give her a loan for her business without my dad's signature. The global rights of women was a passion of my grandmother's, and now it was part of my deep spiritual inheritance. I looked across the room at two independent women that kept our family intact while my dad's career underwent a transition. The more strength each family member has, the stronger the family. I was really proud of my family.

Khalid continued to the concept of the wedding gift in Islam, which is a divorce deterrent called the *Haq Mahr*. I had been challenged in school that in Islam, men buy their wife. I never understood those comments since all the Muslim weddings I had attended were between two people who loved and respected each other. The groom may give the bride a wedding gift at the time of their marriage, known as *Haq Mahr*. With a *Haq Mahr* a woman has financial independence and the means to make her own financial choices. If the groom decides to divorce the bride, he gives up the rights to *Haq Mahr* and the bride gets to keep the money. However, if the bride initiates the divorce, she has to pay back the *Haq*

Mahr. This *Haq Mahr* is a built-in financial deterrent to divorce so that the party that initiates a divorce receives a financial penalty for initiating their divorce. If the decision is mutual, the *Haq Mahr* may be split in half between each party.

The two Irums and the two Saimas joked about snagging a rich guy with a nice big wedding gift so they could go shopping. As I played with my watch, my girlfriends were whispering about getting big *Haq Mahr* and buying lots of clothes. If our parents knew we were talking during the lecture we would get in trouble. My mom was focused on the lecture, so she didn't notice us talking. I looked over at my grandmother, who was taking notes. I guess we would be discussing Khalid's lecture in our next Sunday school class. It was almost time to pray. I knew the lecture was wrapping up. The younger kids were restless. One little boy was crying. It had been a long day for everyone.

Imam Khalid completed his presentation with two Islamic laws about the rights of women and children. He said that if a man divorced his wife while she is nursing their child, he is required to pay her the fair market value of that breast milk since the child is the father's financial responsibility. In the Quran, all financial responsibility for a woman is either on her husband or father. In some cases other male family members may have some financial responsibility if the father or husband cannot provide for her. However, this does not mean that women cannot work. Women can work, and if they do, anything they earn is for themselves (not shared for the family). However, if they choose to use their money to help the family, they may, but they are not obligated to work to support the family.

According to Islamic shariah, everything I personally earn is mine and one half of everything my husband earns also belongs to me. Everything I personally inherit is mine and also one half of my husband's inheritance also belongs to me. On top of that, I am not financially responsible for the bills—that financial responsibility is for my husband along with the financial responsibility of our children. For these reasons, the Quran says that men have a degree of financial responsibility above women. Personally, I love it! These rules suited my personality and were much better than what the state of Oklahoma was offering women at that time. I knew a couple of women at the Islamic center who had gotten divorced and were not treated well by the courts. I hoped that US law would catch up on the rights of women soon.

At the end of the lecture, Irum's dad took the seven of us to meet Imam Khalid. Irum's father, Zahid, was talking about the Sunday school program and how much the mosque had grown. I asked Imam Khalid if women were really that special in Islam. Imam Khalid immediately dropped his eyes. A man dropping his gaze to the floor is a sign of respect for the woman he is speaking to. Even as a teenage girl in the presence of a well-known and celebrated leader, I was taught that I was respected by men.

Imam Khalid's remarks foreshadowed the next election in Pakistan. Little did I know, in five years, Benazir Bhutto would be elected as the first female Prime Minister of Pakistan. Even though Geraldine Ferraro had recently lost in her attempt to become the United States' first female Vice President, he was showing me that women had much to offer in both countries as future leaders.

Chapter 6

CHALLENGED

My struggle in school had always been English class; being bilingual, my vocabulary was not as good as the other kids'. In high school, God added to that struggle with Ms. Parks. Ms. Parks was a petite, older woman, in her mid-fifties, with two daughters at our school. Her older daughter, Sara, was in tenth grade with me, and her younger daughter, Claire, was in eighth grade with my sister Saima. Ms. Parks had reading glasses on the tip of her nose, a nasally voice that made it seem like she was always complaining, and perfectly sprayed salt-and-pepper hair with a pronounced white streak in the front. She was impeccably dressed in her 1980s suits, high-heeled pumps, and long, red nails. She sat at the front of the classroom behind a big, wooden desk filled with books. Behind her desk was a chalkboard, and over the chalkboard hung a painting of the last supper. The first day of class she introduced us to Chaucer. I still haven't figured out *The Canterbury Tales*.

Ms. Parks was Catholic and made it clear that she did not like Protestants and considered them outside of true Christianity. She was not sure how to classify me. After *The Canterbury Tales,* we wrote several papers in class.

I struggled with writing and was constantly counting words to make the word count on an essay. One day before Thanksgiving break, she told us in her nasal tone, "I want you to write a paper on a saint." Granted, at a Catholic high school with a chapel and nuns, religion could enter any class, even English. I was immersed in the Christian belief system, including religion class, going to mass twice a week, and now I had to write a paper on saints. Ms. Parks briefly explained that we could select any saint who inspired us. I asked her what a saint was. Ms. Parks snapped back, "You should know by now." She had a temper and snapped easily, so the students had nicknamed her Sparky.

I went home thinking about Catholic saints. I did not know any but I needed an A in her class. I wanted to have some background information about a Catholic saint. I thought if I could use someone that was also in the Quran, it would be easier to write this paper. On the school grounds near the entrance of the parking lot was a chapel for mass. In front of the chapel was a small, concrete circular sidewalk with a statue. As I walked out of school that day, I passed the white marble statue of Mary, mother of Jesus (pbuh). A light bulb went off in my head. I knew Mary from the Quran and I loved Mary. Could Mary be a saint? I thought I'd ask Ms. Parks the next day.

I came to English early and patiently stood by her desk. "Yes?" she asked in her annoyed, nasal tone. I asked, "Ms. Parks, could I do my saint paper on Mary?" She gasped! She started fanning herself with her hand and exclaimed, "You want to write a paper on the mother of God?" I replied, "Well, Mary isn't the mother of God." Clearly this was the wrong answer. Ms. Parks went sparky on me. She explained the truth about Mary, her truth, the only real truth which corresponded to her beliefs. I also respected Mary but had a different perspective than Ms. Parks. Do I challenge Sparky or concede for an A? I get demotivated when I have to hold my tongue to appease someone else. I explained to her that Mary was honored in the Quran and since I knew a bit about her life, I thought it would give me an edge on my paper.

Ms. Parks was upset. She said that there was no way could I write about the mother of God; I was not qualified and with my beliefs I never would be. She also said the Quran knew nothing about Mary. I wanted to ask if she had even read the Quran—now I was getting sparky! Ms. Parks had a way of letting me know I was the outsider. I just wanted to belong and be accepted the way I am. But, too scared to confront a teacher, I decided to hold my tongue. I didn't mean to agitate her so I offered to do my paper on Eve instead. Ms. Parks calmed down but agreed. She admitted that since I did not know any saints, I could write about Eve. I was happy—I managed to switch from the mother of Jesus to the mother of humanity.

Being at a Catholic high school, Bibles were everywhere and easy to find. I went to her daughter Sara Parks for help; I wanted the official Parks family point of view. Sara led me to the Book of Genesis to get the Biblical version of Adam and Eve. I was really surprised by the story about Eve falling for temptation by Satan and being the first sinner. The Book of Genesis talked about Eve eating the forbidden fruit and then offering the fruit to Adam. Not only had Eve sinned but she had also helped Adam to sin, so it was all Eve's fault. I wondered if that was really true or just written from a male viewpoint. Sara also mentioned that because Eve had Adam eat the apple, women were to birth children in pain. Sara explained that this was the original sin and that since I did not accept Christ as my savior, I would not be forgiven. I was destined to hell for eternity. I had been told I was going to hell before, and it did not feel good this time hearing it from Sara.

I was back to being frustrated. Why was I responsible for something I had no control over, such as the original sin? I didn't know if I wanted kids—after all, I was only fourteen—but I didn't want to have to bear children in pain and carry the burden of a child as a punishment. I did not like being blamed for tempting men. After all, Eve was the mother of humanity, and I felt she was not portrayed in a good light. So I decided to go to the Quran and see how it handled the story of original sin. Somehow the version in the Quran gave me peace.

The Quran's story of creation begins similarly to the Bible and the Torah. There is God, Adam, Eve, and Satan. All Abrahamic religions believe in the devil, and Islam is no exception. In the Islamic story, God asked all of the angels and jinns to bow to Adam because Adam had been given the gift of knowledge. But Satan chose not to bow to Adam as the rest of the angels did.

In Islam, Satan is not a fallen angel but a being of fire known as a *jinn*. Muslims believe that all angels must obey God and that angels do not have free will or the power of choice. So unlike some Christian traditions of fallen angels, Muslims do not believe that angels can "fall." However, jinns, like humans, can be both good and bad because they have the power of choice. The equivalent to a jinn in the Christian tradition would be a demon.

The seventh surah of the Quran, called *Al-Araf*, presents the story of Satan's origins. These are the verses from the Quran I used to write my paper on Eve, or Hawa, the mother of us all, as she is called in Arabic. I wanted to know if I needed a savior. I was attending mass twice a week and getting exposed to the teachings of the Bible. I saw that my Christian friends and teachers were sincere in their beliefs. I had been raised a Muslim for my entire life. I never questioned what I was taught because I followed what my family believed and all our beliefs were similar. I never knew what a gift Ms. Parks and her assignment would be. Here, in tenth grade English class, writing a paper on Eve, I decided that I would be a Muslim. Not because my parents and my culture were Muslim but because Islam is what I believed in. I did not know that these challenges to my faith would make me question my beliefs. I would need to debate within my heart if I was just born a Muslim or if I rationally accepted Islam as the best way of life. With struggle comes strength, and I was definitely struggling in both English class and my faith.

Quran 7:11 - *And surely, God created your father Adam and then gave you the noble shape of a human being, then God told the angels, "Prostrate to Adam"; and they prostrated, except Iblis, he refused to be of those who prostrate.*

In the next verse, Quran 7:12: *God said: What prevented you, O Iblis that you did not prostrate, when I commanded you? Iblis said: I am better than him Adam, You created me from fire, and him You created from clay.*

I absolutely love this verse because I have seen it play out over and over in my life. I was amazed by Satan's logic. Satan's argument is, materially speaking, "I am better than Adam." The argument is totally about Satan's material of fire being better than Adam's material of clay. I had the same thought process. I saw life as material success. I realized I was noticing only money and clothes, not character and blessings. I was at a private school where most of the girls had more money than my parents. They also lived in a much nicer part of town, in much bigger houses, closer to the school. This school was made for the elite of the city. I, on the other hand, was driving forty minutes across town just to attend. On top of that, I was on a work-study program, so I had to clean the art room after all my much richer classmates used it. By the time I had wiped down the easels, cleaned all the brushes, put away the supplies, and commuted another forty minutes back home, it would be five o'clock. My whole day was shot just trying to fit in. I thought if I were richer I would be better, but thanks to Ms. Parks and this assignment, I now knew my thought process was flawed.

Quran 7:13, God said: *O Iblis, get down from this Paradise, it is not for you to be arrogant here. Get out, for you are of those humiliated and disgraced.*

I needed to change. My dad had lost his job and my mom was supporting us. There was financial stress at home. I was so busy wanting more that I had no idea what I had. Next to the high school was the most expensive group of shops in the city known as Utica Square. All the girls from school went and bought Polo shirts, Jordache jeans, and items from Calvin Klein. I was working just to go to school and could not afford many of the status symbols and did not have the right designer labels. I had used this lack of material possessions to make myself feel bad. I just wanted more stuff. I was so busy wanting that I missed noticing my blessings.

Similar to the Old and New Testaments, Satan vows to mislead humanity. After a few verses the story of eating from the forbidden tree appears in the Quran. I was too young to realize the power of these words. As Muslims, we learn that Satan tells us what we want to hear and makes fake promises.

So in the Quran, Surah A'raf verses 19-21, "God says 'And O Adam! Dwell you and your wife in Paradise, and eat thereof as you both wish, but approach not this tree otherwise you both will be of the unjust and wrong-doers.' Then Satan whispered suggestions to them both in order to uncover that which was hidden from them of their private parts before. Satan said: 'Your Lord did not forbid you this tree save you should become angels or become of the immortals.' And Satan swore by God to them both saying: 'Verily, I (Satan) am one of the sincere well-wishers for you both.' So he misled them with deception. Then, when they tasted of the tree, that which was hidden from them of their shame, private parts, became manifest to them and they began to stick together the leaves of Paradise over themselves in order to cover their shame. And their Lord called out to them saying: 'Did I not forbid you that tree and tell you: Verily, Satan is an open enemy unto you?'"

My mind relaxed. Eve did not tempt Adam, and according to the Quran she was not the first one to sin. I respected Eve, and this story gave me a sense of tranquility. I was getting so many different messages from the media, and from the school, about the value of women. I needed to know for my own understanding what the Quran actually said about women. The story of Adam and Eve is also taught in another section of the Quran, Surah Ta Ha verses 121-122: "And Adam and his wife ate of it, and their private parts became apparent to them, and they began to fasten over themselves from the leaves of Paradise. And Adam disobeyed his Lord and erred. Then his Lord chose him and turned to him in forgiveness and guided Adam."

I wanted to have Imam Kareem, the education leader of our mosque, look at my paper before I submitted it. My Arabic was not good, and I used three different translated Qurans to come up with my conclusions on the paper. On Sunday, we piled into our maroon station wagon and went to Sunday School for another fun class with my grandmother. I found the Imam, or religious teacher, and had him read my paper while I attended class. After class was over, the Imam approached me at a break. "I like your paper, and I am proud of your work," he said. I thanked him and told him about the peace I found in the Quran's story of creation. We were in the white cabinet kitchenette with a goldish-yellow laminate floor. I was munching on a samosa and drinking lemonade. Imam Kareen had on the traditional white robe, a trim black beard, and his prayer cap. I knew the call to prayer would sound on the loudspeaker soon.

Imam Kareem asked, "Do you understand the main life lesson of the story?" I answered that women are not lesser than men, and women are not to blame for man's downfall. Imam Kareem said, "I understand how you got that message, and we should look at the intricacies between Adam and Satan. Adam was honored in front of angels and received a demotion from God. Satan also was promoted in front of the angels and given a demotion also." Imam Kareem continued, "The difference between Adam and Satan is that when Adam got his demotion, Adam took responsibility for his part in God's plan. Even though Adam did not totally understand what God's plan was, Adam still said, 'I take responsibility for my actions and ask for forgiveness.' Satan, on the other hand, blamed God for the downfall. Satan not only blamed God but also picked a fight. The life lesson," the Imam said, deep in thought, "is that when a believer has a setback, a believer takes responsibility. However, when someone without faith has a setback, they chose to blame God." I started to answer, but the call to prayer sounded. We wrapped up break and prepared to pray. I took my paper and put it in my bag so I would not lose it, and then went to the bathroom to wash up before prayers.

On the way home, I decided to add Imam Kareem's insights into my paper. I had started the paper with the intention of showing up Ms. Parks. Now I was seeing that her challenge was a gift. Ms. Parks's words charged my anger and got me in motion doing the research I needed to actually learn about my faith. Part of being a Muslim was taking responsibility for my work. I decided to quit blaming her for making me write this paper and appreciate the empowered state I was in. I hit the typewriter and added one last page about taking responsibility as a part of my faith's path.

I loved my religion more than ever. The version in the Quran stated that Adam *and* his wife ate the fruit from the tree, rather than Eve eating the fruit first and then seducing Adam into bad behavior. Furthermore, Adam took responsibility for the act and asked for forgiveness. And in many verses in the Quran, such as Quran 2:37, it is clear that God forgave Adam. I was happy because nowhere in the Quran was the woman to blame. I did not have to bear children in pain and worry about the original sin! Adam took responsibility for his actions and repented to God. The original sin was forgiven way before I was born. I did not need a savior to die for my sins because the original sin was taken care of. But I still had one problem: How do I tell this to Ms. Parks respectfully?

I was still unsure if I should just write about the parts that were similar to the Bible or share my full self with the elation I felt. As a woman, I held no blame, punishment, or responsibility for the original sin. I wrote the paper with my own beliefs and counted the words. I took full responsibility for my thoughts and my point of view. Ms. Parks gave me a B+ and managed to put lots of red ink on all the sections she disagreed with. She did not share my feminist version that said both men and women can be equal based on how they live their lives instead of the label of their religion. Either way, I didn't care—a B+ was a good enough grade on my English paper—but the real gift was finding my faith in Islam. It sounds strange now, but I found my Islamic faith in Catholic School.

CHAPTER 7

ALMOST MUSLIM

"IF YOU SEE THERE TO BE DANGER WITH THE TRUTH, DO
NOT DEVIATE FROM IT. FOR SALVATION IS ONLY WITH THE
TRUTH."

PROPHET MUHAMMAD

I was excited about senior year in high school ending and applying for colleges. Like my friends, I wanted to live my own life and was convinced I would do a better job on my own than with my parents. My parents were not familiar with the US college application process or the required tests. I navigated all the applications myself, found out all the tests I needed, and wrote my own essays without anyone reviewing my work. I had applied to several universities as an electrical engineering major, and the acceptance or rejection letters were coming in. But a war waged at home. I wanted to go away to college, and my parents wanted me to stay home. Their argument was money. My father was still looking for work, and although an education was important, we still needed funds to support the tuition and fees.

My search ended at Texas A&M University, located in the great state of Texas and at least an eight-hour drive from home. I even received an academic scholarship. The scholarship covered my tuition, fees, and some books. I still needed money for room and board. We were still debating between my attending a local university or going away to school. By the time my parents even considered Texas A&M, it was August, classes were full, the freshmen camps were booked up, and there was no on-campus housing available. My dad said, "You don't know if you really want to go unless you see the campus," so just three weeks before classes started, my dad and I took a road trip to Texas A&M. We drove on lazy back roads through small Texas towns like Mexia and Calvert, looking for the school. Using our handy Rand McNally Atlas, we finally found College Station, and we turned onto Main Drive. On the right side were lush green fields and on the left was a beautiful golf course. Straight ahead was the administration building, with huge concrete columns and massive horizontal stairs that were the length of the building. Main Drive was lined with trees on both sides of the road. The summer sun, lighting up the leaves of the perfectly aligned trees, let us know we were now on campus. For me, it was love at first sight. In this strange city, I felt like I belonged.

We visited the engineering buildings and took a tour of campus; our guide David was a huge fan of the school. He spoke of the mascot, the "twelfth man" at the football games, and the many traditions of the school, including the Thanksgiving bonfire. I walked through classrooms, the main student buildings, visited the book store, and ate at the cafeteria. My dad saw my excitement and conceded. He said, "Kiddo, if you can find a dorm on campus, you can come to school here." I was determined I would figure out a way to come to Texas A&M. I had noticed a set of brick arches and asked our guide what the arches led to. David said that was the area for the Corp of Cadets, a mini military school that was on campus. I was intrigued, and I admired the discipline of the military. The day flew by, and it was time to make the long drive back to Tulsa. I took all the brochures, jumped back in the car and said goodbye to David.

The following Monday, I called the offices of the Corps of Cadets to see what was involved in their program. To my surprise, I was transferred to the Commandant's office and spoke to the retired colonel in charge of the program. The commandant was friendly and talked about the life in the cadet corps including getting up at six in the morning, eating breakfast with our units, and all the homework help from upper classmen. He also mentioned that he had space in one of the two women's units, and that I could live on campus with the other female cadets. He called the female cadets "Waggies," a nickname for women Aggies. He also mentioned that we got to wear uniforms in class and march in a parade before each football game. I liked the idea of the daily exercise programs and learning new skills, so I told the commandant that I would check with my parents and get back to him. My parents liked the philosophy of the corps, so we said yes to the military program for college, with, of course, a long lecture from my father.

I told my parents about the uniforms and the military marching band of the school. My father decided to give a history lesson on the military. He started with the Ottoman Empire, where the Muslims used uniforms to tell soldiers apart from civilians. I had to get our Encyclopedia Britannica and look up the Ottoman Empire while my dad told stories he learned in high school about the empire from his teachers. They also used marching bands with the military. When the Ottoman army would enter a city, it would first send in a marching band. The band paved the path for the army to follow. These bands made an impression on the European soldiers who then took the tradition back to their countries. I was headed to the corps with a marching band just like the Ottoman soldiers of the past. But in the meantime, I had two weeks to prepare for this new phase in life.

The weeks were busy with purchasing the required bedding, notebooks, dorm fridge, and trunks as well as saying goodbye to friends. I would need to go to school one week early to learn the routine of the corps and get settled into my new dorm. Just two weeks before my seventeenth birthday, we packed up our little green Datsun and drove down to Texas. We went to registration and got my classes, my dorm assignment, and my beige uniforms. I remembered registering for school in Pakistan, where we had to buy all our books and get new uniforms each year. I was excited; I had boots, exercise pants called fatigues, regular school uniforms, and a formal class A uniform. I even had headwear to go with each set. These uniforms certainly met the Islamic dress code. The dress code for women in my faith requires covering the body, including the arms and legs. We are also encouraged to wear loose-fitting clothing. With the addition of the hat in the uniform, I had a headdress too. My uniform modestly dressed me both as a cadet and a Muslim.

The exercise and discipline started right away. I learned how to make my bed for inspection so a quarter bounced off the mattress. I also learned how to fold my clothes into the tiny closet slots for the items. I got a good night's sleep on Saturday night, but the following night at two a.m. we were woken up with metal cups banging on our beds and flashlights in our eyes. We had to put on our combat boots and run to the middle of the quad with the rest of the corps. The corps commander said a few words and the entire group ran on a five-mile course around campus. We returned to our rooms two hours later, exhausted, knowing we would have ninety minutes of sleep until we had to wake up for morning drill practice.

Along with the military traditions and some crazy customs came a class on the Air Force. Every Tuesday morning at nine, eighteen freshmen gathered to study Ronald Reagan's foreign policy. The current military operations included the Iran/Iraq War and US involvement in Nicaragua. In the war between Iran and Iraq, the US was supporting Saddam Hussein and the Iraqi government. With the lessons on the war came the comments of most of my classmates on how awful and violent Muslims are. I was surprised at the level of hatred some of my classmates had for people that they had never met. I was afraid to say that I was Muslim and even more afraid to say that the images of war on the television did not accurately represent these two nations. Although I maintained an A in the class, I did not enjoy the perspective that everyone who was not just like us was a potential enemy. I dreaded the lessons and began to question my decision to join the corps.

My first few weeks were filled with Chemistry, Calculus, military class, and engineering electives. I would rise at six in the morning, reveille was at six thirty, and then I marched with the unit to breakfast. Since freshmen were known as fish and fish had little mouths, freshmen were not allowed to chew our food nor could we look at our food. I would take my knife and fork, while staring straight ahead, and cut my donut into forty little pieces that I could swallow without chewing. If we got caught looking at out food or moving our mouths, we got push-ups or toilet cleaning. I made sure that breakfast was the only meal I ate at the corps dining hall and ate all my other meals, looking at and chewing my food, at the other cafeterias on campus around my classes.

In Chemistry class, I made a friend with another Muslim girl named Sayeeda. She was a Shia Muslim, and I was considered a Sunni Muslim. I asked her, "What's the difference,?" and she replied, "Not much." She invited me to have dinner with her family that weekend. Her father was a Math professor and her mother was a Biology professor at the university, and they lived about ten miles from campus. To Sayeeda, College Station had always been home. Her family knew what it was like to be a student away from family. She even added that I could bring my laundry and use the washing machine. I accepted eagerly, as free food and laundry without hunting for quarters or waiting for a washing machine sounded wonderful. So on Saturday night, Sayeeda picked me up and drove me to her home for dinner.

Her family was welcoming, and the house smelled wonderful. The women in Sayeeda's family, also originally from Pakistan, wore the traditional head cover, hijab. My family wore the head covers only while praying. As soon as we walked in the door, Sayeeda slipped off her hijab. I realized it was the first time I had seen her hair, all neatly pinned in a bun. As we walked past the living room, I met her younger sister, Amina, a high school junior who also wanted to go to Texas A&M. Her parents were both preparing dinner in the kitchen, and as with Pakistani tradition, I addressed them as Uncle and Aunty. Her mom had cooked a chicken in a tomato-based curry with coriander, turmeric, and garlic. Sayeeda's father was finishing up the basmati rice with green peas. I had not been in a house in six weeks. I missed my family. Sayeeda announced that I also brought my laundry. Her mom said, "Good job. I am so glad you can use our washer." She instructed me to start my laundry now so it would be finished while we were eating.

We sat at the kitchen table talking about freshman year at college from the professors' viewpoint. Her parents were telling us that study habits mattered and that the commitment with which we started our college education would determine our success in school. Her mom continued on what she would look for in passing a student and the flexibility that professors used for determining grades. For example, she continued, if a student came to office hours and showed interest in the class, she was more lenient in grading than a student that made no effort or contact. I added how hard it was to stand outside the professor's door during office hours, waiting for a turn to get help with homework. Aunty suggested I take some other work with me so I could do homework from another class while I waited.

The conversation changed as Uncle asked me, "Sayeeda tells me you are Sunni Muslim." I said yes, and he said it was time for the evening prayer, would I like to join in? I accepted. Amina spread out a cover on the floor to create a clean space for praying. We all lined up in the direction of Mecca and Uncle led the *Maghrib* prayers. I did not notice much difference in the prayers except for the way I placed my hands on my chest and the others were allowing their hands to hang on the sides. After the prayers, we all sat on the floor and individually asked God for forgiveness and assistance. I was praying for good grades and running faster so I could keep up with the spontaneous night runs around campus with my corps unit. After we completed our individual prayers, I helped Amina fold up the floor cover, and we all sat in the living room.

Uncle asked me if I would come to his Sunday morning class in the student center on Islam. His friend Professor Khalid from Egypt was an expert in Arabic and taught how to read the Quran, and then Uncle taught on Islamic practices and mastering religious rituals. The class started Sunday morning at ten thirty and ended with lunch around noon. Getting up at ten on a Sunday sounded like too much effort for me, but I agreed to come to a class to see how it goes. Uncle explained that tomorrow he taught shariah in Islam. I said I was familiar with shariah but did not know much of the details. I heard the term used frequently in conversations, but I myself did not know the laws exactly. Uncle reminded me of my dad, because he took my comment to go into a lecture on shariah. Amina rolled her eyes and went to her room. However, Sayeeda and I sat patiently and listened as Uncle got warmed up.

Like Judaism, Islam has an entire set of laws to live by for Muslims. Islamic shariah is a complete social and justice system that is designed to improve the quality of life and the character of its followers. Islamic shariah, or a way of life, covers six major areas of life, including the protection of religion, the protection of life, the protection of the intellect, the protection of lineage, the protection of honor, and the protection of property. Many of the laws in Islam come directly from the Quran. The Holy Quran tells Muslims what to eat, how to divide inheritance, along with the basics of honoring God. The basis of shariah is justice, mercy, protection, and the benefits of submitting to the laws of God. Shariah not only covers how to behave with other human beings but also teaches respect for all creation, such as the animals and the Earth. Uncle also threw in that shariah applied equally to both Sunni and Shia Muslims. I felt included with his last remark.

RELIGION

He said that it was important for me to be able to explain shariah to those around me, especially to share that viewpoint with the students in my military education class. The stronger your religious knowledge, the stronger your faith, he continued. In Shariah, everything starts with the faith in one God. Uncle said that God was the center of our universe as Muslims, and we declare that we believe in the one true God even sight unseen. Therefore, the first set of laws in shariah is to protect your faith, or your *Deen*. There are certain forbidden actions—such as practicing black magic, worshiping idols or the devil—because they weaken and destroy your faith. Now I understood why my mom would not let us see the fortune teller at the amusement park. I didn't know that believing in the fortune that the fortune teller told me would conflict with my faith, that only God knew my future and my fortune.

Aunty now started to add her perspective, that in Islamic law, all forgiveness belongs to God; therefore, there is no one between you and your Lord. For example, a priest cannot hear a confession in Islam and forgive you. Only God can forgive. When Muslims repent, it is from their heart with no outsider knowing the depth of remorse or shame for their actions. So I asked her about the war between Iran and Iraq. In military class, they had said that the US was siding with Iraq. I told her that on the news it was saying our president Ronald Reagan would host the defense minister of Iraq, Tariq Aziz.

Aunty said the war between two Muslim nations is tragic and that so many people are profiting from the sale of weapons. Therefore, some other nations are supporting a prolonged conflict. Aunty continued that Islam encouraged diplomatic solutions to problems because that protects our faith. Peace keeps faith alive. Everything we experience is from God, so if we are in a tough period, the trial is a lesson or test from God. I interjected, so you believe the Muslims in war torn lands are being tested by God?

Aunty answered that the best resolution is a mutual compromise. If the countries were not being manipulated by foreign powers, compromise will be easier. War and fighting are only for extreme circumstances such as self-defense, Uncle was chiming in. Aunty continued, all Islamic literature discourages war and oppression, because wars cause individuals to lose faith.

I had not anticipated such a deep discussion. I was enjoying the new ideas. Aunty saw my expression. So she continued, in a state of war, individuals witness atrocities and experience pain at high levels. When we see such atrocities, we may ask, "Well if God is so loving and caring, where is God when this happens?" This type of pain and suffering sometimes leads to the loss of faith. Uncle added, "Let's say a prayer that the suffering in both nations does not make any believers lose faith in God."

After a short break, the topic shifted to jihad. I said that on TV it seemed as if Muslims love fighting because of the jihad. I sighed and relaxed, because I received the same explanation of jihad being a struggle for making our egos and life actions in line with the will of God. Aunty added that the way Muslims are shown in our media is similar to the disrespectful language as most minorities in the United States. We are not alone in being shown as violent or barely human. I chuckled at her joke and decided that for my life, I would do something to change the perception of minorities. I did not know what I could do, but the thought had entered my mind. In Islam, peaceful resolutions help keep faith alive. I had no idea that shariah covered so many aspects of life.

LIFE

I asked Uncle, "How can two Muslim countries be at war and yet protect life? He responded that being a Muslim is more than just saying we are Muslim. Our faith is defined by our deeds and the intention behind them. We need to observe a person's actions to see where they are on the faith journey. Anger and manipulation show us that the person is still trying to find a connection with God. And if there is a conflict, there are many peaceful means of resolution within Islamic shariah.

Uncle added, Muslims who resort to violence are like the Ku Klux Klan here in Texas. The KKK feel they are serving God, but violence and service are two very different acts. Taking the life of an innocent person is the same as killing all of humanity. The prophet said that. I told uncle that I had no idea that the prophet took such a strong stance on violence. Uncle said that Islam is about self-control, recognizing an injustice but working within the existing system to create a positive change. Positive change means that society supports the new system and embraces the new ideas. Killing someone just creates anger and pain but does not allow for real change. Uncle stated, with violence, each generation tends to repeat the same mistakes of the generations that went before them.

I always knew killing was wrong but I had a new perspective that killing and war did not help us progress as a society. I would make more effort to honor another soul and give each person the respect that Prophet Muhammad taught us. My generation and my changes would make this world better. Uncle explained that the Prophet (pbuh) also warned us of the dangers of arrogance of two gifts from God—the gift of Education and the gift of Faith. He said that often, when someone that has education, faith, or both, that person considers themselves better than other people that do not possess these insights. I was learning I could have respect for my gifts and compassion for those who have not been given the same gifts. I wanted to be a good Muslim, and as far as being more compassionate, I had a ways to go.

But both education and faith are a gift from God, so having faith should make us humble toward others and grateful to our Lord. I thought about this statement. I considered myself better than most of my classmates because my grades were usually higher than theirs. Now I saw that maybe I had been given the gift of intelligence and engaging in humility was the right path. I could now pray for the gift of patience and compassion and hopefully, God could grant me some patience soon.

Sayeeda said that it is vital to realize that Islam never justifies taking life without due process. In last week's Sunday class, she learned that the Prophet Muhammad (pbuh) was known to say that: "The wiping away of the World means less to Allah than a Believer to be killed unjustly." Muslims believe that God values the life of an individual believer more than the precious house of God in Mecca. Killing is prohibited in Islam—all life, not just humans. Killing or hurting animals for purposes other than to be used as food is not allowed. So I asked Uncle, "Muslims cannot hunt for game?" Uncle confirmed, no, we as Muslims respect animals and show compassion for all life including plants and animals. One of the sayings of Prophet Muhammad (pbuh) is: "A woman was punished because she prisoned a cat and the cat died. Because of this action, the woman was sent to Hell. The prophet explained, that while she imprisoned the cat, she did not give the cat food or drink, nor did she allow the cat to eat the insects on the earth to feed itself." Cruelty to any living thing is a grave sin in Islam.

I knew from Sunday school with my grandmother that Islam had laws that support capital punishment for crimes of intentional murder. But at this dinner I found out about the cruelty to animals. I was proud of my faith for taking a stand for any living creature that was powerless or manipulated. In the case of loss of human life, it is recommended in the Holy Quran that the perpetrator ask for forgiveness from the victims and offer compensation for the loss of life. It is common practice to go to the victim's family and ask for forgiveness when we have hurt them. It is also honorable to try to make amends with either financial compensation or acts of service.

In my life I personally witnessed a situation where the victim's family was asked for forgiveness. My cousin had a paper route and was out early one morning delivering papers with his friend as driver. During the early hours, the driver lost control of the car and ran into a tree. My cousin died at the tender age of nineteen. The friend's family came to my aunt and uncle and asked for forgiveness. They also offered some financial compensation for their loss, but my aunt and uncle did not accept any money. They forgave the friend who was driving the car. I could only imagine the burden this young driver would carry about that day, and hoped that having the family's forgiveness gave him the strength to move on. This is Islam: treating life with dignity and a big heart.

I heard the dryer going off. I had forgotten about my clothes. I was going to interrupt and go get my laundry, but Amina shouted from her room, "I'll get the clothes for you." I was grateful for the clean laundry and for being in an environment that was more relaxed than the corps dorms. No curfews, I could chew my food, and we could speak freely about the ideas that were important to me. Aunty offered me tea. At every Pakistani gathering, there is black tea with cream, cardamom seeds, and sugar. I never developed a taste for the national drink and everyone was surprised when I declined tea. And both Aunty and Uncle asked in unison, "You don't drink tea?" She offered me Texas sweetened iced tea instead, and I said I'd love some.

Sayeeda asked her father, "So we've only covered two sections of shariah. What about the others?" Her father said he would tell us a little more, but it was getting late and he wanted to retire. He told me to come to the meeting tomorrow to learn more. I was fascinated by the lecture, but I had lots of homework. And I added that I still needed to be taken back to campus. Aunty was busy in the kitchen with tea, and Uncle continued his thoughts on shariah protecting intellect.

INTELLECT

Shariah laws preserve the intellect by encouraging education and avoiding intoxicants. Maybe I should have left earlier, I thought. Alcohol and college seemed to be a hot subject in this home. Uncle said that all situations with alcohol needed to be strictly avoided and Sayeeda complained that she would not be able to attend any social events. She continued, "If I am not drinking, why does it matter if there is alcohol there?" Uncle retorted, "Because of the temptation." A heated discussion started, with Aunty chiming in from the kitchen as she brought us tea. I was glad my parents weren't here because they would have panicked if they knew how much alcohol was served at campus social events and how many girls in my dorm room had their own stash of booze. Uncle proclaimed, "Prohibiting intoxicants protects your intellect by not weakening it with damaging substances. In Islam, we are judged by our actions—our goal on Earth is to earn a good life for eternity, so our actions here have the potential to take us to eternity. Often, when someone is intoxicated, they are not in full control of their actions and may make decisions that take them away from the path of God." "The presence of alcohol created the temptation, and the consumption will take you away from God, Sayeeda," Aunty added. Sayeeda held her tongue as a sign of respect.

I always viewed my intellect as a huge blessing. I had often been offered alcohol in different social occasions since high school. I feel blessed that I was able to find groups of people throughout my life that knew how to have tons of fun without drinking. My parents had set the example in my childhood, and I seemed to follow those parameters for fun in life. In high school I was constantly trying to improve my grades and test scores. I needed to keep all the brain cells I had and maybe even develop more. So I couldn't understand the benefits of drinking if it would hurt some of my brain cells. I was a true nerd—every cell in my body and brain was made of pure nerd. But in college it was uncomfortable. At so many events, I was the only sober person in the room. The only activity was drinking and socializing with inhibitions gone. The students I had respected as friends were drunk, making fools of themselves and calling it fun. I began to feel like if I was not drinking, there was no point in showing up. I had started to decline invitations to mixers and look for a sober crowd. I was glad I had found other girls like Sayeeda to spend time with.

I was sipping on my iced tea when Sayeeda whispered, "Let's get out of here. Mom and Dad, we are going back to campus," she said as she put her hijab back on her head. I grabbed my laundry and thanked Aunty and Uncle for the fantastic evening. I gave Amina a hug, and with that, we were out the door. It was dark; Sayeeda's home was large with a lot full of trees. We could not see any street lights or the neighbor's houses. We drove through the quiet farms back to campus. Sayeeda drove slowly and stopped at every yield sign. I could tell she was an extra friendly Texas-raised driver. She complained about the city drivers that were always in a hurry and drove like maniacs just to save two minutes. I smiled—little did she know I was one of those crazy city drivers. We arrived from the back entrance of campus, near the football stadium, Kyle Field. Sayeeda was a perfect driver, stopping at every stop sign and crosswalk on the deserted campus.

She said she was sorry about the heavy discussion over dinner. I said I really liked her parents; they reminded me of home. We reached my dorm, and I was back to my reality. I had two tests to study for, so I was glad my laundry was done. I could see that just like my parents, Sayeeda's parents really cared about her and wanted her to get a good education without getting into trouble. Our two families valued Islam's view on the intellect stating that all Muslims have a right to an education. Having knowledge is of high value in Islamic societies, especially in Pakistan where our parents were raised. The Prophet Muhammad (pbuh) has been known to say, "Seek knowledge from the womb to the grave." With knowledge comes manners, and it is important in Islam to know proper manners for the worship of God and your interactions with your fellow human beings. I was glad I met a friend who knew proper manners with her parents.

I was planning to sleep in the following morning and then continue studying for my tests. However, at eight o'clock, my roommate's alarm started beeping and she hit *snooze* three times. I did not want to get up yet. I was tossing and turning, attempting to go back to sleep. Twenty minutes passed and I failed at falling asleep. I kept thinking about the dinner last night and how nice it was for Sayeeda to be both at school and at home simultaneously. Thanksgiving break was still six weeks away. That would be the first time I would go home and see my family and friends. I felt homesick. Then I saw my laundry. I could take Uncle up on his offer for the Sunday program. After all, it was only a five-minute walk from my dorm. And Sayeeda mentioned that food was involved. I got ready and left for the Sunday class.

Rudder Tower was one of the taller buildings on campus and had an elevator. As I got on the elevator, someone yelled, "Hold the door, please." I pushed the "door open" button, and to my surprise, the football coach, Jackie Sherrill, got on with me. He smiled and said thanks. We rode up to the eighth floor where I got off. As I left the elevator, I thought, Wow, the football team not only has special dorms but the coaches have offices on campus with the best views. I could smell food and followed my nose to the Sunday session. There were about twenty people in the room, half students and half professors. I saw Aunty first, and she motioned me in. I met Dr. Khalid, a chemical engineering professor from Egypt. I also met his wife, Nura, and daughter, Merium. Another graduate student, Syed, originally from Iran, came with his friend Daniel. Daniel was curious about Islam and wanted to attend the session. Aunty kept introducing me to the other students.

Sayeeda gave me a hug and said, "I've saved you a seat." I quickly grabbed two samosas for breakfast and sat with Sayeeda. Everyone had their own Quran. I had one but had left it back in my dorm room, so I shared with Sayeeda. The format was learning Arabic with Dr. Khalid the first hour and Islamic studies with Sayeeda's father, Dr. Nabi, for thirty minutes. We started with a recitation of the holy Quran. Most of the women were wearing hijabs. I brought a white scarf with me and put in on my head. We went through each ayah in the Quran and discussed our thoughts and how the lesson applied to our life in modern 1983. I was learning and reminiscing about all the times I fought my mom on going to Sunday school. Now I was attending voluntarily. I thought, My mom will be surprised this afternoon when I tell her that I am essentially going back to Sunday school.

The Arabic discussion and debates were lively and fun. I was learning from all the different perspectives; we had people in the group from India, Pakistan, Egypt, Iran, and Indonesia. Each country and culture brought their gifts into our group's understanding of the verse. I had thought that I would only show up for one lecture but now considered that I could come back and bring my own Quran to take notes. After Dr. Khalid was finished, Dr. Nabi got up and quizzed us about the lecture on shariah from last week. Since Sayeeda and I just heard him speaking after dinner last night, we were raising our hands and answering correctly. The group was impressed at my extensive knowledge of shariah. But then Dr. Nabi asked, "So what parts of shariah are left to study today?" I went blank. There were six parts, but I did not remember which ones we had not covered. Luckily, Uncle did not call on me. We closed our Qurans and began to listen. The fourth human right protected by shariah is lineage.

LINEAGE

Everyone has a God-given right to know who their natural parents are. Therefore, Dr. Nabi said that changing the family name of an adopted child is not permitted in Islam. Muslims cannot cover up lineage. He was talking about knowing our lineage as a basic human right that is protected by shariah, and there are laws in the system to protect bloodlines. I was looking out the big windows at the campus and thinking of a girl I met in third grade named Mary.

Mary had sandy brown hair and freckles. She and her younger brother would hop the chain link fences between our homes and come play in our backyard. At one point she told me that she was adopted. I asked her what that meant. Mary said that she did not have a mommy and daddy but had foster parents. I had no idea what foster parents were because

Foster was not Mary's last name. After my birthday party, we were playing on the swings in my backyard when Mary started crying, "I wish I knew my real mommy like you know yours." She said she thought about her real mommy all the time and was going to find her one day. Did Mary lose the right to know her bloodlines? It had been a decade since that day, and I hoped Mary and her real mommy were reunited. I came back to the Sunday session in Rudder Tower.

In Islam, we retain the original family name of an adoptive child and do not confuse the lineage by having the child take on the name of the adoptive parents. This way, there is no confusion that the child is adopted and the blood lines of the family are protected. Dr. Nabi continued that according to shariah, every child has the right to know who his or her parents are; therefore, there are no sealed adoptions in which the identity of the parents is concealed from the child. The same rules applied to marriage. For example, married women keep their maiden name and are not required to take on the name of their husband because, when names are changed, lineage gets confusing.

HONOR

Shariah law also protects honor by not allowing believers to slander each other. For example, the free mixing of men and women in Islam is discouraged. Although this may look restrictive to Western standards, this law protects men as much as it protects women. For example, many political figures have lost their careers because of a workplace harassment claim. Whether the story is true or false, scandal spreads like fire. In Islam, this type of free mixing is discouraged and scandal can be therefore avoided. It is recommended that a valid chaperone be present whenever there is a meeting between an unrelated man and a woman. For a woman, a valid chaperone would be her husband, father, brother, or son. For a man, the valid chaperones are his wife, mother, sister, or daughter. Also, valid chaperones are encouraged to protect women at all times.

I was so impressed when my youngest sister, Amina, set up a meeting with one of our local Muslim leaders in 2012. She was in her thirties and wanted to help support the school by offering her business management skills. Amina is a trained consultant and wanted to start some presentations with Islam. The meeting was set in a public restaurant, and the Muslim leader showed up with his wife and two staff members. Even if someone wanted to start a rumor, there would have been no stress on the marriage because both the husband and wife were present, along with other eye witnesses.

In Islam, this law is used to protect both men and women. I have seen several popular political figures from former US President Bill Clinton, David Petraeus of the CIA, and former Vice Presidential Candidate John Edwards suffer blows to their careers when a women from their past came forward. The women claimed that these powerful men displayed inappropriate behavior. I have noticed that when a woman presents allegations against the man, we tend to believe the woman. Either way the man's reputation is tainted. Had these men handled their work relationships in the same manner the Muslim leader set the meeting with my sister, it would make it difficult to accuse them of inappropriate behavior.

In Islam, gossiping about another person is a sin. Even if what you are saying about the other person is true, Muslims are still discouraged to back-bite. Similarly, slander is a grave sin in Islam. We are taught to find a positive spin on a person's behavior because we do not fully understand the story behind their actions and, as believers, we are not the judge of other people. Even if the other person is clearly in the wrong, there are repercussions to exposing someone, such as humiliating their family and friends. Only God is the true judge of people.

WEALTH/PROPERTY

Islamic law is designed to protect wealth and property. Like most legal systems, shariah has rules against stealing and deceiving others. The law protects assets of believers because all assets are given to believers based on blessings from God. What I really like about shariah is the division of assets in a will. Muslims are allowed to have wills; however, if a will is not present, the law divides the assets of the deceased individual fairly among relatives. In shariah, a believer may not avoid giving money to a wife. Just because a believer may not like his wife or preferred giving money to a child instead of his wife, the believer still needs to be fair with his assets. In Islam, our family members have rights over us, and we cannot cheat them out of their right by manipulating our finances.

I have seen many friends have heartaches over property and money when a family member passes. Most of the people I know do not have excellent legal documentation to avoid conflict in dividing property after death. God knew that relationships could be destroyed in handling of money and property of the deceased, so shariah lays down a framework to reduce such conflicts and preserve family relations.

In 2015, my father retired and decided to write a will. I will admit it was a hard conversation to have with my parents. But I was able to ask him how he would like things handled since US law does not recognize Islamic shariah. I was surprised how much I learned about my father in that conversation. I guess I just assumed I knew what he would like because I was always told that the two of us were alike.

I live in a country where the key word is *freedom*. In the United States we all want to be free and support those who fight for our freedom. But what I know now is that true freedom comes from self-discipline and the ability to control ourselves. When we can manage our tongues, our stomachs, and our desires, we are truly free. We do not covet what others have, nor does our behavior put us in situations where we can lose. In Islam, we are taught that if a path leads to something bad, do not even take one step. I never really appreciated these lessons of faith I learned at a makeshift Muslim summer camp I attended when I was eight. I don't remember much about the classes, but I am indebted to the successes all these lessons have provided for me and my kids.

CHAPTER 8

HEADED TO MY DESTINY

"YOU HAVE TO KEEP BREAKING YOUR HEART

UNTIL IT OPENS."

RUMI

Rumi lived in sixteenth century Iran as a famous poet who wrote about love. My Muslim friends sometimes quoted Rumi. I liked his insights and found them honest yet funny. My Muslim friends on both continents protested about the stress of dating and the pains of a non-arranged marriage, known as a "love marriage" in Muslim cultures in the United States. In Pakistan, it is estimated that sixty-five to eighty percent of marriages are arranged, and the custom has experienced a revival in Pakistan after witnessing the high divorce rates of non-arranged marriages. Forms of matchmaking are becoming more popular in western culture too; about half of marriages are initiated by family or friends or through online dating sites. My friends from junior high in Peshawar wrote me letters about the potential suitors that their parents had vetted. These girls followed arranged marriage because it made their lives easier. They weren't pressured to find "the one" and trusted their parents to screen candidates and find someone compatible with them. My aunts used to say that love grows and blossoms from knowing a person over time.

Since I had spent most of my childhood in the US, I had different ideas about how marriage works. With my non-Muslim friends, the concept of arranged marriage had a negative connotation, and they felt dating was fun. I wasn't planning to date to find someone, but I wasn't going to let my parents handle all of the arrangements either. As I graduated from college, I considered marriage at some point in my life, but it was not a high priority for me in 1985.

My parents were very involved in the Pakistani and Muslim communities wherever they lived. My grandmother also volunteered in community service both in the United States and Pakistan. We often sponsored cultural functions and hosted charity events. Between my grandmother and parents, I felt that every Muslim in Oklahoma knew us. Whenever we met a new family in town, they would ask where we were from and trace some acquaintance back to my grandmother or grandfather. This type of heart-to-heart networking is a great way to find suitable matches for your loved ones. My parents were constantly asked by their friends if they knew someone that they would recommend for a potential marriage.

When I graduated from high school, news buzzed happily that Sajeela's granddaughter was completing her studies. People anticipated that I would be looking to settle down in a few years. The marriage proposals started to arrive, often as a long-distance phone call from an acquaintance or someone with a mutual friend. In Islam, marriage is a two-step process. The *nikkah* is the first step and is similar to an engagement in the United States. One of the girls from my high school in Tulsa, Salma, had agreed to a suitor her parents selected. Although there were no plans for the wedding to happen anytime soon, the agreement had been made so that the kids could get to know each other better while still in school. Whenever the other boys would try to ask Salma out, she would say, "I am already married." The boys would just stare in shock. She loved teasing our classmates so then they would look at me and ask, "Are you married too?" I always said of course! The *nikkah* engagement can be for two weeks or a few years, depending on the wishes of the bride and groom.

This period is followed by the actual marriage ceremony on an agreed date with the two families. Since the *nikkah* period could be a few years, parents in our community were starting to look for potential mates for their kids as they finished high school. The timeframe and age of arranged marriages varies. Our family was big into education, so for my sisters and me, it was understood that we would go to college first and get higher degrees. Salma's parents owned twelve convenience stores in Tulsa. They were more focused on business than education and believed in an education with real life experience. Salma was planning on taking over the family business and was looking to settle down before me. Her family was wealthy and emphasized the importance of serving others through products and business. My family was oriented toward charities and serving others through our contributions. Therefore, having such a popular, generous grandmother, I was a finalist on many parents' potential mate lists.

As with other traditional rites of passage, marriage ceremonies are celebrated in many different ways. In our culture, a wedding is a four-event celebration that takes place over the course of a week. The first two events, the henna ceremonies, are smaller and include extended family. There is a henna celebration from the groom's family where the bride's family gets to see the home of the groom and get to know his relatives better. For the next event, the bride throws the henna party at her home, and the groom's family comes. This gives both sets of relatives opportunities to meet each other so they can better support the couple. These henna parties are during the week, where the weekend starts the formal wedding celebration hosted by the bride's parents. In our tradition, the groom is known to arrive at the wedding on a horse, with both the man and the horse covered in decorative flowers and ribbons. The family of the groom walks behind the horse, playing drums and singing wedding songs. A day or two later is the *Walima*, or groom's function, that is a formal party hosted by the parents of the groom.

All four occasions have tons of food. At a wedding, most families want to show that they are generous and are hospitable. The food at weddings is often served in large metal trays and on huge platters that are about three feet in diameter. Think of a wok-shaped dish that can be heated from the bottom. The dish is prepared on a fire pit on the ground with wood and coals. Two cooks, usually young boys, prepare rice and meat dishes using metal spatulas that look like hand-held fans. The weddings I remember as a child were like this, with all the food prepared outside. The guests would sit outside in large tents. Small fans or heaters kept the climate tolerable in the tents. Now weddings are held in hotels with the hotel staff taking care of the decorations and details. When I was eight, two of my uncles were married with these traditions. This meant four functions for my mom's brother, followed by another four functions for my dad's cousin. We celebrated all summer, seeing family all dressed up at different events.

I was a tomboy and rolled my eyes impatiently at the thought of a guy, getting a dress, or the burden of marriage. Being Pakistani, we believe an individual's family reflects the individual's character. My family was known as a "great family," and therefore I was associated with having all the right characteristics of a potential wife. Even though these people had never met me, my grandmother's reputation was impeccable and extended across the global Pakistani communities. My parents were also known for their strong morals, leadership, and character. I am forever linked to their reputation. The community recognized us for our work ethic, our service, and as a family that valued education. So the news had travelled fast that the daughters in our family were in their twenties, finishing college, and must be in want of a husband. Completely unknown to me, my parents had declined offers for an engagement while I was completing college. I innocently had no idea that all of this busy matchmaking was underway in my own house.

One night, I changed my usual location of my daily prayers and instead prayed in the hallway outside my room. My sister and I shared a room, and her clothing and accessories were everywhere. I looked for a clear, comfortable place to kneel and pray, but no floor space was available. I decided to take myself and my prayer rug outside of the room. As I began my nightly prayers, I heard my parents in earnest conversation in the living room. My mother was reviewing the various marriage proposals that had arrived that week—a young man from a "good" family in Indiana and another suitable young man from a family in New York. I abruptly lost focus on my prayer. Marriage proposals and the future of my life were under discussion, and I was not even in the same room!

I finished praying and determinedly marched into the living room, startling my parents. I told my surprised parents that I planned to graduate from college, get a job, and travel the world. I had no interest in marriage, I told them, so tell everyone and anyone who calls that I said no. I proceeded to tell them that I meant "no" forever. "I don't care who they are or how they know us," I continued. With that stalwart declaration, I returned to my bedroom. The angry exchange granted me four years and a college degree without hearing about any unwanted suitors.

While eight hours away from my family, going to school at Texas A&M and visiting new places, I realized that having a family that cared (and sometimes over-cared) was not all that bad. At A&M, some of the other Muslim girls had already arranged engagements—*nikkahs*—and the girls were socializing with their future husbands to establish a base for their marriage. Many of my non-Muslim friends in college were also becoming engaged in their senior year. On weekends, we witnessed marriage proposals at the fountain by the dining hall. There would be a guy dressed in a suit, down on one knee, with a ring. We quietly joked about girls who enrolled in college for an "MRS degree," where they came from small towns throughout Texas looking for husbands. My two cultures were running on parallel tracks. In Texas, as in Pakistan, the message to girls is to first earn an education and then settle down. Or, as many girls in my dorm had planned, go to a big school to meet a great guy and settle down. I celebrated my friends' engagements even while my heart belonged to my engineering classes.

Spring of my senior year at A&M, I had a number of job interviews. I flew to engineering companies in California, Texas, and Colorado while alternately doing interviews with the recruiters that came to campus. I landed a job as an engineer for the Voice of America in Washington, DC. I officially became a federal employee with a salary and a badge, belonging to the United States Information Agency. I saw the glow of my approaching diploma seal, and I did not want to read another textbook or take an exam. During this period, my parents moved from Tulsa to the suburbs of Washington, DC, where my father had finally found a permanent job working for the Federal Aviation Administration. We returned to financial stability. The whole family planned to travel back to Texas for my graduation. Mom had requested that after graduation, I, too, come to Washington, DC, and live with them. I gladly fulfilled her request by becoming a federal employee just like my dad.

My parents and sisters drove twenty-four hours to College Station for my graduation. Road trips are in our blood. My aunts and uncles came from Tulsa and Dallas for a mini family reunion and my big day. And my grandmother wouldn't miss my big day even if it meant a twenty-four-hour flight from Pakistan. My parents spent the first day in Texas helping me pack up everything except my cap and gown. The following day, everyone attended the evening graduation event where the Ambassador from Mexico to the United States gave an address. And with that forty-five-minute speech I was granted my degree and headed off to a family dinner at Red Lobster.

The following day featured the engineering department ceremony. Once again my entire family showed up with proud smiles and lots of camera flashes. As hard as it was to leave my "home" for four years, I knew that I had been given a foundation to build my life. I was grateful to all my professors and friends that had invested their energy in me and was glad that God chose them to cross paths with me.

For the final time, I walked back to my dorm from the engineering center. I finished packing up my Datsun B210 with my whole college life. I bid farewell to the amazing university and my dear friends. I followed my parents' car out to the freeway. My family embarked on another memorable road trip on Interstate 40 from Texas back to Virginia. I watched the highway signs fly by as I remembered the football games, the Thanksgiving bonfires, and the all night study sessions that I was leaving behind. The farther we got from Texas, the more I realized that life would not be the same carefree existence again. I was no longer a student but an adult with a real job where I would actually learn how to be an engineer.

After driving for two days, we arrived at our apartment in Falls Church, Virginia. My parents were in temporary housing while their home was being built. As a graduation present, my parents gave my sister and me a trip to Sao Paulo, Brazil, to visit one of my uncles who was working at the Pakistani embassy there. I planned to spend a month in Brazil and begin my new job when I returned. My grandmother, my uncle, and Mary Ann, one of my engineering friends from A&M, accompanied my sister and me for the month. We all looked forward to relaxing and connecting in the tropics of Brazil. I had never visited South America and wanted to check off Brazil from my bucket list. I did have a few worried moments that my grandmother had some connections in the southern hemisphere with a "good suitor" for me. My sister and I hoped no guys from great families would drop out of a palm tree or swing by for dinner. Luckily, my uncle and grandmother wanted to rest, so I had a relaxed trip of sightseeing and unwinding from finals. I knew Sao Paulo was my last long vacation before my new career as a radio frequency engineer for the Voice of America.

I was a young woman engineer on a path to make a mark in the world. My day filled up with ionospheric models and learning how shortwave radio signals propagated. On lunch break and after work, I explored the city of Washington, DC. I spent my lunch hour every day as a tourist in the capital of the United States of America. The first week at the Voice of America, I often ate lunch at the National Gallery of Art café, followed by walking along the Washington Mall. The city bustled with motorcades and politicians driving by in limousines. Many politicians' and presidents' photos hung on the walls of the local restaurants. In the springtime, the city filled with the cherry blossoms, and in the summer I explored the Smithsonian Museums and Chinatown with the tourists. Often our efforts at VOA were rewarded with lunch at a fancy new restaurant on Capitol Hill. The Voice of America attracted many visitors too. Lines formed at the studio entrance on Thursdays and Fridays, especially in the summer. Visitors could listen to fourteen different languages being broadcast on our antenna system around the world. We had programs in forty languages, and at noon Eastern Standard Time, all our studios hosted news announcers. I believed in the VOA's mission to foster cross-cultural communication and understanding of different viewpoints. VOA represented the artistic creativity, scientific advancements, and regional traditions of the United States along with our view of international news. I designed the radio antennas that made our transmissions work.

I learned how to design antenna systems, run propagation models, and even write testing software. I initiated a computer program that visually showed the improvement of radio coverage if Congress would invest more money in Voice of America's relay stations and antennas. My travels made me realized that seeing is believing. I thought if they could only see the impact of the upgraded antennas and transmitters, Congress would approve our requested funding. My world maps with visual representation of the new and improved radio coverage worked. We were invited into the Director of Engineering's office to watch on C-Span as Senator John Glenn held up my propagation maps in front of Congress and showed the other Senators what Voice of America radio achieved. I got to watch the vote as funding was approved for Voice of America's modernization program. Our team of five engineers cheered as the vote came in. I was a minority, an immigrant, a Muslim, and one of only two women, yet I was thrilled to see my ingenuity acknowledged by my team and our Congress. My faith taught me that I was blessed by God with the gifts of intelligence, and I was grateful for the privilege to be a part of the team that designed the new antenna system for Voice of America's mission to communicate directly to the people of the world using radio.

I met other engineers who became my friends. After work, we celebrated birthdays, went to holiday parties, and met each other's families. At times I did feel decidedly "single." Most of the engineers were married, buying homes, and building a future family. There were not many young engineers and thus not many single people to meet and hang out with. Furthermore, I had moved back in with my parents. Traditionally, young Muslim girls live with their families until they are married. I enjoyed paying no rent and eating free food, but I was not meeting new people as I had so easily done in my student days. After four years away, I was much more appreciative of the warm and supportive family that I have. Interacting with the people I loved at our nightly dinners was a novelty that I had missed at college. Life with no real responsibility and a paycheck gave me more options, and I decided to study for a master's degree. I was so excited to learn that the federal government would pay for part of the degree, so I thought, "Why not?" I would have two wonderful social worlds, with more college friends and still having my family with me.

I came home one Wednesday evening, and my mom informed me that some friends were joining us for dinner on Saturday. My parents are social butterflies, so dinner parties on the weekends were frequent events that I remembered from childhood. My parents loved the social interaction and time to relax with friends. They were also people "connectors" and knew individuals in different social circles, whom they would invite to make new contacts. Whether a person was running for office, celebrating a religious holiday, or visiting from out of town, my parents always seemed to be the first people to call.

The following fall weekend all the leaves were turning colors on the trees. The green, lush foliage of the Washington suburbs had some yellow hues of fall. The weather still had the hot and humid temperatures, but the nights were getting cooler. We shifted into our very familiar entertainment mode. Saturday morning dawned, and I could smell my mother's usual grand dinner menu. Dainty pieces of dough balls were being fried on the stove as *gulab jaman* dessert balls. She was a master at having all four burners and the oven going full swing. Fabulous aromas of spices and meat were dancing in every room of the house. Another burner displayed our pressure cooker with the top making a rhythmic sound of steam leaving the pot. That was an easy guess, chicken curry with turmeric, coriander, garlic, and paprika. The other burner had the deepest and largest red pot in our home. My mom used it to make basmati rice with green peas. My mom was in her zone, and every kitchen counter had a cutting board, a serving plate, or food waiting to be caressed in my mom's talented hands.

My dad was cleaning up the main areas of the house with the vacuum cleaner. My sisters and I set the table. All of our dining room cupboards were empty. We laid out the fine china and the even finer silverware. The cutlery was my great-grandfather's and had been handed down generation after generation in its original red velvet box. My sister and I carefully removed the serving spoons and wiped them with damp towels before laying them intricately on our small yet elaborate table. The entire family was well practiced in the exciting rush of the pre-dinner party preparations. Each of us had different roles. I was the designated dessert chef. Since I was eight, I had been interested in baking. I baked cakes, cookies, pies, and baklava and made puddings and cheesecakes. I practiced different combinations in my cakes, starting with adding pudding to the batter or even folding in whipped cream. If my dessert trial went well, I would prepare it for the party, and all our guests would comment on how amazing the dessert tasted. This weekend, I was back in my cherished role, and I perfectly executed my famous pineapple upside-down cake that I had learned at eight years old.

My sister Saima and I took a break in our living room. My mom came in and asked if we were ready. We both said yes. My mom then said, "So are you wearing *that*?" I was in casual jeans with my long, brown hair pulled back in an unglamorous but very functional ponytail. My sister wore khaki pants and a faded shirt. We had not dressed up since it was my parent's dinner party, not ours, and I had anticipated that my sister and I would hang out in our rooms, watch TV, and make a brief appearance to grab some food. Obviously, no need to change clothes. "Why would it matter what I wear?" I bewilderedly asked my Mom. I immediately sensed that unknown plots and plans were underway. My mom responded that since guests were arriving, we should both at least look a little better dressed. My sister left the room to change, but I had to ask, "Do these people have some sons our age?"

My mom hesitated. Her hesitation was all that I needed to see. This encounter would be the first of many official "let's meet the young man's family" events. While I understand that my parents meant well, I was simply in no mood for a prospecting visit. My mom insisted that it wouldn't hurt to meet some people. I felt stranded. Earlier in life I could hide behind college or launching my career. But now, I thought that I did not have any excuses and was completely unprepared. I ran upstairs to commiserate with my sister. The two of us decided the best course of action would be to sabotage the process. That night, we were gracious hostesses and met with the family. Afterward, my parents asked us what we thought of them. I knew my parents were really asking if we would consider the son as a potential husband. I did not like games, especially games that encroached on my freedom. In response, I firmly stated that I hated the potential and I was going to bed. I impressed myself with my skills of avoiding the discussion. But I knew that in the future, I needed to up my game.

Saima returned to our bedroom and we decided on a plan. The next few months, we created grand diversions to avoid meeting anyone that we did not already know. As the months passed, we refined our subversive and exasperating tactics. We were women on a mission: stay single, live rent-free, and have fun! Once at a similar dinner party plan, my mom realized that we were out of milk and asked me to kindly run to the store and buy some for our guests. I went to the store. I came home in total stealth mode and put the milk in the fridge. Then, still in full stealth mode, I walked back to my car and did not return for hours. I attended a movie and finally arrived at home at the late hour of eleven o'clock. My parents were miffed and embarrassed, and they had looked for me everywhere and wanted to know how the milk showed up without me. Apparently, a missing hostess did not phase our guests. They were more interested in meeting the family and assessing our values and character. My presence in that sense was not missed. Despite my lack of punctuality, the undaunted family still sent a marriage proposal. Many of my local friends were undergoing similar situations with their determined parents. They enjoyed the process. My friends graciously charmed and entertained potential suitors, and decided on whom they wanted to marry. But I am a rebel.

Nonetheless, despite my subversive tricks, the requests continued to arrive for potential suitors to meet my family. This tireless pursuit seemed to be a standard process of growing up in a Muslim household. I was wearying of dodging meetings. I told my parents that they were welcome to meet whomever they wanted, but I would not be available. My intense schedule of working, hanging out with friends, and watching television would not permit such frivolous diversions. My long-suffering mom was constantly asked, "Have your daughters found anyone yet?" My parents were persistent, convinced, as most parents are, that they somehow knew what was best for the children that they have borne and raised since infancy. Their persistence, in turn, taught me how to be more persistent. We were one big, happy, persistent family with each of us dutifully toiling toward our own goal.

My parents persisted, and my sister and I moved into high gear— literally—on our avoidance tactics. Once again, our parents scheduled "visitors" to join us for dinner. Prior to the dinner, my sister and I were out of the house, running an errand, and by chance stopped for gas before driving home. We had to walk into the station to pay for the fuel. Inside the gas station, we noticed an elegantly dressed family of five. Their mom wore a traditional *shalwar kameese*, with a young daughter of about twelve gorgeously arrayed in a long dress of bright cotton. They were in the station to use the restrooms for final primping. The two guys that looked like they were in their twenties were dressed in suits and ties. Both of the young men were adjusting their ties and combing their hair.

My sister warningly whispered in my ear, "I bet those are our dinner guests!" I whispered back, "Let's stay inside and pretend to shop so we can follow them when they leave." The family piled back into the car and pulled out of the station to the stoplight. We followed cautiously. The car turned left and headed toward our home, turning into our neighborhood. My sister knew the routes around our house, turned sharply to take a short cut, and floored the gas pedal, speeding us on our way. We weaved through the familiar streets that we knew much better than our guests. Meanwhile, since this event was during the life before Google Maps, our guests had to read each street sign and determine which way to turn. My sister and I arrived at home as the other car was coming up our street. We screeched into the driveway, jumped out of the car and ran into the house. I saw my dad standing expectantly and persistently in the entry hall as we burst in. I hastily said, "Dad, this is a setup! I'll be in my room all night." I stayed in my room all night, stubbornly reading a book. I had a great evening, and I hope our guests did too.

Pakistani tradition holds that daughters live with parents until marriage. We were raised with this tradition, and I had never really questioned the concept. As many American families are now experiencing with their boomerang Millennials, there are pluses and minuses of living at home as an adult. No rent and great food were a trade-off for living with my parents' rules. But I realized whenever I was with my parents, in their eyes

I was still a child. I was leading my own life but still under their roof. I had to balance respecting their wishes and my need for independence.

As I reminiscence, and as a parent with my own daughter, I now realize that my parents had a point. It was good to keep my options open. Another Saturday night, they went to a new couple's home. They asked all of us to come with them. Muslim cultures are centered around family, and having dinner together is common. I checked out our home pantry and the refrigerator. The options were slim so I opted to join my parents. For the second time, I did not see this coming; the couple had a daughter, Asma, who was older than me, and two sons, Amir and Qasim, that were about my age. We ate dinner and played games in the basement for the evening. To my surprise, I thought that Amir was, in the parlance of my twenties, cute.

The next day, Asma called me and suggested that we hang out at the mall. It sounded like fun, so we went to the mall on Sunday afternoon, shopped, and had lunch at the food court. Over lunch, Asma confided that her brother Amir really liked me and wanted to meet me again. Since he had already had the cuteness factor, I agreed. Asma asked if her mom needed to call my mom for permission. I did not think there was a need for a formal meeting yet. I said no, that I would meet him at a café, and the three of us would spend time together. When I returned home, I told my beleaguered mom about our planned meeting. She was thrilled!

Three days later, I was scheduled to meet cute Amir and Asma at the café outside the mall. As I left the house, my mom gave me the usual, "Are you really going to wear *that*?" She rolled her eyes and said, "You know, Honey, these things matter." I sweetly replied, "Yes, Mom, I am just having coffee, not marrying the guy." My mom let it go since I was willingly meeting a guy of a family friend. I kept my good jeans and white button-down shirt for this occasion. I walked to the car looking like I was headed to buy groceries instead of a sort of coffee date. Maybe I could scare off this guy with the real me. I rebelled against women being judged by their looks and figured my lovely personality would have to do the trick or he wasn't worth it.

I got into my Honda and drove to the mall. I walked into the café and saw Asma and Amir sitting at a table by the window. As I walked in the door, they both stood up. Asma was dressed in a cute pantsuit, and Amir had on dark slacks, a white shirt, and a red tie. I think my mom and Amir were on the same thought process of this being a type of date. I gave Asma a hug and Amir smiled and nodded. He was being a good Muslim guy, but he also brought a bouquet of flowers for me and was a really sweet young man. Muslims don't date in the American sense; we usually have an escort when meeting with a member of the opposite sex. Asma was an excellent escort and cheerleader for her brother. We talked for what seemed like a fast three hours getting to know each other's story. We talked about the books we liked and where we had travelled. Asma was a great escort, sitting at another table all alone, reading a book and occasionally glancing toward us. I got a sense of Amir and what was important to him, such as being close by so he could help his ailing father. I was interested in getting to know him better. I guess he felt the same way and invited me to dinner the following Saturday night.

When I returned home, my mom was there with twenty questions. I knew that Amir's mother and my mom were friends. I wanted to support my mom, but living at home meant always feeling like a kid that had to answer to her parents. I didn't want my mom to start naming her grandchildren, so I skipped the part of meeting with Amir again. Instead, I went to my room and asked my sister to be an escort for next Saturday night. She said, "So what's going on?" I said, "Just come next Saturday, and you can give me your feedback too."

The following weekend I went out with Amir to a Mexican restaurant with amazing food. This time I brought my sister Saima, who sat alone at another table, having Spanish rice and a taco salad. Again, Amir brought me a gorgeous bouquet of white roses with a big red bow. I had only mentioned once that I liked white roses. Apparently he had listened. We chatted about his job and his family. I told him that my sister and I planned to travel to Hawaii and Australia soon. My mom had a part-time job with an airline, and I took full advantage of being a dependent of an airline employee. I told Amir that I enjoyed his company and would call him when I returned from my trip to Australia. Saima had finished eating and was sitting at her table alone, so Amir motioned her to join us. He asked us about what our plans were for our upcoming trip. The three of us discussed what we knew of Australia, although none of us had actually been there.

After dinner, I took my roses and walked outside. Amir escorted me to our car and opened the door for me to get in. Saima drove us home. As soon as we pulled out of the parking lot, she said, "I like him, but what do you think?" I said that meeting him three times was not enough to decide either way for me. "So no butterflies?" Saima asked. I said "No, no butterflies." Then she said, "Well you better think of something to say to Mom. You know Mom and Dad will call you picky if you don't marry this one." "I know, Saim," I said. "Let's just focus on Australia for now."

I continued to trot around the globe. My sister Saima and I embarked on road trips between the international trips. With my job, I attended conferences all over the country and even a few conferences in Zurich. I lived my dream of seeing places that I had only read about in books. The exposure to new countries taught me that there was more than one "right way" to accomplish a task. And even with all the unique foods and traditions, deep down we were all the same. We wanted to be loved, be accepted, make a difference, and leave this world a better place for the generations that followed us. I spoke to Amir when I returned from my trip. We met at our usual coffee shop. He again spoke about the future. By this time, I had turned twenty-two, and Amir was almost thirty. He was more ready to settle down than me. I told him that I would like to stay friends. I said that right now I wanted to prove to myself that I could not only do the job but that I could be a great engineer like my dad and grandfather. Our families kept in touch, but we did not.

I was too busy with my fun, full life. I was halfway complete with my master's degree, which I had accomplished in two semesters. And Amir had given me confidence that when I was ready to get married, there were some really amazing Muslim guys in my parents' community. The idea of getting married just didn't seem like a huge life change that I was seeking yet. I had gotten so many blessings from parents and a grandmother who showed me how to live with joy and service. My dad demonstrated to me that I could be good at math and a successful engineer. My mom gave me the passion for travel and my own type of art—photography. I could see past all the covert match-making efforts and see that, somehow, God would take care of my future.

My co-workers had heard me complain about my nosy parents. George, a seasoned engineer that had learned shortwave radio in the army, was a mentor for our group. The other five members were fairly new graduates that were learning engineering at their first job. George listened to my rant about the unplanned covert dinner parties and said, "You know, my parents are gone now. Maybe you should think how much your parents are concerned and willing to put their necks on the line for you. You got your nerd skills from your father and the ability to see the world from your mom. I know it's hard to live with your parents as an adult, but they are only doing what they think is right." George added that in the northern area of town he lived in, many immigrant families from Central America functioned the same way.

I had to agree; my family lavished us with love and an education. George was giving me a view from the parent who loves their child. From my parents, I learned how to have a generous heart, to serve others, to be kind, and that caring about others is paramount. My parents were determined to set up their daughters' futures with good families, leading to a happy life. They put us in cultural dance shows, brought us to community festivals, and even bought us expensive tickets to attend fundraisers. I, on the other hand, kept finding new ways to fill up my schedule with one great reason after another for why I simply could not be home for dinner parties. I decided to ratchet up my efforts with graduate classes and convert my degree progress from part time to full time. Full-time classes meant spending most evenings in class and most weekends in study groups. My family-based events would have to suffer, and that was by my design.

When I was in high school, I used to type my dad's résumé (yes, on a typewriter, with correcting tape!). Luckily, I had upgraded to an electric typewriter, so that was better than the manual ones in school. But I typed my dad's resume over and over again while he was looking for a job. My talented father had a bachelor's degree, two master's degrees in civil engineering, and an MBA, so I always remembered thinking one day I was going to have three degrees. I had no idea that the degree was going to change my life and destiny forever.

I had been working for almost a year, and now it was Memorial Day weekend. I was in the elevator of my parents' building, going up to our apartment, having just finished playing at the pool with my two cousins who were eleven and nine. We lived on the top floor of a fourteen-story building in the northern Virginia area. An older gentlemen and two guys about my age were already in the elevator. They must have been moving in, I guessed, since that was the only way to get into the service elevator in the basement. My eleven-year-old cousin turned to me and said quietly, pointing to one of the guys my age, "What if you end up marrying that guy?" I laughed. After all, there are six of us in an elevator—not the time for a private conversation. The other party got off on the eighth floor, and we continued up. I told my cousin, "You don't marry some guy you see in an elevator." I never really thought about that elevator ride again except for the fact that even my eleven-year-old cousin was attempting to set me up.

I started my Masters of Science in Electrical Engineering that fall while still working full time. So, I would work a full day and then high-tail onto the DC metro all the way to the suburbs and take classes for another six hours. It kept me out of the house and out of the line of my parents' dinner parties. Life was good and progressing fast. And then I took a class in stochastic signals, and a nice guy sat in front of me in class. I think it was the guy from the elevator.

I walked into the stochastic signals class that first day and sat in the second row. One of the girls who walked into the class one day looked really familiar. Understand that being an engineering major at that time, there weren't many girls there, so anytime you saw a girl in an engineering class, she was easily noticed. I thought, She looks like one of the engineers I went to school with in Texas. Then I dismissed the thought—after all, what are the chances that someone from Texas would have moved to Virginia and also attend the same graduate program as me. I looked back a second time and she mouthed to me, "Did you go to Texas A&M?" It's a small world, but it was about to get even smaller.

After class, Lisa and I gave each other a hug and got details on how both of us had ended up in Virginia. I introduced her to Dan, one of my coworkers in the class, and she introduced me to one of her coworkers, the guy who was sitting in front of me. That is how I met Tariq, the guy my cousin checked out in the elevator. The four of us started a study group. Working full time and going to school was difficult enough, so we would meet on the weekends and get the homework done as a group study. If one of us was struggling, the other three would help out. We kept in contact as we all muddled through our degrees with some of the same and some different classes.

The following semester, I decided to travel to Europe. Seeing the Eiffel Tower in Paris and eating pizza in Italy was a dream of mine. While I was at Texas A&M, I planned my dream vacation in my head. In school and before I had a "real job," I had plenty of time but no money. I was broke, working on grants and loans, and I daydreamed about visiting Europe. Now I was finally earning money, but I had no time between working full time and my full-time graduate school schedule. So, again, my dream of traveling and sightseeing in Europe had been put on hold. Then one of my former roommates, Pam, called me from Texas and said, "In October I am going to tour Europe, and I want you to come." Seven countries in a whirlwind eleven days. Pam and I had read travel brochures on France and Germany since sophomore year at A&M, so I said, "Why not?"

Being gone for eleven days meant that I would miss my midterm review, though, and then I'd fly home from Paris the day of the midterm exam. To make my plan work, I asked Tariq to take really good notes at the review. In the late eighties, we still predated email and internet use. I asked Tariq to hand-deliver the notes to my parents. So this classmate, whose handwriting was a little questionable, took awesome legible notes. He captured all of the material from the review, and went to my parents' apartment. When I landed from Paris, I was immediately prepared for my midterm. Tariq was so concerned about my doing well on the test and my completing my master's. It reminded me of my dad's commitment to my success when he tutored me in trigonometry back in high school.

As the semesters continued, Tariq, Lisa, and our friends from school would hang out after school. Sometimes it was doing homework, other times it would be the movies or an office party. Both Tariq and Lisa were contractors, and their work functions were so much better than our government employee parties. I would tag along as another engineer and enjoy the venue. We all became great friends, and we all progressed toward our master's degrees together.

In the meantime, as with Muslim tradition, my mom and grandma still were looking for suitable candidates for an arranged marriage. On Saturday evenings I decided to study. My excuse would be that I was going to the library to study and I would not be able to make the dinner party. My parents said that their friends were bringing their kids and enjoyed having us there. But things were still "off." I noticed that none of my parents' usual group of friends showed up; these were new friends with older sons. The parents assess the strengths and preferences of their children and find suitable people to marry. After all, who knows a child better than their parents?

But I was mad. Why was I not informed about the intentions of these guests? Plus, just to bug my parents, I told them I was never getting married. Back to studying. I had class and none of my work was done. The next evening in class, I was still frustrated and in walked Tariq. I started venting about my evening disagreement with my parents, and he quietly sat and listened. He let me say whatever was on my mind and suggested a movie this weekend to take my mind off of living at home after college. Most of my classmates were guys and I would hang out with them after class, so it seemed like a regular request. We headed to the movie theatres on Saturday afternoon. And that's when he dropped the bomb on me and said, "I thought we were more than just friends." I don't know why he got this idea since most of our interactions were either in class or in groups.

I assured him that he was just another classmate to me. He kept persisting and invited me to movies and made dinner at his home for my friends and me. Tariq is a great cook. We got to know each other better and became good friends. My friends and family also met him and thought he was kind. He made an effort to meet my parents and get to know them. As the friendship grew, it blossomed into a romance. When Tariq brought up the idea of marriage, it felt more like spending time with a good friend. Eventually we got engaged, and a year after that we were married.

Tariq has been taking care of me ever since. Just making sure that I have had the little things that I needed to get through life. After we had kids, he has been an amazing father. One of the things that we see in traditional Muslim cultures is that men like playing with their kids and spending time with their kids. My husband worked his way through college as part of the Naval Reserves, and to make ends meet, he also worked as a cook at a large restaurant chain. Because of all his experience in restaurants, he was great at making meals. He would always cook for the kids, and the kids loved eating what he made because it tasted so much better than what I made. And so not only would he cook them dinner but then he would sit down and feed them dinner when they were babies. The kids loved it. Even now when my kids come home from school they ask what is Dad making for dinner. And I'd say, "I can make you a turkey sandwich." I remember my thirteen-year-old son rolling his eyes and saying, "Mom, I'll just wait for Dad to come home."

My husband's other major pastime is sports. If there's a sport, he's watching it. Basketball in the spring, football in the fall, all year round—ESPN is his channel. When the kids started playing soccer, my husband was at every game and most of the practices. I liked to drop them off at practices but my husband liked to stay there and watch. He even coached some of my daughter's basketball teams and soccer teams when they were short on coaches. I see a lot of the same behaviors in my cousins and in my uncles: being there for their kids, showing up, and having a work-life balance that includes coming home after a workday and having family time.

My sister has said that since we don't have any brothers, my husband is the closest thing she ever knew to having a brother, such as the time he helped her paint her house to get her house ready for sale. With my brothers-in-law and my husband, you see Muslim men really taking care not only of their own parents, because that is a tradition in the culture, but also taking care of the wife's parents because they honor her family. I see that a lot with Tariq. In fact, half the time when my parents call they ask for him (and just say hi to me).

Three decades and four kids later, despite all the match-making schemes by my parents, sometimes you just marry the guy from the elevator. At the wise age of eleven, my cousin was right.

CHAPTER 9

ADULTING

"THERE ARE TWO BLESSINGS, AND MOST PEOPLE EVALUATE
THESE BLESSINGS INCORRECTLY: HEALTH AND FREE TIME."

PROPHET MUHAMMAD

I often wonder how simple my life would be if I lived somewhere where everyone looked and thought like me. But that is not the path that was chosen for me, and I in turn chose the path of raising my kids as Muslims in the United States. I see now that I did the same thing to my kids that my parents did to me by making them different. When I was in school, being different meant being excluded, so now I know that my gift is the ability to include.

My advice to any mom would be to raise kids with faith. Yes, we all like our labels of Muslim, Jew, Hindu, Buddhist, Christian, and Sikh, but having a strong religious background also strengthens our kids' moral foundation. The label is not as important as the values we impart to our children. The biggest gift we can give our kids is the power to believe in a God who is bigger than us. The certainty is that there is an intricate order to our lives and that we do not have to worry about every detail to make life work. A strong faith means less stress because we have the power to give things to God to handle.

As a mom, there is a huge sense of relief when we see our kids make good choices. I was blessed with a faith that challenged me to become better every day. Islam has a huge prohibition on lying. With my kids, especially, I watched my tongue. My son had a way of pushing my buttons and, as a punishment, I would put his video games in time out. I remember looking into his big, brown, disappointed eyes and saying his video games were going in time out for three days. The little voice went off inside my head and said, "Hey, are you really going to be able to keep your word on this?" I remember thinking, He is going to have a ton of energy and I am going to miss the video game coma. I knew I probably did not have the energy to follow through on three days. So, I corrected myself and said to my son, "Your video games are going in time out for three hours." I felt it was critical that in all conversations with my kids, I had to keep my word. If I said it, even if I did not want to do it, I still kept my word.

As a result of my faith and self-discipline, I have four teenagers in the house right now and very little stress. I can trust my kids because they can trust my word. They witness first-hand the value of honesty and the act of keeping our word, even when it is inconvenient. The Quran drilled into my head, *control your tongue*. Sometimes after a long day when I am tired and the kids are full of energy or fighting, I struggle to stay calm and say nice things. I remember one time I was so frustrated with my son that I told him to go to his room and think about hitting his sister. He came out five minutes later and said he was bored. I told him to go back to his room and make a drawing. The house was peaceful and quiet for thirty minutes when I got a sick feeling in my stomach that my son was too quiet. I ran up to his room. When I walked in, he was drawing on the walls. I gasped and asked him, "What were you thinking?" He innocently said "Mom, you told me to draw." He was right. I wish I had been more specific and had instructed him to draw on paper. Now I think twice about speaking while tired or angry. I make sure I can actually keep my word and say only what I am willing to commit. I am still a work in progress and slowly improving.

I wanted my kids to believe in one God and have the peace I have experienced. That is why I chose to raise them as Muslims, even when they would stick out or feel pain. Yes, it is painful to be different. I have had countless days of a child coming home from school and hearing the hurtful things a teacher said about Islam or something on the news. My daughter took a world government class that included studying the government structures of six different countries. One of the countries was Iran. The teacher made several derogatory comments about the government, and my daughter came home and told me. Yes, I acknowledged, Iran had had some issues like every other country with poor treatment of women. And no, not all so-called Muslim governments are perfect, but I did not like the attitude that one peoples' ideas are superior to another peoples' ideas.

I don't always know how to handle every situation. So I asked my daughter how she felt when the teacher said those things. And she replied, "You know, Mom, I thought he's talking like a guy who's never been to Iran or he would have known better." The wisdom I learn from my kids! My super smart daughter recognized his ignorance and was still able to learn from the teacher despite his limitations. She found the good in the teacher and did not let his comments lead to a judgment of him as a person. We all have limitations, even our teachers. I was grateful my kids have been exposed to different people and viewpoints; by visiting Pakistan, Turkey, and Qatar they can have their own perspective despite the TV news. I want my kids to know that being different is okay. Unique is more valuable than cookie-cutter, and our uniqueness will open more doors than it will close.

I am glad our kids have the confidence to be themselves and still respect others. My daughter's writings are fantastic. She can use her voice and still keep her dignity. I am proud that my kids have found their own ways of being heard without making someone else guilty or wrong. Islam helped me raise strong, empowered, confident kids. I owe these skills to the life of the Prophet (pbuh) and the lessons of my faith.

I would want my kids to remember two things from me. First, there are two ways to have the tallest building in town: One way is to build the tallest building, and the second way is to tear all the other buildings down. I taught my kids that when someone attacks, they are revealing their own insecurity. If we attack someone's faith, we need to strengthen our own faith. My advice to my kids would be when it comes to faith, education, and life, build the tallest building so you don't need to worry about tearing someone else's building down.

The second lesson I want to leave to my kids is: If you can spot it, you got it. The only weaknesses we see in others are the weaknesses we see in ourselves. Our life is a mirror, and if we feel that someone is irritating or mean, then we somehow feel we have that quality. When I get angry, I ask myself *what character trait do I need to develop or improve?* I have done the same with my coworkers and my kids. Negative emotions are just a signal to guide us on where our own character needs strength. I was so impressed with the strength of Prophet Muhammad (pbuh) and his patience with so many different people. Now I realize that it was his character that made him patient. I work on my character regularly so I can model for my children the way to inner peace.

To work or not to work? That was my question. I wanted to be supermom and "you can count on me" mom, but also have an amazing career. I had spent most of my life studying math and science, graduating with an engineering degree, then writing a master's thesis on computer architecture, and finally working as a systems engineer. Being an engineer was my identity. A systems engineer is the person that takes different software programs, types of computers, and makes different pieces work as one system to achieve the goals of the clients. I was the bridge that taught the different hardware and software pieces to communicate together, and I helped "glue" all the different parts together. Think of it like building a house—there is the electrician, the plumber, and the carpenter as the different pieces to make the house. A systems engineer is the general contractor that tells each of them where to put their wires, pipes, and walls so the house is designed correctly.

I was also a systems engineer in life. I took the different pieces of two cultures, my religion, and my goals and integrated them into working with harmony. But I was stuck. I had been married a while and now we were thinking of having kids. I had watched other women in my office "balance" work and family. I felt they gave up on both sides. My friend Sandy's kids spent so much time with a babysitter that they were fluent in Urdu, a foreign language Sandy did not even know. On the other side were the stay-at-home moms that seemed to be existing for their kids and tight on money. I wanted to have it all—money, kids, freedom, and achieving my goals. I was in limbo and looking for inspiration.

And my inspiration came from the oddest of places. I was invited to a fundraising dinner. I was an engineer and did not particularly enjoy social events, but having a soft spot for charity, I decided to go. The plan was to eat, donate, and run. After dinner, as I was preparing my getaway, a speaker came on and started speaking about charity. The speaker mentioned that Muhammad's (pbuh) wife, Khadija, had practiced charity and had impeccable character. Khadija was a wealthy widow living in Mecca, and not only did she have a successful business but she also used the funds to help those around her.

Khadija knew that money could not buy character. She had noticed the same qualities of honesty and compassion in Muhammad (pbuh) and sent him a wedding proposal. The inspiration I need had come. Khadija had it all—marriage, kids, a business—and still made an impact on our world. I needed to be more like Khadija, embracing all the gifts and options God had laid out for me. Khadija would be my role model. What hit me most was that Khadija and Muhammad (pbuh) both went against the grain. In a society that had lost its moral values, they stood up for what was right. And when the social condition did not empower women, both of them showed women that they deserved it all and that God honors women. So I decided to study a little more about Khadijah.

Khadijah lived in an era when the Catholic Church was debating if women had souls. Her home of Arabia was not much more enlightened. The male-dominated culture had yet to learn the value of women. Sons were preferred to daughters because sons could protect the family and bring in money. And in this culture, Khadijah, a noble woman, decided to run a trade business and hire employees. She had hired Muhammad (pbuh) to take her caravans to Syria for trading goods. She knew of his reputation of being honest. When presenting the merchandise, not only would Muhammad (pbuh) tell the buyer of the benefits of the item but also any flaws. Her other employees told her of Muhammad's (pbuh) unique business style, and she was impressed. In a society of deception, Muhammad (pbuh) was so honest that people bought from him because they could trust his word. Muhammad (pbuh) would go on to do more for the empowerment of women than anyone in modern history.

Khadija was in her forties and had been married before. She was not looking to get married, but she was impressed by Muhammad (pbuh) and decided to send him a marriage proposal. This could only be a match made in heaven because she was wealthy and he was poor, she was forty and he was twenty-five, and she was his employer and he was the employee. Muhammad (pbuh) and Khadija were happily married with six kids until Khadija died. She was the love of his life.

I was getting excited now. The vague memories of Sunday School and all those hours of learning religion that I never thought would matter to me actually seemed relevant now. I was an engineer, a wife, and a Muslim. I had forgotten that my faith showed me that the first woman to become Muslim had both a family and a business. On top of that, Khadija is historically referred to as Khadija bint Khuwaylid, or Khadija daughter of Khuwaylid. So when she got married, Khadija did not take her husband's name. I was realizing that the support and validity that I was seeking was already given to mean through my faith in Islam. There was the tug to change my name after marriage and conform with my American friends and co-workers. However, I wanted to keep my maiden name. I liked my name—why did I need to give it up? God had shown me that women were powerful and earned their own money but were still regarded highly as mothers and wives. Even Khadija, in 595 AD, got married and kept her name.

I loved engineering, but in a male-dominated field, I was constantly proving that I was a worthy engineer. Even with a master's degree, I was often asked to make copies or order lunch. I even had one manager that referred to me as our "lady engineer." We were in a meeting once, and he introduced my designs as the radio system designs from our lady engineer. I had been working for a long time and was looking for advancement and respect. I knew that I would never get to the Vice President level because in most engineering companies, there was only one "Pink VP," and that was the Vice President of Human Resources. When I left engineering in the late 1990s, there was still a large pay gap between men and women. I had spent fourteen years trying to prove that women were great engineers. I had several awards for amazing designs. My radio system designs were presented to the United States Congress by Senator John Glenn. But I knew that even though I had taken all the same classes and had the same degrees and experience of my male counterparts, I still had to prove I was just as competent.

I decided to look for something more flexible. I wanted a business like Khadija's where I could have both finances and flexibility. At that point, direct sales came into my life. I met a girl in our apartment elevator who was selling the cosmetics I was using. We struck up a conversation, and Jeanine asked me if I need some more cleanser. I told her yes, so she invited me to be a guest at her meeting the following Monday night, and I accepted. I was going to get a makeover and more cleanser. It sounded like fun. There I met women who were building businesses, making money, helping other women become empowered, and having flexible schedules. I was looking for female role models and certainly needed more self-confidence. I thought, if I could learn some business skills, maybe I could be more marketable as an engineer.

I did jump in. I went with my gut and said yes to selling makeup! Sales was not easy, and my engineer personality did not help. I was into facts and figures and computers that did what I told them to. Working with women instead of computers was another world for me. I would question my ability and wonder if I could ever take a business off the ground. I was constantly teased by my male co-workers about being a "ding-dong lady," and inside I wondered if all the evenings and weekends that I was putting in would ever amount to anything. I thought, Why can't I be like everyone else and just work a day job for the rest of my life? I was still trying new paths and stretching myself. My friends asked me if I was crazy, and frankly I wasn't sure that I wasn't. But I was relying on my Muslim history, my role models of Muhammad (pbuh) and Khadija and their example: to be honest, care about people, show respect, always take the high road, and trust God, and everything will work out.

The sales training did help my engineering career. I learned how to sell my designs and implementation ideas. I also learned to see upper management as my customers and decided to reformulate technical designs into easy concepts that management could understand. Management was constantly rejecting our requests, and with my new sales perspective, I saw that management just didn't understand our technical language. I was getting promotions at work and I was building a business. I had earned the use of two cars in my sales business while working full time as an electrical engineer. I was ready to try life without a job, without a boss, and without a commute. I wanted to make my own mark on the world by raising my kids on my terms. I felt like I had built a credible business and like Khadija, I could now have a business, a family, and an impact. Khadija helped so many causes with her wealth but was also an amazing wife. A famous *Hadith* (or saying) of Prophet Muhammad (pbuh) would honor Khadija as his wife: "She believed in me when no one else would, she accepted Islam when people were rejecting me, and she helped and comforted me when no one else would lend a hand."

Both sales and Islam forced me to grow. Islam said that education was important and to continue to learn and grow to improve my faith. Sales taught me that I need to improve my skills and my thought processes to succeed. I was blessed to be put on a path of constant personal development and discovery that led me to seek mentors for both my faith and my business. I was blessed to learn how to empower women. I was able to show other women how to invest in their own businesses and get back more time with their families. I knew the frustration of working with lousy bosses, driving long commutes, and getting excuses instead of promotions. When I announced I was quitting my job as an engineer, I got no support. My co-workers asked how would I pay the bills, and my friends said, but what about your degree? I knew what I wanted but had not fully developed my inner strength, so I turned to the best source of support I knew—my faith.

In the Quran, there are several verses that talk about trusting God and letting go of fear. I never really understood them. But then I had never really had to take a leap of faith. It was a leap to let go of all my engineering family's "get-a-secure-job" mentality and go for something I had no degrees to do. Furthermore, my new path would put my financial destiny in my own hands. My success depended on my ability to help women grow. But then I thought that Muhammad (pbuh) also invested in women and changed the lives of all Muslim women, even when it rocked all of the social and cultural beliefs of the day. Islam gave women the right to vote, the right to own property, the right to initiate divorce, and the right to be respected by men. I would use the skills I had learned and back them up with Muhammad's (pbuh) example of giving women everything they deserved. I had the support I needed to start a new path.

Working for myself was an adjustment. It took tons of self-discipline. I knew I had made the right decision the day I was at another sales leader's home planning a retreat. There were ten women sitting around a large table in a basement. We were all taking notes on how we would schedule a motivational retreat for our sales team members and which person would teach the different concepts to be covered. I was the new kid on the block, and there were several other women there with more experience, higher clout, and were making more money that me with my new "just-went-full-time" business. One of the top performers at the table got up to get coffee and turned to me and said, "Would you like me to get you some coffee?" I was in shock! What, I am no longer considered the coffee girl? The respect and belonging I had wanted in all my engineering jobs just showed up at this first meeting. I was so glad to feel like a valued member of the team. I could be myself and not have to work to be one of the guys.

I had overcome one obstacle, but there were many other mental obstacles that I would face. My next challenge was whether a stay-at-home mom with a business should have a nanny. I was bringing in some money but not tons, and my kids were little and needed regular attention. I would start making phone calls or writing a newsletter and keep getting interrupted over and over. Could I justify the extra expense of someone watching my kids when my hours were flexible, I worked mostly in the evenings, and I was usually at home? The answer came from an unexpected source—I remembered that Islam loves education.

I had learned to read Arabic script when I was twelve. Learning to read an alphabet at twelve is not as easy as when we are younger. I wanted my kids to easily and effortlessly read Arabic, particularly the high level of Arabic used in the Quran. I found a lady that was willing to come to my house and teach each kid to read. I was glad to have a break to get some work done during the day, and the kids got to learn something new. The teacher went from four hours a week to twenty-four hours a week. And I ended up with my nanny or teacher. Having the extra support, a clean home, and someone to give the kids lunch helped free up my time, and my business succeeded even more.

My goal is to show my kids the living example of a good Muslim. I do my best to practice the faith. One night I told the story of Amina, Prophet Muhammad's (pbuh) mother, to my children. I reminded them that having parents is a blessing, while Muhammad (pbuh) lost his father before he was born. My son asked wide-eyed, "So he never even hugged his daddy?" I said yes, but you get to hug your daddy whenever you want. I continued to tell them that at the age of five, Muhammad (pbuh) would lose his mother. On her deathbed, his mother gave a prayer that every parent wants for their child: "Everything that is alive is one day going to die, and nothing new comes into the world except that it gets old, but I have left good in you." Then I said to my children, "There is so much good in you too." I went on with the tale, stating that after the Prophet (pbuh) had lost both parents, an angel turned to God and said, "You have taken his father and his mother; who in the world is left for this boy?" And God replied, "I am here for him. I left myself for this boy." I wanted my children to know that God is always here for them and would love and protect them when I could not.

My desire for my children is to see Islam as a thriving, relevant lifestyle and an integral part of their journey on Earth. I want to always be my best as a parent. And when I make mistakes, I take responsibility. There are times of frustration when I feel that everything that I have taught them is going in one ear and out the other, but I feel that eventually the example of how they were raised will follow them forever. In Pakistan, I grew up with the example of my aunts having businesses, having domestic help, and raising a family. I wanted to set that same example for a mom here in the United States. In the end I feel that I succeeded as a stay-at-home mom who had money to say yes to fun camps and travel. And I also am a work-at-home mom who has time to volunteer at school and coach their sports. My kids and family are my priority, but as shown in Islam, I can also be a force for good and make a positive impact in my community and world.

CHAPTER 10

MY PILGRIMAGE

"THOSE PEOPLE WHO SHOW NO MERCY TO OTHERS WILL
RECEIVE NO MERCY FROM GOD."

PROPHET MUHAMMAD

In November of 2008, I found myself at the airport boarding a plane for Jeddah, Saudi Arabia. I had no idea what to expect during the *Hajj*. I had visited Mecca about twenty years earlier, but I did not go during the Hajj. At my first visit, Mecca was totally quiet and roads were clear. We performed the *Umrah* ritual, which includes all of the steps of the pilgrimage of Hajj, but it was not during the Hajj season. I remembered Mecca as a peaceful town in the middle of the desert with wide-open roads and lots of houses. In the twenty years since, the city had totally changed. Also, the city's population grows by two million people for the two-week period of Hajj. The airport was crowded, the highways were jammed, and all the hotels were packed.

We arrived at Jeddah Airport with thousands of other Muslims; the airport is like a city unto itself to accommodate the pilgrims that come at the same time every year. Half the airport is indoors and half of it is outdoors due to the mild desert climate. The modular design allows the airport to grow to the outside for the Hajj and Ramadan seasons and then retract to a normal size for the rest of the year. Even though it was late

November, the weather was a pleasant seventy degrees. After a long flight and about four hours clearing the airport authorities, we waited for our bus to take us about eighty-three kilometers east to Mecca. We had not eaten since the flight and it was approaching midnight, so many of the airport shops had closed. But being Hajj season, some of the shop owners stayed open to serve the pilgrims. The shopkeeper showed us gratitude and told us that it was an honor to serve pilgrims. I was touched by their kindness and felt welcomed in their city. My twelve-year-old son was hungry, and my husband has a way of always finding food; the food shops went out of their way to make sure my son was taken care of. Everyone began to congratulate him for performing the Hajj at such a young age. My son beamed from ear to ear in his two white towels and flip flops. To the outside observer, it may seem that all the men performing Hajj has just stepped out of the shower. The theme of this event is that we are all equal before God. The airport was humming with eager Muslims showing their humility before their Creator. This memory of the electric night air in Jeddah and feeling of so much joy will be burned in my heart forever.

We had arrived from the States, but flights from Pakistan, Turkey, Indonesia, China, and many other countries were landing with us. The whole world was joining us for this amazing religious journey. All these pilgrims were now on the exact same six-lane highway to Mecca. The gas stations we passed had about sixty gas pumps to keep all the vehicles filled up. I had never seen so many pumps in a gas station. It felt like the whole country was on standby to help pilgrims, from the immigration officers to the bus drivers to the Saudi army that was helping with crowd control. We stopped at several checkpoints along our journey, and at each checkpoint we were greeted with a smile and congratulations for taking on the challenges of the pilgrimage to Mecca.

We checked into the hotel at about 1:30 in the morning and got our hotel rooms. All hotels in the world boast about rooms with a great view, but our room in Mecca had the best view I've ever seen. The hotel room came with either the city view on one side of the hotel or the *Kaaba* (the house of God) view on the opposite side of the hotel. We were lucky enough to get a room with the latter view on the twenty-first floor, overlooking the entire mosque and the Kaaba. It was the first hotel room where I didn't have to figure out which direction to pray in because I could just sit by the window and look directly at the Kaaba.

By this time it was two a.m., and I thought it would be a good time to go to the mosque, since I assumed it would be nearly empty. After all, the city should be asleep and I was on US time, so we were wide-awake. I was wrong. There were people everywhere; the mosque was packed even at my two a.m. arrival. I had to make my way through crowds just to reach one of the seven doors. Once I entered, there was hardly a place to sit. Imagine a building the size of four professional football stadiums bursting with worshipers at two in the morning. I wanted to make the traditional greeting the mosque. This greeting meant walking seven times around the perimeter of the black cube in the center of the mosque, the Kaaba. If the mosque had been quieter, I could have performed this ritual in under five minutes. However, in the current conditions, it took me over an hour just to walk with the crowds. We struggled to get through the crowd and decided to stay until the first morning prayer at four a.m.

Hajj was an incredible show of community. The mosque was filled with over a million worshippers by four in the morning, all humble and dressed the same before God. There were some people praying, some washing up in the well of *Zam Zam* (the well providing water to the house of God) to prepare to pray, and others reading the Holy Quran. All Muslim men must dress in two white cloths similar to towels. Women, on the other hand, may wear regular clothing that is loose and easy to pray in. Nothing can be worn to signify wealth, education, or any kind of status. No watches, fancy sandals, or stitched clothing. Everyone is just a human in the eyes of God.

I had three days before the pilgrimage to explore Mecca as a tourist. I spent the daytime sleeping and the nights in worship. I sat quietly during the worship time, reflecting on my life and memorizing parts of the Quran. I wanted to spend as much time as possible in the actual mosque, but with the crowds this was difficult. Even though our hotel was across the street, it took me about an hour to get in and another hour to get out. The stories of others that had done the pilgrimage crept into my thoughts. I began to understand the challenges of Hajj. For example, as a sign of respect, it is customary to take off our shoes in a mosque. That means that we were walking barefoot on hard marble floors for our entire time at the mosque. And finding our shoes in the many shelves that surrounded the seven entrances was difficult. Often this involved circumventing the Kaaba, or house of God, in the middle of the mosque or walking between the hills of Safaa and Marwaa. With the large crowds, it would be about five miles of barefoot walking inside the mosque each day along with the walk to and from the hotel. I quickly realized that waiting till I retired, like many people do, to come to Mecca would be tough. My son was bouncing along with no problem. I guess his years of soccer and gymnastics really helped with the fitness required for this journey.

Since it was hot during the day, my goal was to pray all night and go to sleep after the morning four a.m. prayer. Many believe that prayers in this mosque are given one hundred thousand times the credit of prayers in other locations. I had a long list of what I wanted to pray for, starting with the health of my family through giving thanks for all my material possessions. Each time in the mosque was unique. At times I was with my family, but many times I was with total strangers, praying as one. Americans have a different definition of personal space than many other cultures, so when praying with strangers, I was often sharing my prayer rug or crammed between groups of people. Walking on the first level of the mosques was so tight that if I had lifted my feet, the packed crowd would have carried me.

We visited Mecca for a few days and then took the long drive to Medina. Medina is the second most holy city in Islam and is about four hundred miles north of Mecca. When Prophet Muhammad brought the message of worshiping only one God, the pre-Islamic Arabs were very upset and started persecuting Prophet Muhammad (pbuh). Prophet Muhammad (pbuh) had to migrate to Medina to avoid getting persecuted and killed. This move from Mecca to Medina was called the *Hijrah* and is the beginning of the Islamic calendar. In Medina, Prophet Muhammad (pbuh) established the first Muslim community.

It is tradition to go to Medina to the Prophet's Mosque and say forty prayers. With five prayers a day, that's eight days of praying in Medina at the second largest mosque in the world, known as The Prophet's Mosque. The Prophet's Mosque is known for its famous green dome and black-and-white striped arches. Growing up as a Muslim, I had heard stories about these places since my first day of Sunday school in the makeshift mosque on Ash Street in Denver. Actually walking in the hallways and touching the walls seemed surreal. Was I really in these exotic lands that I had been reading about in books and on websites my whole life?

This mosque also contains the grave of the Prophet Muhammad (pbuh) in an area called *Al-Rawdah*. To the left is an old building with one window and one door showing what is remaining of the Prophet's home. The home of the leader of Arabia and the founder of Islam is a small ten foot by ten foot room with one window and a door. Inside the humble home are three unmarked graves. One is for Prophet Muhammad, one for the first Caliph of Islam, Hazrat Abu Baker. Abu-Baker was also a good friend of the Prophet before Islam. The last one for the second Caliph Omar. Prophet Muhammad (pbuh) wanted to make sure that his followers only honored God and would not make an icon out of the Prophet's (pbuh) grave. The Prophet (pbuh) and the early followers wanted the attention to go only to the worship of the one true God. They took extensive measures to keep out of the limelight by living and dying in humility. Outside the home is the area that would have been the garden. It is known as the *Rawdah,* or gardens of paradise. The area is highlighted by the green carpet, in contrast to the rest of the mosque that has red carpets. We were able to pray in the *Rawdah* for a short period of time due to the crowds at the Mosque. The humble home and small gardens reminded me that I needed to focus on not only this life but my next life, like those who came before me.

In Medina, we enjoyed great meals, great friends, shopping for souvenirs, and attending amazing religious lectures over dinner. My biggest surprise came when I left the gate of the Prophet's Mosque. Just outside the gate was a Starbucks coffee shop. My son jumped and ran to the Starbucks. We stopped momentarily to enjoy a Frappuccino before returning to our hotel. During the evening meals we would listen to lectures from religious leaders on what to expect the next day and how to fulfill our religious obligations. We were reminded of the customs and rituals that the Prophet performed and the intentions behind them. One such ritual was to pray for our salvation, and another custom was not to overindulge or waste food. I enjoyed the friendships and the historical lessons. Our tourist section of the trip was concluding, and it was time to prepare for the actual Hajj.

After being a tourist for a week and a half, we started the Hajj. I was a little apprehensive because this was the "hard part" of the journey. We boarded our buses and headed back toward Mecca to the Tent City of Mina. Once again, we went through checkpoints, and the buses were boarded with locals offering us juice and snacks. When I was there twenty years earlier at a time with no pilgrims, this trip was about four hours. With all the traffic and checkpoints this time, it was about twelve hours. I am grateful for a bus driver that stayed alert the entire time and kept us safe.

The level of excitement among my fellow pilgrims had increased exponentially. I could feel the energy change on the bus. We were beginning our pilgrimage with this four hundred kilometer trek south toward Mecca. It is tradition to stay in tents for three days. With millions of pilgrims, I had no idea what the food or bathroom situation would be. We were placed in tents by national origin. Some tents were pretty basic, but others, such as South Africa, had red carpets, chandeliers, and amazing food spreads comparable to a five-star hotel. I was in a large tent with forty other women sleeping on futons.

Now I understood what was hard about the Hajj—dealing with all different types of situations without getting emotionally triggered or upset. My husband and son were in the men's tent next door dealing with their own issues, like sick pilgrims. Because he was twelve years old, my son thought the days at Mina, living in a tent, were the best part. He loved the food, the tents, and the adventure. The tents were a maze. If we walked to the left we would end up at the food rooms where they had cold drinks and snacks for us. My son saw this as a fun game: Where would we end up this time? One alley went to the bathrooms and another alley went to the buses. Even within our tent compound we would get lost.

Many pilgrims had travelled by foot across the desert. Some had been on boats for months just to make the journey. The lucky ones, like us, came on airplanes. We were blessed that we had tents, but many of the poor just slept on the streets for the three nights. Many had make-shift camps on the side of the road. Others that had driven slept in their cars or in the back of their trucks. These pilgrims were determined to complete the Hajj, and no obstacle stopped them. Their commitment to their faith was clear, and we pray that God accepts their Hajj.

The major day of Hajj occurs at the mountain of Arafat about three miles away from Mina, opposite from the direction of Mecca. We loaded into our three group buses at three that morning. The night before, we were warned several times that if we did not leave before four a.m., we would be stuck in traffic and miss the prayer at one p.m. The distance was a mere three miles but, with traffic, could take over eight hours. I thought the guide was exaggerating, but I was wrong. Most of the pedestrian were flying through the night faster than our bus. We came to a new tent for the day on the Plains of Arafat.

Arafat had amazing signage. Huge billboard signs told the pilgrims the boundaries of Arafat by marking off the four sides of the plain. We were lucky to have a guide, but many of the pilgrims from other countries were looking for a spot on the crowded field. Muslims believe that Arafat is the location that Prophet Adam and Eve came to when they descended on Earth. Our tent was made up of bamboo poles with canvas sides and a roof. There were several other groups sharing the same tent area, and the sections were segregated by the bamboo and canvas wall. The floor was dirt. I had a small piece of cloth and a prayer rug. We could hear everything in the different sections, so I knew the group next to us had come from California. Everyone was excited. I was filled with anticipation. This was the day I had travelled fifteen thousand miles to experience.

We were greeted by the staff and intermittently visited by beggars. We had never seen so much traffic or people in our life. The sidewalks were full of pilgrims all dressed in white. The bathrooms were a little better but also had long lines. After we freshened up at the tent, our staff appeared with lunch. Rice with camel meat was the meal. I had never tasted camel, but I found that it was well prepared and tasted like lamb. Everyone found a spot in the tent.

After the second prayer of the day, the main part of the pilgrimage began. We stood for hours and prayed for forgiveness of our past sins, for blessings in this life and the next, as well as salvation. Arafat is the rehearsal for the Day of Judgment, when all of humanity will stand before God and have our lives reviewed. In Arafat, you reflect on this day, and repent for any wrongs you may have done. If you perform a perfect Hajj, that is performing all the acts and never thinking or feeling negative emotions, then all your sins till that point in life are forgiven and you will be as a newly born child.

I spent hours praying for my family, my friends, humanity and our world. In the months preparing for this journey, I had made a plan of everything I would do during these precious four hours at Arafat. I had a list of everyone I would pray for. I had a second list of every blessing I would thank God for. And then I had a third list of extra prayers that I wanted answered if I had time. I had also bought and was planning on using a book of prayers that the Prophet Muhammad (pbuh) used to use at Arafat. The prayers that I heard around me were so heartfelt and powerful that often people were crying. I went outside for a few moments, and I was looking at millions of people, all dressed in two white towels, in the Valley of Arafat, praying together. It was a moving experience and something I will never forget for the rest of my life.

I had spent weeks planning for this day, but I feel as if the day just flew. Before I knew it, sunset came and it was time to leave.

When we returned to our tents, the air was filled with the smell of spices being used in preparing the evening meal. Each of the countries was using different spices as far as my nose could tell. The cultures were all so different. The women's dresses were different. Even our skin colors were different, but we felt as if we were one. The whole world was together participating in the same act. We were all praying as one, living as one, and worshiping God as one. I had read in the Quran over and over again that humanity was all connected. But on this day, I witnessed how humanity was one.

CHAPTER 11

RAMADAN REFLECTIONS AND A MATURING FAITH

"THE MOST BLESSED HOUSE AMONG BELIEVERS IS THE ONE
IN WHICH AN ORPHAN IS CARED FOR. THE WORST HOUSE
AMONG BELIEVERS IS THE ONE IN WHICH AN ORPHAN IS
TREATED BADLY."

PROPHET MUHAMMAD

REAFFIRMING FAITH: WHY I FAST

After a million childhood messages that I needed to drop some weight, I would say I started my fasting not as a Muslim filled with the love of God, but more as a type of diet mechanism. I figured that I could use this month to detox and balance out my weight. Ramadan was an exercise in getting through a tough month. Since I could not eat or drink water, I found other ways to amuse myself. I would get lost in a book or rent three movies and "kill" six hours of fasting. I was not thinking about anything or anyone except my own struggle and how I could "check off" the list that I had fasted that day. I was a teenager, and I approached my faith and fasting with the teen mentality of just getting by.

Sometimes, I would shift my days around if fasting was in the summer. Sleep in late and stay up late. That way instead of feeling the fast and the struggle, I could sleep through most of the day and then get up in the afternoon a few hours before it was time to eat. I would then eat from sunset into the night and stay up late because I could eat and drink. I was modifying my day to minimize the hardships of fasting. Again, as a teenager, I did not have a strong faith.

Over the years, my faith has evolved. I think one big spurt of growth came after having children and thinking of the type of role model I wanted to be for them. I had started the habit of listening to CDs and tapes in the car while driving. When I was first married, I received a cassette series as a gift. The series covered the many rights of a Muslim wife in Islamic marriage. These tapes sat on a shelf in my house for a really long time. Until the weekend I decided to paint the dining room.

I knew I would spend the whole day painting the dining room, so I took out my boom box and popped in the first cassette tape. I was laying down the plastic sheet to save the floor and removing all the window treatments while being fascinated by how little I knew of the rights of women in a Muslim marriage. I continued removing all the plates around the light sockets and removing all the dining room chairs. By this time, it was time for cassette two of the eight-cassette series. I put in the second cassette and played both sides. As I taped the trim, primed the walls, and painted the walls, my ears were getting filled with Islamic wisdom from the ages.

I fell in love with the cassette series and discovered the author, Dr. Jamal Badawi, had made tons of cassette series on different aspects of Islam. I was hooked. So my Islamic education started at Sunday school on Ash Street, and as an adult I continued my education with Dr. Jamal Badawi's series of tapes. In the era before the internet, I bought all his cassettes I could find at local shops in the area that sold Asian spices and Halal (Muslim version of Kosher) meat. I was constantly looking for book sellers that would have the next round of cassette tapes for me.

Birds of a feather flock together, and believe it or not, my two younger sisters were also cassette tape collectors. One of them offered me cassettes by another speaker, Humza Yusuf. So with my well-developed habit of listening to cassettes in the car instead of the radio, I started listening to a series called "Purification of the Heart." Yusuf talked about how to get anger and jealously out of our hearts and the benefits of having a pure heart. I slowly began to realize that my faith was more of a "going through the motions" and "checking off boxes" type of faith. I was a Muslim when it was convenient for me and I was more concerned with myself than loving God. After eight years of cassette tape priming, God had made me ready to raise the level of my faith.

I have heard people talk about getting hit with a bolt of energy when they fall in love. I guess that day in the car, listening to "Purification of the Heart," I got hit with a bolt of energy and fell in love with God. I suddenly saw the shallowness of my faith and how my heart was not fully engaged in what I was doing. I didn't decide it was time to change. I just changed.

My entire life I had prayed two of the five daily prayers and felt bad for doing only two. I could not even remember when it was time to pray the other prayers, but now in the afternoon all I can think is, Have I said my prayers? It kept happening to me over and over and over each day. If I did not pray, I would start to worry that my prayer was missing. This was so new to me, that after living so long in neutral and saying how hard it is to pray, I became a faithful five-prayers-a-day person overnight.

That was the beginning of Ramadan 2004. I had four kids that were eight and under. I was busy and had little time for myself. But that is the exact time in my life that I got the prayer from God. The prayer and the renewal of faith made me realize how shallow my fasting had been. My faith was just a checklist that I went through daily without fully engaging my heart. Without the prayers to back up the fasting, what was I doing? I was not fasting for God but using Ramadan as some kind of a social diet. I was blessed to be given the gift of seeing my actions so clearly at a young age.

My next big leap of faith was Ramadan in 2007. I had earned a new pink Cadillac and had it for a mere twenty-four hours when a young girl making an illegal U-turn hit my car. Although she had left her license at home, she was driving four friends to a party that night. My car was ruined, but I had no idea how things were about to get more interesting. All four girls made up a story to the police officer so instead of their friend being punished for an illegal U-turn, I got blamed for the accident and got a ticket for reckless driving. The four girls versus one of me told the officer that they were not making a U-turn and merely driving straight. I was in shock—I didn't get speeding tickets, I didn't get parking tickets; I was an engineer rule-follower who read directions and specifications and followed them. How did I get here?

Stress does funny things to us. I was stressed out for three months waiting for the court date so I could tell my story. I played the scene over and over in my mind. I couldn't stop thinking of the accident, and even though it was a fender bender, how could I get a ticket for reckless driving? I was very careful while driving.

In order to sleep those three months, I started reading the Quran before going to bed. The words on the page would jump out at me. I would read till two in the morning and be relaxed enough to sleep. Because of the fender bender, I ended up reading the Quran cover to cover with translation and descriptions about seven times.

Reading a book over and over is like watching a movie over and over. The second time I read the Quran, I noticed messages that I had totally missed the first time. By the fifth time, the wisdom and the structure were just jumping off the pages. For the first time in my life as a Muslim, I felt empowered. My whole life people would say "The Quran says so" or "You need to do this because it is in the Quran." Now I clearly knew what was in and not in the Quran. My perspective had expanded, and I felt confident for the first time in my Islamic knowledge. The Quran got me through a stressful summer waiting for the trial for my ticket. The Quran is the reason I was able to sleep peacefully at night.

The morning of the trial came, and I felt pretty stressed. But I had forgotten that the truth sets us free. I had an attorney who spoke to the District Attorney. After sitting in court for forty-five minutes, the judge called my name. I was amazed because they were only on last names starting with B and my last name was an M. I was asked to go outside the courtroom where the District Attorney said my ticket was dismissed. He had no idea why I was given the ticket in the first place and said that the evidence from the accident did not support the other driver's theory. I was free to leave.

I felt so free! I was elated, leaving the courtroom and the accident behind me. But what I didn't know was that I was given a greater gift. God had used the accident to wake me up and bring me closer to my faith and the Quran. Reading the Quran at night had become such a habit that my kids would sometimes sit with me and have me read out loud to them. Then one night when I was too tired to continue reading, my daughter asked if she could read and I listen. Great idea! From then on, all four of us (the baby was too little to read) would take turns reading the Quran together at night.

I began to love the stories. With each repetition I would notice new details and wisdom that I had not seen before. I felt so alive because I was growing, and on top of that I got to watch my kids learn to read better. Since I lived in the US for most of my life, I did not get the same cultural and social exposure to Islam as my cousins and friends that were raised in Muslim countries. But with my new habit of reading the Quran over and over and over, I finally had the base level of knowledge that my cousins and friends had absorbed from being immersed in that culture.

This year, in the middle of Ramadan 2016, I feel truly alive and blessed because I am fully fasting and praying for the sake of God and not for my own gains. I am glad that I had a car accident in 2007 because it was a small price to pay for a major advancement in faith. I feel lucky because some people wake up with cancer, some people wake up with the death of a loved one, and I was woken up to my faith with a fender bender.

Ramadan has continued to be a blessing for me. Each time I use the month to grow my faith. For Ramadan in the summer of 2012, I decided I would take the kids on a trip to Australia, however they could "earn" the trip by memorizing Surah Rahman in the Quran. This Surah is long with about eighty verses; I was intimidated about memorizing that much Arabic, but I knew my kids had developing brains and it may be easier for them. Three days into the month of fasting, it became clear to me that I had asked my kids to do something that I myself was not willing to do. I felt like a bad mom and decided that if they could memorize seventy-eight verses, so could I. I set off with all my subliminal learning techniques and got started. At night, I would play an MP3 file of the surah throughout the house so the kids and I fell asleep to the beautiful and melodious ayahs.

I felt blessed that my kids pulled through the challenge. I even finished the memorization of all seventy-eight verses. The task gave us something to share as a family and got the kids off their phones. My belief that memorizing the Quran is difficult melted away. Although I have forgotten some of the surah, my kids still have the ayahs dancing in their heads.

Why am I fasting today? I am fasting because I believe in God and because fasting makes me appreciate all the miracles around me.

My son graduated from high school this year, and we had a party for his friends at a local restaurant. The party was, of course, at 8:30 pm because it fell during Ramadan and sunset was at 8:35. That evening, my husband was away, so I took one kid to gymnastics practice, one kid took the mini-van and drove to basketball practice, and two of my kids were with me. I was driving around all evening and was on my way to the restaurant to pay the bill for the party.

As I took a ramp off of the parkway toward the restaurant, I heard a loud bang on the rear passenger side of my car. My son was sitting there, and I asked if he was okay. I thought I blew out my tire so I slowed down to see if the car was wobbling and my tire was flat. The car was driving fine. Now I was confused. Did I drive over something and mess up the tire or not? A few lights down the road, the light turned red. I jumped out and looked at the rear passenger door. It was dark and everything looked fine. We went to the restaurant, celebrated with my son and his friends, picked up my other son from the gym, and had a nice evening.

The next morning, I could see my car in daylight. There were two mini-dents in the door and some white fur in my tire. I think a baby deer ran into the side of my car. But we were not harmed, and my tires were fine. I prayed that the deer not be hurt or in pain and was grateful because it was so dark and I had not seen anything approach my car. That was week one of Ramadan.

As a graduation gift, I got my son a ticket to visit my sister Saima in New Mexico for a week. On their way home from the airport, a baby elk ran into the side of my sister's car, jumped in the air, and landed on the hood, shattering the entire windshield. Everyone was fine, and my sister's life was spared. It's Ramadan, and all I see are blessings. Little things that could have been life-changing pivotal moments are ending up as blessings for us. The police officer said that if the elk had jumped any higher, it would have landed on my sister, killing her. I am reminded about how fragile life is and how much God is looking out for us. Just a small change in a split second and the outcome can go anywhere.

Sometimes, I focus on everything that is going wrong. I sometimes play superwoman and I lose at being perfect. I take on too much and forget about taking care of myself. While wallowing in self-pity, I watched a video, looking for hidden blessings from God. The video told a popular story from the life and example of Prophet Muhammad (pbuh). Once a poor man came begging to the Prophet (pbuh). The poor man said that he and his wife had nothing. The Prophet (pbuh) asked, "Nothing?" The poor man replied yes and went on to say, "All I have is this blanket that my wife and I sleep on." The Prophet (pbuh) told the man to sell the blanket for an axe. The poor man returned with an axe. The Prophet (pbuh) then told the poor man to cut wood and work. The man was able to earn money. I realized that in those moments when I felt I had nothing, I could still put in a little time and energy and create a blessing.

I went for a new outlook. Instead of focusing on all the car problems and beating myself up for not being good at selecting food or delegating, I make a list of what is working well right now. I have a hard time asking for help. But what this example of the Prophet (pbuh) has taught me is that it is better to empower someone that to give a handout. He let the old man learn that a blanket is a blessing and that gift can lead to more favors from God. I felt better because I released all the guilt I had about what a good mom should do, like homework. I decided to teach my children that they were smart enough to figure out their own homework without my help. And that even when we think we have nothing, we still have our bodies, our limbs, and our ability to work. I think about this story often.

WHAT AM I THINKING?

Ramadan 2016 has fallen over the summer solstice, so it is some of the longest fasts of the year. I started my first fast with a headache from dehydration, and I was feeling tired all day. After fasting for a week, my productivity goes down to half and I am usually frustrated because I am a "doer" and I like to get things done. But now my faith and Ramadan are about compassion. All I can think of are the millions of people that share our planet and go without food every day. I have so much empathy and patience for those who do not eat. When I do not eat, my brain is just not as sharp. One time when I was fasting, I locked my keys in the trunk of my car. My brain just does not think that well without proper nourishment.

Today I am praying for kids that have to go to school hungry every day and still learn, think, and take tests. How do they do that every day knowing that the next day, the next week, and the next month will not be any different?

When we don't eat for a while, two things happen; first, we can smell food a mile away, and second, we start to think about when we can eat again. Half of the exercise of fasting is to control our bodies physically and avoid food and water, but the other half of the exercise of Ramadan is to control our thoughts. My goal this Ramadan is not to zone out by watching TV or taking naps but to feel the fast fully and empathize with those who do not get to eat. I have also decided that I will be praying for the hungry instead of obsessing that I am feeling hungry.

My second goal for this Ramadan is to give charity. Feeding our friends, feeding our business associates, and feeding our community is a huge part of this month. So I am focusing my charitable contributions on organizations that give food. I am getting divine help in the form of letters soliciting contributions in the mail every day. I open up all the charities' requests and select those that help feed hungry people or teach farming skills and food preparation to those who do not have access to good, wholesome food. When I find a charity that meets my Ramadan criteria, I write a check and put on a stamp.

I am also proud of my kids for fasting and taking their final exams this week. Finals week is never easy, but without food and water, an exam is even more challenging. Our local public school is great and my kids receive "Ramadan passes." The Ramadan pass allows them to go to the library at lunchtime instead of the cafeteria. This is an amazing gift since looking at food while we are fasting is difficult. It brings back memories about when I was in school at that age. I remember being in sixth grade one Ramadan, and I was on the service team that month. My job was to hand out milk to each student at the end of the cafeteria line. For forty-five minutes I watched child after child approach me with a plateful of delicious food. I would give each child a milk carton and some would reply "thank you." I was only twelve years old. It was one of the toughest weeks of my life, smelling all the aroma of food and knowing I would not be eating till the evening.

Finally this Ramadan, I am focusing on gratitude. I am grateful for a religion that stretched me both as a child and an adult. I spent four decades in a country that did not understand fasting. I was questioning the practice myself. I really believe that the Quran is the word of God, but comments about how harmful fasting was and the effects on the metabolism had gotten to me. My weight was up. "Insulin resistance" is what my friend Jennifer had called it. My father's side of the family had diabetes, and I thought maybe I was headed that way.

I had tried every "sensible" nutrition plan. But this Ramadan, I got the best gift of all. I ran into a book and some research that said the best way to break insulin resistance was fasting. The book spouted the benefits of the detox process and the lowering of insulin. Ramadan 2016, I became a believer all over again. All the answers I was searching for were in my faith. I just needed a little more trust. For the first time in my life, I felt like fasting was an honor and privilege. I quit focusing on the brain fog and the thirst. I embraced a tradition that honored the human body, that nurtured the body, and I would never listen to another negative comment about fasting again.

I was irritated that I had to take this full circle path to come and embrace the power of fasting. I decided to listen to the Quran on the app on my cell phone. The *ayats* covered the battle of Badr during Ramadan in 624 AD. The pagan Arabs lead an army of one thousand against an ill-equipped Muslim fighting force of just three hundred civilians. The pagan army not only had more men but also better weapons and training. They attacked the Muslims during Ramadan, when they were fasting. The battle should have been an easy win for the pagan Arabs when the odds favored them by a factor of three to one. But as history goes, the Muslim army overcame the odds and won the battle. My thoughts considered that faith can conquer anything. But two details stood out to me on leadership. I saw the story of Badr as a stepping stone to level up my skills as a mentor and coach.

The first lesson I learned is that during the battle, Prophet Muhammad (pbuh) as a leader was fighting shoulder to shoulder with his followers. So in a position of power, we do not ask for special privileges but we model the behavior we want our team to perform. The second lesson I felt had been written directly to me. I liked to help too much and sometimes prevented others from learning their own lessons. During the battle, the man next to the Prophet (pbuh) had his finger cut off. As he lost his finger, the man expressed his pain by saying the equivalent of "ouch." Muhammad did not stop guiding the man even in such a dire situation. The Prophet (pbuh) did not abandon his role as a teacher and mentor and told that man that if he had praised God instead of saying "ouch" it would have been better for the man. I also wanted to be a leader that always operated in a manner of elevating and developing people.

Every Ramadan, I measure my life. A year had gone by and I wanted to be better. I asked for gratitude, and God gave it to me. My heart is overflowing. I was taught to respect the poor and hungry for my entire life and I now have the self-discipline to reach my own health goals. I learned this discipline by having the willpower to pray on time and the self-control to fast even when I was thirsty. I realize now that I am created to be strong, compassionate, and kind. I get to take a month out of every year to remember what type of person I want to be and where I am headed after death.

To pay it forward, I decided to sponsor an orphan. My family had all their quirky uniqueness and idiosyncrasies that allow me to love them. I also have had the opportunity to eat every day of my life. From now on, Ramadan is my pay-it-forward month. It is my timeout to give away the blessings I have taken for granted my entire life. I am hoping all my future Ramadans are as blessed as this one. My Christian friends end a prayer with Amen; in Islam we say Ameen.

CHAPTER 12

EMPOWERED OR OPPRESSED?

"IF A SERVANT COVERS THE SHAME OF ANOTHER SERVANT, ON
THE DAY OF JUDGEMENT GOD WILL COVER THEIR SHAME."

PROPHET MUHAMMAD

I am a doer and an achiever. I ran a half marathon and then trained for a full marathon. I decided to have a large family with four kids and also run a business at home. I feel that being a Muslim is part of the reason I am driven. However, the media and newspapers only choose to show Muslim women in dire circumstances without giving value to their community. I am grateful for the support of my family of all my ventures and adventures. My grandmother was a huge influence in how I chose to live my life. My mom ran a successful business, and my sisters, Saima and Amina, are the two most intelligent, savvy women I know. Even in Sunday school, the Muslim women in history had influence and power

But I still get asked often, "Does Islam oppress women?" I find ways that Islam empowers women and gives them the foundation to build a great life, and I resolved to share the experiences I have had with Muslim women. I started thinking of all the strong, smart, and funny Muslim women in my life and how much they have supported me.

Then I turned on the TV. Another story on the news about how Islam does not support women or that women are oppressed by the faith. Of all the speaking I do on Islam, I get the most questions about women. The most common question is, "Why do women have to wear a scarf?" The question is usually followed up by whether women have any rights in Islam. I feel sad when I see how women are portrayed in movies and media, but especially for Muslim women. Maybe the pain of those portrayals is what makes me want to change this perception. The Muslim women in my life have been fun, successful, accomplished, and ambitious. I've traveled the world with these strong, sensible, and empathetic women. I thought of all the amazing Muslim women that live all around the world that have impressed me and influenced my life.

Nafisa and Naheed started junior high with me at Presentation Convent in Peshawar and were soon my two great friends. I would never have guessed that forty years later we would still be close. At the age of twelve, they both knew that they wanted to be doctors. After college, I took a trip back to Peshawar. I had just been engaged to Tariq and shopping for a wedding dress. Both Nafisa and Naheed were in medical school by then. I was only in town for a few days, and we all wanted to maximize our time together. I decided to go to school with them for two days so we could see each other and I could meet all the guys they had been talking about.

Pakistan is not known for central heat. Only the rooms that we are using are heated or cooled. It was December, and it was cold. I put on several layers of shirts and sweaters. To look like a medical student, I borrowed a white lab coat from Nafisa. Naheed's dad came to pick me up, and I spent my first day of vacation as a pretend medical student. I walked into a classroom with forty cadavers on metal tables and six students gathered around each body. The classroom was kept cold, and the dissection was already in progress. All the students had long tweezers and would pull veins and muscles out of the arm when the professor read the Latin name. I had never experienced real cadavers. All I smelled was formaldehyde and death. No one else seemed to notice the sterile, frigid, grim scene. I felt sick, so I took shallow breaths.

I was an extra at our table. Nafisa and Naheed were dissecting away. I was trying to survive the smell. I think the cold helped. They said that since it was cold, I was lucky. These cadavers smelled much worse in the summer. Every once in a while, a professor would come through. Most of the assistants did not recognize all the students, and in my borrowed lab coat uniform, I fit right in.

Dr. Qurashi was different. In her late fifties with salt-and-pepper gray hair, she looked straight at me and asked, "Who are you?" I was surprised; her eyes were intense and so was her question. Nafisa, always rescuing me, came to my defense. "She is a visiting medical student, ma'am." Dr. Qurashi was not convinced. She glared at me and asked where I went to medical school. My mind went blank. The only medical school I knew of in Pakistan was the one I was at. Nafisa jumped in again and let Dr. Qurashi know I was in med school in the United States. Dr. Qurahsi stared me down with her dark eyes and glasses on the end of her nose. She made a sound of disbelief and walked away. This was my first and last day of pretending to be a medical student.

Nafisa and Naheed's influence has shaped my life. I was not a great student when I met them, but they taught me how to study as well as how to be a great girlfriend. Nafisa took the family route, had kids, and also worked for the army. Naheed, on the other hand, preferred to stay single, and she worked in the hospitals. For my fiftieth birthday, the three of us were going to be together again. The three of us share the values of education, and to me, travelling is the best education. We decided to take a girls' trip to Singapore, Brunei, and Hong Kong. Ever heard of the Sultan of Brunei? I had too, but I didn't think the Sultan was actually real. Once again, I was planning another adventure with my girlfriends.

I wanted to visit Brunei, with a friend there and a niece in Singapore, I could vacation and see the people I love, too. Right before the holidays, the three of us decided to meet in Singapore as our embarkation point for the girls' trip. I arrived first due to time zones and flight schedules, then

Nafisa showed up at the hotel twelve hours later. I started my first day in Singapore with lunch on the famous Orchard Road at a Spanish Café. We were trying out a new app on our phone named WhatsApp at the café between courses at lunch. The internet was good, then spotty, then good intermittently. We had left our kids with our husbands and were trying to let our families know that we were safe and having fun in Singapore.

Even in December, the city was warm but decked out in more snowmen and wreaths than I had ever seen. We decided to stroll through the National Orchid Garden while we waited for our other friend to arrive. Nafisa was well informed and had made a list of all the places she wanted to visit. I was enjoying the lush greenery and koi ponds while cross-checking my Singapore list against hers. The botanical gardens were filled with people practicing yoga and jogging the winding paths. There was even a moss chandelier in front of the book store.

Our first stop, according to Nafisa's research, was a Hindu Temple. My friends and I attended our first Hindu service in the Temple of Sri Mariamman. Islam teaches respecting all religions. Only God is the true judge. Even though Hinduism is very different from Islam, we all wanted to learn new traditions and experience the unique culture of the temple.

The temple was colorful. Statues of Hindu gods with flutes and arrows surrounded the roof. The statues were layered in an ascending trapezoid. We walked through an archway into a brick courtyard. We took off our shoes, similar to when entering a mosque. There were several individuals just walking around in the courtyard. I did not know what was going on. Ever the curious tourist, I was people-watching to see what was happening. There were flowers, candles, and offerings. The main shrine was in the middle of the courtyard. There were some men in turbans and white, flowing pants working in the shrine with lamps of incense.

A bell started ringing, and everyone from the courtyard began lining up to enter the shrine. The believers lined up, but we hung back, watching. All the Hindus had their hands cupped and were standing patiently.

There was a couple with three kids in front of us. The kids were standing at the rope, and the parents were just behind them. Three men came from the shrine with incense and ashes. They placed ashes on the woman and then her husband. The kids got the ashes on their foreheads next. About seventy people lined up on both sides of the rope—all were praying. They received their blessings. This ritual reminded me of Ash Wednesday at Catholic school. The family of five made a gesture of gratitude and left.

I asked one of the men with incense what was the purpose of the ritual. He said it was to ward off the evil eye. The evil eye is prevalent in many Asian cultures and even in Islam. The concept is that if someone is jealous of us and wishes to harm us, they could cause us misfortune. So Muslims also pray that they are protected from the evil eye of others that do not wish them well. Some Muslims will give extra charity in protection from the evil eye. I discovered I had something in common with the people at the temple. I, too, wanted to ward off the evil eye.

Three Muslim women from Brunei, Pakistan, and the US were on a girls' trip visiting a Hindu temple in Chinatown Singapore. . . . amazing. I took a few last pictures to remember my visit. We got to the door and found our shoes. We were all somber; the ceremony was over, and Nafisa was calling an Uber as we silently waited. The ceremony was moving. The sun had set. Singapore was lighting up in the dusk. Barefoot on the beach weather in December, I was inspired by the Asian architecture. And it was Christmastime. The buildings were lighting up. All the structures were decked out in Santa and Frosty, in a city that celebrated halal food, with Buddhist monks and Hindu temples. Different cultures and different faiths from different continents blended perfectly into one amazing day. Singapore knew how to celebrate its diversity.

While our kids were having fun at home with their dads, this was a girls-only trip to get away from career stress and responsibilities. The three of us were playing tourists while reliving memories of our life together in junior high. It felt like we were fourteen, in school again at

Presentation Convent in Peshawar. We spent the days exploring and the evenings designing our next adventure. The next day we decided to see the Buddhist temple. We were lucky to have seen the service at the Hindu temple the day before. The Buddhist temple, called the Tooth Relic, was massive, with several floors and an elevator. Some floors allowed tourists and others were roped off for observance. As tourists, we took in the sights and took tons of pictures. Since it was located in the heart of Singapore's Chinatown, we decided to end the temple visit with some food and shopping. I loved the blend of Chinese and South Asian culture in the foods.

After lunch, Nafisa, Naheed, and I headed to the afternoon prayer at the mosque, Masjid Al-Falah. Later we took long walks through the botanical gardens and chatted while watching the waterfalls in the Cloud Forest. Our time in Singapore flew by. Being in Singapore reminded me of being a junior high student with my friends, when all we had to worry about was what we wanted and taking care of ourselves. When was the last time I didn't have to worry about what everyone else wanted to eat or where the kids had left their socks? I didn't even have to clean up after anybody. We were enjoying the freedom of having "just us girls."

After five amazing days in Singapore, we flew to Brunei. I boarded my first flight on Royal Brunei Airlines and saw the newspaper Borneo Post in the seatback pocket. I heard of Borneo and knew it was around here somewhere but I had no idea that I was headed to the Island of Borneo on this flight. On the map, Singapore looked so close to Brunei. But we had a big section of the Pacific Ocean to cross. Our flight was very bumpy, and we flew through storms in the pitch dark. In the middle of the night, we landed in Brunei officially known as Brunei, Dar Es Salaam. In Arabic, Dar Es Salaam means "the house of peace" and is often used as a name for someplace beautiful. The name of this serene island nation literally means the abode of peace, and I would enjoy five relaxing days with my friends in tranquility.

Nafisa, the army doctor, worked at the local clinic near her home in Brunei during the day while her husband, Samir, helped with their two sons at home. Samir had retired from the army earlier and was enjoying his retirement while supporting his wife and her career as a Lt. Colonel. Samir went out of his way to make sure we felt welcome in his home and made sure we went to the local grocery market and got the food we wanted to eat. Nafisa and Samir showed us the entire town of Bandar Seri Begawan from the restaurants to the museums. Samir even took us on a boat ride through the water village, Kampong Ayer, in the middle of the Brunei River. My favorite spot in Brunei was the lavish Empire Hotel with the lovely Zest Café. The food at the Empire Hotel was divine, making Brunei seem like a slice of heaven. There were not many places I wanted to return to, but the Zest Café made my list of places worth a second trip.

I think I love travelling because I love learning. In Brunei, we visited a park for a morning hike. The park had an intricate stone patio with different types of stones to be used for a foot massage. The locals were taking off their shoes and walking on the stones based on the inlay design. My friends and I decided to act like the locals and walk on these stone paths barefoot. While the locals had no problems with the stones digging into the heels and balls of their feet, I was in pain. Obviously this type of foot massage was an acquired skill, and I was not prepared. Since my trip, I have acquired a genuine plastic foot massager that works in much the same way.

Brunei had the island feel of time standing still and no one rushing. We had time for everything, even ample time to pray. I had often seen pictures of a beautiful mosque with a gold dome and a large pool in front with a huge ceremonial boat in it. I never believed it was real. I had even heard about the rich sultan who owned the boat. But now I was standing at the entrance of the famous Omar Ali Saffuddin Mosque.

The white pillars and gold domes looked like a fairy-tale palace. We were near the equator, and the sun was out. It was time for the afternoon prayer and people were filing in. It was hot, and with the white marble floor and the sun's reflection off of the white building, it felt even hotter. We went inside to the cool interior. The people of Brunei are probably the most friendly and kind people I have ever met, and their mosques reflect the beauty of their hearts. Everyone was smiling and willing to help. Even with the language barrier, the locals made an effort to make us feel welcome and at home in their mosque. Because they knew we were from out of town, they wanted us to know they cared about us. Brunei was the best implementation of Islam I had seen in a long time.

Not only was the Mughal architecture stunning but the water fountains and inlaid stonework on the mosque grounds were also done with love and care. We walked into the magnificent structure and saw the intricate mosaic on the inside of the gold dome. The mosaics were bright blues, reds, oranges and greens. The light from the outside came in through little openings, giving the dome a glow. The columns inside were all marble with ornate gold capitals. The inside mirrored the composition of the outside—white with gold on top. The floors were covered with beautiful woven rugs with the square designs showing us which way to pray.

On the back wall were robes and head scarves for women to borrow for the prayers. I prayed my first prayer and pulled out one of the Qurans on the shelf to read a little. I was in total serenity and started to contemplate, How can I retire in Brunei? Needless to say the mosque was beautiful and world famous. But as an engineer, I have to add that was the most organized and efficient mosque I had ever seen, filled with super kind, smiling, and helpful people. I knew I would remember this prayer for the rest of my life. I wished I could stay there forever. The mosque had a unique energy. The place filled me with peace and a sense of gratitude. Brunei is heaven on Earth.

While I was sitting and admiring the mosque's beauty after the afternoon prayer, I started noticing more details of my surrounding. I was looking up at the dome. The prayer leader, or imam, was giving a sermon. My mind came back from the mosaic to the sermon. I started to focus. The imam was talking about patience. I still had not mastered patience. There is something about getting away from everything in our lives and just reflecting. I was reflecting on all the hassles I had overcome to arrive to this place. I started thinking of all my struggles. I looked down at the Quran and started to read. I was waiting for Nafisa and Naheed to finish their prayers. I play a game sometimes when I am searching for answers and looking at a book. I ask God, make me open the book to the perfect page. I opened the Quran to a section on the Prophet's (pbuh) birth. I read a few verses, and then I started thinking of Halima.

Halima lived in the deserts of Arabia at the time of the birth of Muhammad (pbuh). She would take care of babies for the rich Arab families who lived in Mecca. The families in the city felt that city life was too hectic for their babies and the babies would be stronger when raised in the desert. I guess the debate of city life versus country life has been going on for a while! Brunei definitely had the feel of the country life with a slow pace, light-brown, sandy beaches, and the ocean as far as our eyes could see. I sat there on the pine-green carpet with rectangular prayer rugs leaning against a strong, white marble pillar. Halima was my message from God in this mosque.

Shortly after the birth of Muhammad (pbuh), several families from the desert came to Mecca to select babies to raise in the desert. The desert women caretakers preferred to take children from well-to-do families because their pay for rearing the child would be higher. On that day, however, Halima, riding on a donkey, was having issues. Times had been tough, and food supplies were low. It was hard to feed all of the empty mouths, including the animals'. The donkey did not want to walk fast and was tired from the trip. Because of her journey on a slow, difficult donkey, she was the last to arrive in Mecca. All the choice families' children had been spoken for, and the only child that was left was Muhammad (pbuh). Muhammad's (pbuh) family was not wealthy, and his father had died. No father meant not much money; the child was considered an orphan.

The city Arabs valued these desert families' values. Living in the desert would allow the child to connect with nature. Furthermore, trade caravans came to Mecca and brought the goods, traditions, and languages of other nations. The diversity in language introduced slang terms into the speech in the city. Going to the desert allowed the child to learn proper Arabic and then come live in the city to learn the variations. Another benefit of desert life was creating an alliance with another family. This is similar to the concept of having godparents in the United States. But above all, the Meccan Arabs valued resilience. Life in the desert is tougher and required more endurance and flexibility. The city Arabs wanted to teach their children coping skills early in life.

Halima stood and looked at the orphan. She wanted another baby to come play with her children. Halima decided to go for it. She took responsibility for Muhammad (pbuh) and agreed to raise him in the desert. Halima had a big heart. Her decision was made out of charity. She told her husband that maybe some blessing may come from helping this baby. Halima was about to be blessed, indeed, but she had no idea what was in store for her.

What an amazing lady! I had just realized that her life's lesson was in front of me for four decades but I never saw it. When we are having a difficult day we should do a little charity and think about potential blessings. Sometimes, the delays of a slow donkey are the miracles to give us the perfect gift. I started seeing delays in my life as gifts. I sometimes felt like I had the slowest donkey in the tribe, but I didn't really think that being slow could be a blessing. Hitting the big five-oh had made me wonder if I had achieved everything I wanted in life at this age. There were times I thought I should have been further along by now. Was life passing me by, and was I just getting left behind? I felt as though I were the one with the slowest donkey while the others reached success first and got the best rewards. But I began to see there were times in my life when being the last to arrive had actually set me up for a miracle.

I was going to enjoy my next fifty years and stop thinking about what could have been. I was going to live by the story of Halima. The slow pace was still a pace, after all. I knew I had plenty of room to grow. But instead of feeling left-behind and discouraged, I was feeling some hope. I remember a lot I bid on for a house, where the agent did not file the contract. That lot went to someone else, and I was forced to pay more due to a price increase. I ended up with a new lot ten times better than the one I originally bid on. There are gifts in the delays of my life. God's timing is always perfect.

My mind wandered to a time we had bid on a house for my in-laws. The real estate lady was dishonest and increased the price of the home overnight, the day we walked in to sign the contract. We protested to the owner of the development, but he said that the realtor told him the properties were undervalued and he decided on a twenty percent increase starting that day. We ended up getting another house that was in a better neighborhood and closer to the river. Later we found out that the development we originally had signed papers for had mosquito problems from the man-made canals the negligent developer put in. This delay had been a gift from God. Sitting in the mosque made me see many of my detours as blessings in disguise. I looked back down at the book. I thought of Halima in the desert, working to support her family by taking care of wealthy children.

Halima had also started noticing blessings immediately. With Muhammad (pbuh) in her arms, she started her trip back home to the desert. Her donkey suddenly had tons of energy and was running faster. Halima not only caught up with the others but was now leading the group. They kept asking her, "Halima, did you get another donkey?" She said, "No, this is the same donkey that brought me to the city." Her desert tribes would not believe her. They said, "Your donkey is going so fast it seems like a new animal."

The miracles continued as the produce on her land began to grow faster than that of her neighbors. Halima was a strong and charitable woman. I needed to strengthen my charity. I needed to see my place in life differently. I wanted to take the focus off of myself and put my focus back on serving others. I was totally immersed in Halima's life. People were walking around me and putting books back on the shelves. My friends, Nafisa and Naheed, were still praying in the mosque in Brunei, but I was mentally in the desert of Saudi Arabia. The stories of Islam were made up of strong women. And having a charitable heart made us strong women.

Halima was not the only strong woman. The Prophet's (pbuh) mother, Amina, was a strong woman, raising a child alone after her husband died during her pregnancy. The Prophet's (pbuh) wife, Khadija, was a strong woman who hired him as an employee and then used her business funds to support and benefit his dream of calling people to worship only one God. Prophet Muhammad (pbuh) surrounded himself with strong women. And I saw that I had too. My friends were doctors who were supporting their families and making a difference in their communities. They were healing people at all times of the day and wanted to bless the world with good health. It was the strength of these women that made me want to excel in school and eventually led me to being the math whiz I am today. Even the current Queen of Brunei, Saleh, was working on women's issues and making a difference where she was born. My lessons from Omar Ali Saffuddin Mosque were to trust God's timing and to surround myself with strong women.

With Singapore, Brunei, and Hong Kong visited in a single year, I was ready to relax. As I returned home, I thought there was no need for a renewal of my passport. My passport was scheduled to expire as it was almost ten years old. It was chock-full of visas from all over the world. I had no immediate plans to travel, so there was no need to go through the hassle of taking new pictures, downloading the application, and going through the headaches of passport renewal. I let my passport expire. After so many trips, one year of just being at home, hanging out with my family, would be a treat. That was my plan—to trust God's timing and do nothing.

Nothing actually goes as planned. My passport expired in July, and I was relishing shorter trips within the state of Virginia, where I could have an adventure with my family and return home at the end of the weekend. We visited colonial Williamsburg and watched the ponies swim at Chincoteague Island. I wanted my children to experience the beauty surrounding our home. However, just fifty-seven short days after retiring my passport, I received a call from my mother. My mother had gone to Pakistan to clean out my grandmother Sajeela's house and get things in order, since my grandmother had recently passed. The trip was to be for a month to get the house ready to rent out. My mother had made several trips to Pakistan in the past. She travelled there about once a year. Her going to Lahore and hanging out at my grandmother's house for a few weeks was normal for us. However this time she had sent us several emails and text messages saying that she was sick.

I had started my own business while working full time as an engineer. I dabbled in leading a seminar on empowering women and talking to schools about the diversity in Islam. The business gave me flexibility and total control of my own schedule. I had relished this freedom earlier in the year. In January, due to inclement weather, the local school had closed. But a snow day wasn't a scheduling challenge anymore.

Receiving a call from my mom was not only unexpected, but there was worry in her voice. She had had an upset stomach for ten days, then she had finally gone to a doctor and received a diagnosis of typhoid. I had no idea what to do. I called my father. Our family was on the phone all night. I called my sister, then I called my other sister, then I called my dad again. I was on the phone till almost one in the morning. One of us needed to go to Pakistan and help my mom come back. Someone needed to be a strong woman. Mom was too weak to travel alone.

I had no idea why I was being taken back to Pakistan so soon. It was a busy week; my schedule was packed with kids' activities and my business. An unplanned trip with no passport or visa is tough. Just to get the right documentation, I had to buy a plane ticket showing I was leaving the country within twenty-four hours. I then had to get a doctor's note from her doctor, stating that my mom was ill. I took both documents to the US passport office on I Street in downtown Washington, DC, and got a passport made in four hours. I took my new, shiny passport and drove to the Pakistani embassy eight miles away and got an emergency visa. I drove home in the lovely rush hour traffic, packed, and went to bed. The next morning, my husband dropped me off at the airport, and I boarded a plane to Pakistan.

I arrived at Alama Iqbal Airport just seventy-two hours later. All flights arriving from the Middle East land in the dead of the night. I know each time I land at the airport it is two in the morning and the humidity of the city is the first sensation walking off the plane. The airport was packed with crowds of people, but the streets on the drive home were deserted and dark. With such short notice, my cousins Atif and Imran showed up at three a.m. to greet my flight. They drove me home and said my two favorite words, "Anar (pomegranate) juice?" I said, "It's almost four in the morning—do you think the juice guy is open? Imran responded, "Well it's almost time for morning prayers, so yes, let's go home via the juice guy." This is Pakistan; people are there when I need them and so is fresh juice after a twenty-hour flight. I walked in the door and laid down on the coach. I vaguely heard the call to prayer but did not have the ability to move. My mom woke me up and gave me a hug. We both went back to sleep.

I was in the middle of training to run a marathon. There was a park across the street from my grandma's home that was tranquil and large.

The park was not only beautiful but it had a two-and-a-half-kilometer gravel course around the circumference. When I woke up, I knew I had to go and greet my favorite place to escape. There were four gates that entered the park, and one of the gates was on my grandmother's street. This was Pakistan, and I forgot how well women are taken care of. So I was escorted by a neighbor the two-block walk to the park. I entered the gate and took a deep breath. The sounds here are loud, not just the street and market noises on the way to the park but also the birds. I could hear the birds singing, and judging by the chirping, there were several birds.

I started running the two-and-a-half-kilometer course while my mom still slept and rested. I decided to do four rounds in the park. Each time I finished a lap, I was feeling grateful that I had made it this far and that my mom was feeling better. The park's course was gravel and much easier on my knees. Ten kilometers seemed like a good idea. The greenery of the park, the happy people sharing the path, and the fresh air made me relax. I was feeling grateful for the trip. Grateful that I had decided to come even though a last-minute trip is never easy. Since I was in training, I was trying to improve my pace for the marathon. I was walking and running to improve my time every time I passed the clocks at the gates. I was trying to beat the duration since the last time I had passed the same route. I even made a new friend in the park that day.

Hajra came up behind me and said, "I've been trying to keep up with you." She was in an *abiya*, or a long, black robe, and had a pink *dupatta*, or a scarf, around her head. No one wanted to be sunburned, so most men were wearing caps and the women wore glasses and head covers. She immediately asked me if I was new. How did she know? I wondered. Did I really stick out this much? Hajra was a sweet woman in her forties, and she had three kids roughly the same age as mine. She commented on my running-walking technique again. "You've been walking and running so fast. I was so impressed, I wanted to keep up with you." She spoke in fluent Urdu. She decided to join me for the next circle on the track. I found out about her family. Her husband had left for work and then she was going to get home. After her quick exercise walk, Hajra was going to help her daughter get ready to go to college and then take the other kids to school.

I told her that I was visiting to take my mom back in a couple of days. I mentioned how rushed my trip was and all the appointments I had cancelled to come. One of the appointments was for a haircut. I had been waiting till the last minute to get my hair cut so it would be in ideal condition for an event the next weekend. Hajra mentioned that her sister lived in the same neighborhood and owned a salon. She would be happy to get me an appointment if I had the time. I told her I was rushed but would try to fit it in. We had a great conversation, and I made a new friend. It's so easy to make friends in a beautiful park. We came to Hajra's gate, and she said goodbye.

After I was done with the fourth round, I decided to go home and check on my mom. The sun was out now, and it was getting hot. The gardener was sitting and waiting. I asked if he had stayed the whole time. He said no. He said my mom was awake and wondering where I was. I walked out of the black, metal gate with the gardener. The gate led to a shopping center. Lots of cars and motorcycles were parked everywhere, and some mechanics were working on cars. There are several cute shops, an optometrist, and even a Dunkin' Donuts embedded in all the chaos. The Dunkin' Donuts was my sister's go-to breakfast spot for coffee every day of her visits with my grandmother. Next to the donut shop is a small hole-in-the-wall Pakistani food store that specializes in samosas and chapatis for breakfast.

My two-day stay was a whirlwind. But the purpose of my trip became clear. I realized that life is never too busy to support family, and I was a strong, independent woman who could support my mom when she needed me the most. With jet lag and travel exhaustion, I walked into my grandmother's home. I immediately started to miss her. Every single wall and piece of furniture held her memory. My mom would try to eat and get something done. She got tired easily and spent most of the time lying the couch.

I called Nafisa, telling her, "I am in town and sad about my grandmother." Nafisa was always as adventurous as me. She had just returned from Brunei and started a new position in a town nearby. She said she would leave her kids with Samir and come visit for a few days. Naheed still lives in Peshawar, where we went to elementary school. Naheed could not make it on such short notice, as she lived on the other side of Pakistan. But I was back in my grandma Sajeela's home, and my best friend, Nafisa, was on her way.

My mom lay on the sofa, dozing in and out of sleep. I heard a sound at the gate, and a car with the Uber logo honked outside. Out jumped a familiar face with a small, black backpack. Nafisa marched in carrying her belongings and my favorite dessert made out of carrots. Nafisa, as a doctor, checked on my mom's breathing and temperature. After she told us what to expect as Mom recovered, she announced, "Let's eat!" We started munching carrot *Halwa* (cooked carrots in sugar with ricotta cheese) and drank tea. I am not a fan of tea so I searched the empty house for some coffee. I was not in luck. The house had been cleaned up for new renters.

I had posted on social media that I was in town. I got a quick message from my nephew Omar, "Can we come visit?" I said sure, and he replied that he would bring his mom later that day. I was chatting with Nafisa and my mom, and I replied to Omar, "Bring your mom *and* some coffee," with a smiling emoji.

Omar arrived with his mom, who is my cousin Yasmin. Yasmin was shorter than me. Her hair was short too. Her loving eyes smiled as she saw me. I could always see love in her eyes. At five feet even, I hardly knew anyone who was shorter than me. But tiny Yasmin had a sense of power. She always wore platform shoes that matched her outfits perfectly on her petite feet. Today was no different; she was dressed in all pink.

As a child, I was proud of my older cousin. In the seventies, when in the United States most women did not work, Yasmin was in Pakistan getting her degree in nuclear engineering and working to bring efficient power to Pakistani homes. She was short, and she was deaf in one ear. None of her limitations stopped her. She got married. After a few short years, the marriage dissolved. Yasmin became a single mom of two amazing kids, her daughter, Amna, and son, Omar. She kept working as a nuclear engineer and supporting her kids both financially and emotionally as a single parent.

She took her kids to the zoo every Sunday. Sunday was family day. Whenever we visited, Amna and Omar would say, "Let's go to the zoo." And we did. Although the zoo was pretty run-down compared to the ones I was used to in the United States, Lahore Zoo had some unique benefits. It offered both camel and elephant rides. It also had a white tiger exhibit and an elephant show. We would follow the zoo with snacks at a food cart. I was proud of Yasmin for being a single mom that could balance both family and career. It was nice having another female engineer in the family.

Yasmin was also an investor. She made a living and then made a life. On her own income, she bought her first house. And then she bought another home. She not only supported her two kids through advanced degrees in college but also bought and sold real estate. A few years earlier, she had sold her home to a commercial builder. The transaction gave her enough money to purchase beautiful new house in an up-and-coming area near her son's college. The house represented Yasmin perfectly, classic design with modern amenities. Her new home was impressive with the Mughal-Era, ornate, hand-carved wooden doors and posh carpets. The home had many features such as motion detectors and cameras that made it both ornate and technologically advanced. Now as a retired nuclear engineer, she was enjoying her grandkids and a stress-free, blessed life.

I love to say that success is caught not taught. We make the world better by our example. The Muslim women in my life have been models for me. Yasmin set an amazing example not only for me but also for her daughter Amna. My little niece had grown up strong and smart just like her mother. She excelled in grade school and high school. Amna led her class in tests and set the bar for others to excel in education. After completing college, she sat for the Civil Service Exam in Pakistan. The test is brutal. Amna studied for months to prepare adequately for the exam. She succeeded. She received the highest test score in the country and had her choice of civil service jobs. She is now married with three kids of her own. And like her mother, she has a powerful career in the government. I follow her on social media as she goes to conferences in Europe and the Middle East.

Yasmin and Omar were getting ready to leave. We said goodbye as the sun set. The sky, radiant orange and blue mix, morphed into a dusky gray. I walked to the gate with Yasmin and Omar. They got into a white car. "Is that a hybrid?" I asked. "Yes," Omar replied. Everyone was going for natural gas cars, and this was helping the environment. I took a breath of the clean, fresh air. The natural gas cars were working because the level of smog in the city had improved. My phone buzzed. I got a text message.

While I was still hugging Yasmin goodbye, my mom's cousin Amber showed up. Everyone was making their rounds of goodbyes to my mom for her trip back. We visited with Amber, another single woman supporting herself with her investments. Amber's mom had run an interior decorating business and taken the profits to invest in real estate. Amber now owned a large home that she had sectioned into four rentals. She was receiving income from each section of her home and using it to fund her lifestyle and travels. She had just gotten a new car and wanted us to check out her new wheels. It was pretty dark outside now. The porch light and gate light barely lit the driveway. Just then the power came back on. How fun, all the gate lights brightened and the flood lights came on, and her car was glowing. She had a pearl-white Honda with a manual transmission. The car still had the new car smell, and she was waiting for her tags.

Her visit was short and sweet. She was on her way to a ladies club meeting where they were raising money for funding new schools. Amber had lived in Lahore her whole life and knew everyone, so she had been selected as the main donation solicitation person for the fundraiser. But the visits to bid farewell were just beginning. A few minutes after Aunt Amber pulled out, my other cousin Tariq showed up with his wife, Rabia. Their visit was also quick. But we had power now, hot tea, lights, and a fan. The house was feeling much more comfortable. My cousin ran a business exporting carpets and his wife, Rabia, was a principal at a local high school. They had five daughters who had all gone to college, gotten married, and were working everywhere from Singapore to Canada. I was amazed that, being in town for just two days, so many people had made time to drive across town to see me.

I had been texting everyone that I was in town earlier that morning. I had just received a reply from another old friend, Naeema. She knew the two words needed to kick off a girls' night out—"Pomegranate juice?" Of course! My two lifelong favorites are chocolates and fresh pomegranate juice. Naeema must have just left work. She was a professor at a local university, teaching social media marketing. Her students, who included my nephew Omar, said she was tough. I texted back that pomegranate juice was a definite yes! I would be free in about an hour, and Naeema offered to come pick me up. I texted that we will be ready. "We?" Naeema asked. "Who is we?" I told her, Colonel Nafisa was in town. Naeema was even more excited. She had news to share with us, and the much-needed fresh pomegranate juice awaited.

At about seven thirty, there was a honk at the gate. It was really dark now, and I knew the power would go out again. I wondered why Naeema did not come in. Jet lagged but excited, I got ready to leave. Nafisa and I grabbed our purses and headed out. "I'll be back late, Mom," I said as I walked to the gate. My mom was looking tired with all the visitors, and she was relaxing on the couch. She needed rest.

We walked onto the marble patio and then down the brick-laid driveway to the gate. The brick walls were eight feet high. Our gate was heavy gray metal with two posts with lights on top. I could see some light on the other side through the gap in the bottom of the gate. I opened the gate, and there was Naeema in her car. "Why didn't you come in?" I asked. And then I froze. I was not prepared for what I saw.

Bouncing around in Naeema's passenger seat was a baby. The child looked about nine months old and was sitting comfortably in the front seat with no seat belt. I was in shock, after living in the United States where I was used to car seats, seat belts, and infants in the rear seat only. In the big seat, the child looked tiny. I forgot that in Pakistan we could see a family of seven on a motorcycle. So Naeema pulling up with a nine-month-old baby sitting in the front seat, just hanging out, with no car seat or seat belt, was surprising. It reminded me of the seventies in the US when my little sister Amina was born. We could take her anywhere in the car, and all you had to do was make sure that when you took the turns, she didn't roll over. In my surprise I asked Naeema, "Who is this?"

His name was Aiden, and he was Naeema's son. Naeema and her husband, Arshad, had been trying to have kids for a while, but things had not worked out. I recalled her talking about her struggles with infertility procedures for several years. I felt for her sense of longing to have kids of her own. But last year, things changed. Naeema's sister generously had a baby for her. I was amazed. Such an unselfish sister and such a cute baby—I could tell Naeema was overjoyed. Just in that moment the call to prayer went off again. The mosque was next to the car, and the loud speakers had enough power to vibrate the entire car. We all paused to listen to the call to prayer and reflect. Naeema came into the house with the baby. We each took a bathroom to clean up for the prayer and then met in the living room. We prayed the night prayer together. God comes before pomegranate juice. All I could think of in the prayer was Naeema's sister giving up a baby. My mind drifted to Prophet Moses (pbuh) and his mother also giving up a baby. I realized that I was surrounded with such strong women and that our faith taught examples of strong women. I got up from the prayer slowly, with joy for Naeema filling my heart. Aiden was still jumping around on the sofa.

Naeema was not the first to get a child from a sibling as surrogate. I had known two other Pakistani couples that had used a sibling as a surrogate. In Pakistani culture, the thought of a sister having a child for us did not seem odd. I was really happy for Naeema. She was glowing with her new role as a mother. Nafisa and I jumped in the car. We were so excited to meet this new addition to our girls' night. Naeema was talking about how she was so tired and had no sleep. Nafisa and I had kids in college. No sleep and no sanity—those were the good ol' days. We started giving Naeema parenting advice.

Naeema mentioned that there was a new mall in town called Pacers Mall. Did we also want to go to Pacers? I said sure, I was interested in pomegranate juice, Pacers mall, and our favorite Chinese food hangout, Yum, that had crispy beef on the menu. Naeema said, "Let me call Arshad so he can watch Aiden while we shop."

We left the house again to see Arshad's motorbike parked next to Naeema's car. Arshad hopped in the passenger seat and held baby Aiden in his lap. Nafisa and I jumped in the back seat with Naeema at the wheel. They had recently taken a trip with the baby up to the mountains in Kaghan, a valley in the Himalayas. We chatted about their trip and what they saw. I asked Naeema how it was being a mom and travelling with a baby. She started to tell us about all the diapers and the night feedings. Nafisa and I laughed. Nafisa has two kids, and I had four. We kept telling Naeema and Arshad, one kid is hardly any work. With one kid, you never have another child around to torture the baby.

Naeema and Arshad were planning Aiden's first birthday party. Nafisa and I both told them to do something small because it is rough on a baby to have a large party. Naeema and Arshad were thinking big, with ponies, balloons, and a huge cake. I said if you do those with a one year old, the birthday is for you, the parents. If you want to do something like that for Aiden, wait until he is four. We were discussing alternate first birthday party ideas, such as a family photo shoot, when we arrived at Pacers Mall.

Pacers was huge, about the size of a small airport. We entered the giant complex and drove around looking for parking. It was a Tuesday night, so even though there were several cars parked, we found a spot not too far from the main entrance. Arshad took out the stroller and put Aiden in his carriage. We all started walking toward the mall with Arshad pushing Aiden. There was a light security check to get into the mall.

The shopping center was totally white and immaculate. We were greeted by two sets of escalators and an elevator. Arshad took off in the elevator with the baby, headed for the food court. To have an elevator meant the complex could run on power generators alone. I thought, How many generators do they need to keep this place going? With all the load shedding in Pakistan, we had lost power four times already today. Pakistan is conscious of its energy footprint and does not encourage the over-consumption of resources. Resources such as electricity and water are monitored for a controlled rate of consumption. Because of the lack of rain, we were in the middle of "load shedding," where the power companies regularly shed their loads throughout the day. For a while the power and water would be running, and then load shedding would start and we would lose electricity or water for an hour. The mall had been designed to conserve power so it could run on generators alone when the main power grid switched off.

Naeema, Nafisa, and I started looking at the boutiques. I had come to just experience the mall, but now I thought of doing some shopping. After all, who knew the next time I would be back? May as well embrace the potential shopping opportunity with my two shopping assistants. Naeema and Nafisa were telling me the most popular stores and what the specialties were. Some of the stores also had promotional items, and some allowed for a little bit of bargaining. I was looking for some gifts for my kids and maybe a stylish white shirt for myself. We were hopping from boutique to boutique, with occasional texts from Arshad on the status of Aiden. I tried on a ton of white shirts, and of course I found some I liked. Getting Naeema and Nafisa's approval was more challenging. "This one looks too long," "I don't like the fit," "The collar is too high." I was certainly getting a full serving of fashion advice.

After spending too much money on things I really didn't need, we received a text from Arshad that Aiden was hungry. We also wanted to make it to the Chinese restaurant before it closed at eleven that night. We left Pacers as Arshad pushed Aiden's stroller. Aiden was squirming by now, and Naeema offered him a bottle. With everyone back in their original positions in the car, Aiden sitting on Arshad's lap in the front seat, Naeema started driving off toward a part of town known as Gulberg. Gulberg had a strip of high-end restaurants, and at the end of the strip was one of the best Chinese food places in town. The restaurants were from all over the world, including the popular chains in the United States, such as Hardee's, and from South Africa, Nando's Peri Peri chicken. We were interested in a more local fare, from Pakistan's neighbor, China. All of us were bouncing over speed bumps on the quiet street, passing beautifully lit restaurants with valet parking for mini parking lots. I was observing how different safety rules were in Pakistan and the United States. Not just in the car but the way the motorcycles were weaving in and out around us.

Traffic had eased up this late at night. I was observing things that had changed since my last visit four years ago. We turned into the tight eight-car parking lot of the Chinese restaurant that was full of way more than eight cars. The valet parked the car. The restaurant was full of bamboo plants and items from China: the carving of a jade dragon on the hostess stand, and the chopsticks at the table were covered with Chinese symbols. The waiter came over, and we started to order. We wanted crispy orange beef, one of our favorite dishes. We started off with some soup and some rice on a big Lazy Susan sharing food. Aiden sat in his high chair, checking out the white rice and big bowl of fried fish chips. He was enjoying the appetizers along with us.

I was getting tired. But the company was great, and I picked Naeema and Arshad's brains on marketing operations for my business and speaking presentations. Arshad wrote a book on branding, he gave me some branding options that would fit my goals. Naeema added her ideas on social media for developing followers. Why don't you make videos on YouTube so people can see your personality. That's a brand in itself Naeema said. Then she explained how to post the videos when there was the highest number of people on platforms such as Facebook. We kept eating and discussing business propositions. Marketing was usually outside of my comfort zone, but now I was beginning to understand some basics. Maybe I could hire someone to help with my marketing. Arshad knew some virtual assistants. The thought of paying a virtual assistant in Rupees really sounded appealing. Good Chinese food always helps me think.

When the check came, I tried to pay for dinner, but Arshad insisted on paying. With typical Pakistani hospitality, he insisted that we were guests and it had been a long time since they had seen us. I had eaten too much. It was a slow, too-much-food-in-my-stomach walk to the car and then off toward my grandmother's home. It was about midnight, so the streets were quiet and the shops were dark. However there was one little light on at the Gulberg Boulevard circle—the pomegranate juice guy. I was told he stays open till three in the morning. Must be my lucky day. We pulled up to the curb, and the juice guy appeared. We ordered four pomegranate juices in disposables. Disposable cups are the equivalent of saying we want the food to go. I gave my usual order, pomegranate juice, no salt, no sugar, no ice, no water. I wasn't going to risk drinking ice or water from the market.

The juice guy ran back to another man sitting on the sidewalk with three blenders. The shop is just a hole in the wall. The blender man sat next to a column covered in papier-mâché fruit. The same fruit had been there since the seventies, when we first discovered the place, though by now the juice guy was famous. Normally, there would have been eight or ten juice boys running up to parked cars to take orders, but it was midnight, and there were only two order takers running around. Our juice came and Nafisa said, check it. I took a sip of the juice. Perfect, he had gotten the order correct. Just plain pomegranate juice, no additives, and the cup was room temperature so he had not added ice. This was the good life—friends, shopping, and pomegranate juice at midnight.

I was determined to sleep that night. I was fired with adrenaline and falling over at the same time. However, the next morning started the same way when I was awakened by the call to prayer at dawn. I got up to pray and was wide awake. So what could I do while the rest of the city was getting up? I stood in the garden, watching the light change the vines climbing up our walls. Nafisa and I decided it was time to go to the park and run around. We walked through the dimly lit streets toward the park. It was light out, but the sun was not up yet. The shopping center was quiet, with the exception of the bakery and the breakfast stores. Some of the shopkeepers were cleaning the sidewalk and the storefronts to prepare for the day. We kept walking toward the gate of the park. I had on my Fitbit—six thousand steps already. I wanted to be in good shape for my upcoming marathon. I told Nafisa that I was going to push myself for endurance running today. We walked toward the main gate. After the main gate was the back of the hospital my grandmother had started and the wing she had dedicated in her father's name. Nafisa agreed to stay with me for the warm-up rounds and then go to check on my mom.

Soon I was jogging alone in a park full of smiling strangers. "*Asalaam Alikum*, may peace be upon you," one woman said as she looked at me. I replied, "And also on you." The park soothed me. I would be returning to the States that night, and Nafisa was taking a bus back to her home. So many details still remained for closing up the house and getting my mom ready to travel. I kept running as another woman bid me *Asalaam Alikum*. I looked at the flowers and at the peacocks. Everyone is praying for peace for me. I needed peace this morning, and I felt God had answered my prayer. I will miss this park. I will miss the strangers that walk the circumference, wishing each other peace. I headed out the gate, and the ticket collector said, "Ma'am, may peace be upon you." I replied, "*Wa alikum, Ma salaam*, and may peace be upon you too."

I crossed the bazaar and decided a little local food would be great. I stopped by a boy making chick peas in one vat and frying flat roti in another. I asked for two orders of the most delicious greasy and spicy bazaar breakfast, *halwa puri*. I received the contents in three plastic bags and smelled the freshly made spiced chick peas and the *halwa* made out of sugar and Cream of Wheat. I will have a party in my mouth for breakfast. I felt relaxed after a nice walk in the park and knowing my mom was with my best friend, the doctor.

When I got home I announced, "Nafisa, I have breakfast." I asked my mom how she was doing. Nafisa said, "Your mom cannot eat any of this." I said, "Yes, but the two of us can eat all of this." Bazaar food is my guilty pleasure. Over the dining table we discussed the plans for the day. Nafisa went over the medications my mom needed and made sure that she would be ready for the trip. I kept nodding and making sure we had the right medication in our carry-on luggage. My mom felt better and decided to eat. She ate the gluten-free toast and tea with coconut milk. The cook walked into the dining room and said, "*As Salaam Alikum*." I replied, and then she asked, "An omelet, ma'am?" She saw that we had food from the bazaar and expected me to say no.

But I said, "Yes, I'll take an omelet. I don't want to miss out on the extra thin veggie omelet you are famous for." The cook smiled and said, "Thank you, ma'am." We started discussing the plans for the day. Nafisa had to leave that evening, we had company coming over for lunch, and my mom had errands to run. There was only one car. I was eating my omelet as Nafisa and my mom sat and kept me company. I saw my hair in the mirror. I started complaining about my hair and how I really needed a haircut. Nafisa chimed in with her hair needing a keratin treatment. It reminded me of Hajra, the lady I met in the park yesterday. Her sister owned a salon a few blocks away. Nafisa and I could go over there without a car. That would be amazing.

I went on Facebook and Google, looking for the salon Hajra had described. I didn't have her number; I just knew her sister's name, Saleema, and the approximate section of town the salon was in, on the main street in C block. We were in A block, so not too far to walk. I found a couple of places online and had Nafisa call to see if an Saleema worked there. Bingo, our third try we found Saleema's salon. Nafisa said we were friends of her sister Hajra—a slight exaggeration—and that we were leaving town tonight. Saleema agreed to see us before lunch.

I didn't know what to expect. We walked through the crowded boulevard circling the park until we hit C block. C block had the ladies club, and some of the land the ladies club owned had been donated to my grandmother. My grandmother had raised funds with events at the ladies club to build a hospital. Walking past the hospital reminded me about a trip I made ten years ago when my daughter did the ribbon cutting on the new wing. We kept going past the hospital and club looking for Saleema's place. Saleema's home was easy to spot with the large "Ladies Salon" sign on the front. By this time, Saleema had already spoken to Hajra about her new "friends" who were coming over for treatments. We walked into what was the first level of Saleema's house. Each room was a portion of the salon, with the front section for haircuts, a section for pedicures, and the far right for massages. There were about thirty girls, working dressed in all-black pants and salon logo shirts. We were greeted at the door by a young lady named Azra, who was Saleema's assistant. Saleema offered us the works—a manicure, pedicure, and some highlights. I had a conference the day after I got back, so having multiple treatments sounded great. Maybe having to cancel all my appointments for this week was a blessing in disguise. We were given robes to change into in private rooms.

Saleema was indeed a business woman. I told her I did not have much time. So she had one girl working on my hair, one giving me a manicure, and a third girl for the pedicure. Nafisa opted for the same. We were sitting in the seats, joking about our days in Brunei and how we would have to go back to reality tomorrow. Today, again, was a husband- and kids-free, girls-only type of day. I was relaxing while one girl massaged my hands and another one was massaging my feet. Saleema came over and offered us tea. I opted for green tea with honey. This was the life—my mom was better, my best friend was in town, and we were hanging out in the spa. In two short hours we looked and felt like new women. We walked out of the spa ready for lunch.

My Aunt Bano was coming over to bring us food. She knew my mom was sick, so she had made a special meal with fish. I started to help my mom pack while we waited for Bano to show up. I was sorting old photographs that my grandmother had. It was so hard to go through so many memories and realize that my grandmother had been keeping pictures of my kids and me for decades. There was a horn at the gate, and the bell rang. Bano must be here. I went to wash my hands before lunch. Bano showed up with a burst of energy and her huge, loving smile. She was carrying two covered dishes. "How are you, my sweetie?" she asked as I gave her a hug. "Sometimes the unexpected events in life are the best," she added. I am so glad I was able to come because I was having a blast seeing everyone.

Bano was divorced and raised three kids by herself. One of her daughters, Jasmine, was going to join us for lunch but was running late.

Jasmine soon bounded into the house. A bundle of fast talking animated energy, Jasmine has a beautiful heart and caring soul. She reminded me of a fairy that fluttered from spot to spot. She sat down for lunch but didn't eat much. Jasmine was a vegetarian and had a little rice but wasn't interested in much else. She kept talking about her job and her co-worker who was going to join Jasmine in her own graphic design business. Jasmine was playing with the rice on her plate. I asked, "Won't you be hungry at work?" She mentioned having some food in the car. She pulled out her phone and asked if I wanted to see her designs. "Sure," I said. She pulled up her Facebook account and showed me some of the flyers she made. I passed the phone to Nafisa and then my mom. Jasmine had to get back to work. She left with the same whirlwind she arrived in.

I was back to talking to Bano. Bano and I liked to sew. We used to sew together when I was in junior high and high school. We had the same body shape—short and plump. All our clothing needed adjusting, so we decided to make our own clothes the way we liked. Bano mentioned that she had made the shirt she was wearing. She was living in the same house her parents left her and using the same sewing machine her mom had. It was an old Singer that was a manual sewing machine. We used to sew by swinging the bottom section of the machine back and forth. It was a good accessory for the load-shedding society we were in. Bano could keep sewing even when the lights were gone.

She was also involved in charity organizations. Like my grandma, who had made a hospital in C block, Bano was building wells in villages. She had started with the village her mom was from and made a well in her memory. The well was huge, and not at all like I imagined it. It was a large, sixteen-foot-diameter cement tank above ground with twelve faucets around the perimeter. Below the tank was the actual well that pumped water into the tank. She was building her fifth well in yet another village. She was part of a group that was actively fundraising for wells in villages. Bano took personal interest in the wells and would drive out to the middle of the country and look at the progress of the wells. She was driving out to a new village to see about their water needs tomorrow. She would assess the size of the well the village would need to be self-sufficient. She was becoming a bit of a well expert. I gave some of my money to her for her new well project. Lunch ended, and we said good bye to Bano.

Successful and loving women filled my trip. My grandmother, whose philanthropy changed the lives of the kids and the doctors at the hospital. My mom, who wanted her three daughters to have careers and choices just like Prophet Muhammad's (pbuh) wife Khadija. My cousin Yasmin, who became a nuclear engineer to bring electrical power to Pakistan. Her daughter Amna, whose career in the civil service helped bring resources to women in villages. I walked in the park with Nafisa, a medical doctor and a colonel in the army. Her medical advice and military connections had helped my family on many occasions. Then there was Naeema, working as a university professor teaching her students and me how to market our businesses on social media. Not to mention Naeema's sister, who gave up her baby so Naeema could have a child.

The strong emphasis on charitable works also showed up in my aunts Amber and Bano, each living off of her investments and generating enough income to give back and leave her legacy even as a single woman. I thought about Hajra, a supportive mom who wanted her children to have an education and who referred me to Saleema, a dynamic businesswoman who employed over fifty young girls in her home. Some of the girls in the Salon were Muslim, and others were Christians. Both religions worked side by side in harmony for a common goal of serving clients and learning the skills of a good beautician.

It just occurred to me that I had collected an incredible group of brave women who was making an impact each in her own way. I felt relieved. In my heart I knew that the media images of Muslim women could not irritate me anymore. The media may portray a typical Muslim woman as oppressed. But I know from my travels that the majority of Muslim women I know, like the women in Islamic history, are empowered.

Chapter 13

PEACE

JAHIMA CAME TO THE PROPHET, PEACE AND BLESSINGS BE
UPON HIM, AND HE SAID, "O MESSENGER OF GOD, I INTEND
TO JOIN A FIGHTING FORCE AND I SEEK YOUR COUNSEL."
THE PROPHET SAID, "DO YOU HAVE A MOTHER?"
JAHIMA REPLIED YES.
THE PROPHET SAID "THEN SERVE YOUR MOTHER, FOR
PARADISE LIES BENEATH THE FEET OF YOUR MOTHER."

Our words and the descriptive language we use create our culture and country. What we boast about represents what we value as a society. In the United States we claim to value education, health, and our children's future. However, we do not put our best resources to the very things we want. Our football players make more money than our teachers. Some of our farmers are losing money if they do not produce cheap, mass-market food. I envision a society where we actually put our capital into our values. We can explore other identities that would make us powerful yet venerated.

In the United States we pride ourselves on being a military superpower. Most other countries use different terms to describe themselves. Pakistan strives for hospitality and great food. We Americans are gratified with our defense strategies and implementing our global foreign policy. Our defense contractors are rich and well connected with the best technology and access to resources. China is both a military and manufacturing superpower. Japan uses the terms of technology superpower as their self-definition. But what if we were a different superpower? We can be an educational superpower, where instead of spending half of our tax dollars on weapons, we invest in knowledge. Instead of being at war, we could come up with the most innovative memory enhancement and subject mastering skills. We could have free education for everyone with teachers who would be among the higher paid professionals in our society. We would give the best riches to the people that spend six to eight hours a day investing their thoughts and influence into our newest generation. Imagine a society that taught enhanced memory skills, where we spoke multiple languages, and where we constantly improved ourselves by learning something new. "Come to America and we will educate you for a better life" would be our national motto.

We could use the word superpower in another way, such as a medical superpower with the message, "Come to the United States and we will heal you." We can focus our tax dollars on the best medical breakthroughs, conquering diseases, replicating organs, and increasing brain function for anyone that visited. Our specialty would be in healing via a nurturing environment and soothing emotional support. We would be known for the best mental health in the world. We substitute questionable prescription drugs with holistic relaxation techniques, and our health salons are world-famous for rejuvenation and eliminating pain. Our slogan could be, "Come to America and live healthy, happy, and stress free."

Like Japan and China, we could also focus on technology, or our superpower could be superior food. "The United States of America, the country that feeds the citizens of Earth." We could spend our money finding innovative ways to grow nourishing, energetic foods while keeping our environment green. Our food could be used as medicine, and we would not be addicted to junk foods, fad diets, and magic pills. Our farmers would be revered for keeping us healthy. A new slogan for our country could be "Come to the America, where you won't go hungry."

There are different directions our word choices and the values behind them can take us, but we have settled for being the one that has the military strength to force our foreign policy on others. To maintain the value of being a military superpower, we constantly need a super enemy. In the past we had some real enemies, and when we heroically defeated those enemies, we needed some new ones. Sometimes, enemies were in short supply and we decided to create the enemy. The United States is the only country where we joke that if you want to boost the economy, start a war. Most people hate wars, and we want to hate them too, but a "good" war does boost defense spending and therefore creates jobs. We have many other avenues of creating jobs, yet we seem to prefer war over creating amazing products.

After World War II, enemies were in short supply. We entered into long-term conflicts in both Korea and Vietnam. After South Asia, we discovered Central America and decided to engage in conflicts in Cuba, Grenada, Guatemala, El Salvador, Nicaragua, and Panama. These conflicts focused on the Latino population, and we started using our words to describe both the people and their culture in derogatory terms. These conflicts were followed with another long boycott as well as with military action in Iraq that resulted in the death of over half a million Iraqi children, as stated by former Secretary of State Madeleine Albright:

> Madeleine Albright (then U.S. Ambassador to the United Nations) appeared on a *60 Minutes* segment in which Lesley Stahl asked her, "We have heard that half a million children have died. I mean, that's more children than died in Hiroshima. And, you know, is the price worth it?" Albright replied, "I think this is a very hard choice, but the price, we think the price is worth it."[4]

---

4   https://en.wikipedia.org/wiki/Sanctions_against_Iraq

At home, we started off with our internal conflicts. Our forefathers built this country on the land of the aboriginal people and cultivated their crops with African slaves. We continued our Native American turmoil, taking their land and erasing their culture. Henry Ford, the inventor of the automobile, stated, "Any man who thinks he can be happy and prosperous by letting the government take care of him better take a closer look at the American Indian." I grew up in Colorado, and my father worked with the Native American nations. I personally witnessed their grievances and mistreatment. I also was bussed as part of an initiative to desegregate schools in the 1970s in Denver. I learned firsthand in elementary school about racial tension between African Americans and Caucasian Americans. I experienced the difference in treatment between the two races. In 2011, blacks were incarcerated at a dramatically higher rate than whites (five to seven times) and accounted for almost half of all prisoners incarcerated with a sentence of more than one year for a drug-related offense. In 2011, my forty-year mark in the United States, the statistics were still the same as they were four decades earlier; all the initiatives to end racial prejudice did not give our minorities social justice. After the Native American nations and African Americans, we as a society decided to turn our wrath to the immigrants.

We labeled the Native American peoples as heathens, and then the African Americans as criminals, followed by calling immigrants violent. The twenty-first century key word for Muslims is "terrorists." The other minorities enjoyed a brief respite period as Muslims took the lead role of evil people. Current media and new stories revolve around horrible scenes of violence and bloodshed in the Muslim lands. I told many friends and coworkers that I wanted to write a book about Islam and about peace. Yet the question continued to loom, "But what about the terrorists? How can you say Islam teaches peace?"

In December 1989, my supervisor asked me to attend a radio conference for the International Telecommunication Union. I spent three days in Geneva, listening on shortwave radio to different representatives present their views while I represented the Voice of America and ironically voiced our concerns on radio frequencies and interference in radio signals. I enjoyed working as an engineer during the day and playing a tourist at night. On December 21, I flew back to Washington DC through London Heathrow.

I had a four-hour layover in London and planned to continue my tourist routine for a few more hours. However, when I exited the plane, I noticed that the airport was really crowded with lots of security guards, who were very visible in uniforms of black pants and white shirts. I found my departing gate so I would be familiar with the gate when I returned from my four-hour English layover adventure. A security officer approached me and asked if I was on this flight. I said "Yes, I am flying back to the US today." He responded, "On this flight, Pan Am 103?" I was even more surprised when he asked to check my passport. He went through the passport page by page and put a red stamp on one of the pages near the front. I asked him why transit passengers needed a stamp. He said, "Don't you know, this is the one-year anniversary of Pan Am flight 103 that exploded over Lockerbie, Scotland, last December 21? You know, the terrorist attack by the Muslims." I told him of my plans to visit London, and he explained that today the airport was under a high security alert.

No security alert was going to stop me from seeing the sights, so I attempted to leave, heading to the exit. I saw line to enter the airport going out the front doors and onto the sidewalks. Maybe the security guard had a point. I didn't think I could take the tube to downtown, see the sights, take the tube back to Heathrow, and clear the lines in my layover. I decided to sit and wait at the gate. There was a TV in the waiting area showing pictures of Lockerbie, Scotland, and running footage of the remains of the Pan Am 103 from last year. I felt uneasy. I did not want to fly on this plane after watching footage of an airplane blowing up. I decided to pray for the best.

An airport employee came on the public announcement system and announced a one-hour delay for a security check. I started to wish I had gone out exploring instead of watching the news. An hour and fifteen minutes later, another delay announcement came over the PA system. I continued to watch the news. Now the weather report indicated a snowstorm headed to Washington. We were scheduled to arrive early in the evening, but with the delays, we were arriving after midnight and in the middle of the snowstorm. After a stressful airport stay and a normal but tension-filled flight, we landed at Dulles Airport in the middle of a huge snowstorm well after midnight. Luckily the roads, though snowy, were passable, and I made it home.

The next day the comment the security guard made about Muslim terrorists kept going through my head. I decided to do some research on what happened to Pan Am 103 and why I spent a long nine-hour layover at London Heathrow. An apparent precursor to Pan Am 103 happened in July of 1988, when the US accidently shot down Iran Air flight 655, killing two hundred and ninety people including sixty-six children. We did not apologize for the incident to the Irani people for several years, and even refused to discipline Captain Rogers of the USS Vincennes for his rash behavior against a civilian airliner. Furthermore, the United States had also bombed Libya, killing many innocent victims including accidentally blowing up the Embassy of France and erroneously bombing several civilian neighborhoods in Tripoli. I wondered why the news flashed horrible images of the Lockerbie bombing but forgot to cover the acts our United States government performed leading up to the event. No photos of the innocent bodies of the sixty-six Muslim children appeared on any media source. The tattered neighborhoods and blood-covered bodies in Tripoli were strategically omitted. We erased our own horrible crimes against Libya and Iran, while painting their retaliation as a wrongful act. Blowing up a civilian airliner is wrong regardless of race, religion, nationality, or wearing a uniform.

I remember the bombing in Oklahoma City in 1996. The first few articles about the bombing blamed Muslim terrorism and Middle Eastern groups. For three days, we as a nation believed that some turban-wearing, violent terrorist had penetrated the US heartland. Many of our neighbors that looked Middle Eastern were attacked and harassed for looking like someone that would blow up a building.[5] However, when we discovered that the all-American former soldier Tim McVeigh had committed the act, the term *terrorist* disappeared. No Caucasian churches were searched, and we did not immediately implement security restrictions exclusively for white males purchasing fertilizer. Apparently, the use of fertilizer as a weapon is limited to this one act committed by an individual, and therefore did not implicate anyone associated with the race, religion, or nationality of Tim McVeigh. So all blue-eyed American males continued to have the freedom to purchase large quantities of fertilizer and rent trucks.

Mass shooters in Columbine, Sandy Hook, and the 2017 Las Vegas shootings were not labeled as terrorists. In August of 2019, the violence continued with domestic shooters killing victims in the El Paso, Texas, Walmart, followed by another mass shooting in Dayton, Ohio. No churches were raided nor was the Anglo-Saxon American group scrutinized.

I fully agree that Muslims are all too human, nor are Muslims excluded from social and economic challenges. However, just because we have decided to label different races in derogatory terms does not mean those races are prone to more violent behaviors. So when I am asked if Muslims are terrorists, my canned response is: "Yes they play one on TV. The ones in real life are nothing like what is portrayed in the media." People are quick to believe gossip and adopt negative prejudices. Our need to hate has lead the United States to lose the reverence in which our nation was once held.

5   https://www.latimes.com/archives/la-xpm-1995-04-22-mn-57460-story.html

In my opinion, our greater challenge is the decline in character that has occurred globally as we focus our media and attention on the poorest behavior of human beings. We have allowed our media to put a camera on humanity's sewage with the euphemism of "being informed." In business we see role models of successful brilliant CEOs who steal from their employees' retirement accounts. Our sports news is filled with gifted and talented athletes who are abusing substances to cope with basic life. The famous celebrities who are amazing performers on the big screen are often rude and vulgar in real life. Our politicians are strong and powerful leaders who cheat on their wives or abuse their power by giving handouts to their friends. As a mom, I'd love to show my kids an example of a "famous" or "popular" role model that I can endorse as an example of honesty, dignity, and excellence in emotional management. I am still searching for that individual, so I redirect my kids to my main three role models, Muhammad (pbuh), Jesus (pbuh), and Moses (pbuh), for lessons in flawless behavior.

What if we were to focus on good behavior and random acts of kindness? We need a world where we can make someone famous for service, love, and generosity. I want to thank the countless people that God sent into my life at different points to show me the beauty of humanity and that one person can make a difference and make someone else's day. To the news media that believes "if it doesn't bleed, it doesn't lead," I counter with, "Let's make good acts go viral." We need to be Viral for Good. Even if we are poor and have little power, we can still impact another person's life in positive ways.

I'll start with a soul I met in Peshawar, Pakistan, in 1979 named Rahim Gul. Rahim Gul helped me with a problem I had with our cook's dog. In 1979, while living in Peshawar, our maids had found a stray dog and brought him to the cook, who named the dog Dabu. Through Dabu, I would meet Rahim Gul. Dabu was a crazy dog, but somehow Dabu was our dog. In eighth grade, I lived in Peshawar, Pakistan, attending the Presentation Convent School, and living on Karakul Lane. Karakul was a nickname for my grandfather; the town knew him as Karakul, so when he bought the section of land in the University Town portion of Peshawar, the adjacent street was named after him. When I moved into this house in 1978, the home had a staff of a cook, two maids, and a resident crazy dog named Dabu.

Dabu had a mind of his own; he would come and go as he pleased. The dog left for days and would come back looking like he had been in a fight with another dog. Then when he found his way back to our house, our cook nursed him and fed him, and the girls gave Dabu shelter in their modest home. Like any stray dog, Dabu's coat was dull and dirty, yet he walked around the three-sectioned compound like he owned the place. If we ever came home and Dabu was in the driveway, Dabu would not budge. Dabu made our home his home and always arrived promptly at mealtime, expecting a full, extravagant dinner. Despite being poor, the cook shared his food with this senile dog, and the girls working in our home had compassion for the homeless animal.

Dabu continued the disappearing acts and returned with some sort of injury or scratch on his nose. As soon as Dabu healed, he returned to picking fights with strangers, both dogs and human. For this reason our house was notorious. Dabu chased down passing bikers. Despite the walls, the gates, and the doors, nothing seemed to contain him. He also scared the milkman and the mailman. He chased them down and tried to grab the milk or mail. Both of them complained about the dog. Neither of them would deliver items to the house without either the cook or the driver coming to the gate. I think my uncle let Dabu rule because when he put his mind to it, Dabu was an effective guard dog.

My relationship with Dabu was not the greatest. He was usually dirty, sleeping in the middle of the driveway and then snarling when the driver made him move to park the car. This "Dabu Show" continued for about fourteen months until one evening. As I was bringing groceries into the kitchen, Dabu bit me. I ended up with four canine marks in my right leg and was taken to Peshawar Hospital, and working in the emergency room was Rahim Gul.

Character is everything in Islam, and when I think of the thousands of Muslims I've met around the world, I would say Rahim Gul embodies the character of the average Muslim. Rahim Gul took care of me and my dog bite. The incident reminds me of all the kind people in my life and how well cared for I am.

Decades later, I still remember Rahim Gul because of his kindness and generosity. He reminded me of the story from the Holy Quran. One of the many memorable characters in the Quran is a dark slave named Luqman. In the Ayat, a stranger asks Luqman, "Why are you so popular?" Luqman told the stranger that the secret to being well-liked by everyone is by behaving as follows: lower our gaze, watch our tongues, eat what is lawful, be chaste, keep our promises, fulfill our commitments, be good hosts to our guests, respect our neighbors, and not get into other people's business. According to Luqman, these behaviors and the underlying character made him attractive to others.

Like Luqman, Rahim Gul, a medic, also cared for people. We showed up eight p.m. at the hospital facility, after all the doctors had gone home. Even though the place was empty, Rahim Gul decided to stay late for emergencies. I was in pain. The ride to the hospital had brick-paved roads that were uneven and bumpy . . . not the best feeling when my leg had four holes in it and I was trying to keep weight on my uninjured leg. My uncle drove up to the ward door, and I hobbled into an eight-bed ward with semi-clean beds, a dirty floor, and some limited medical equipment.

Rahim Gul was probably in his forties but looked much older. His skin was tanned from sun exposure, and several of his teeth were missing. From his clothing and hands we could tell he did not have much money. All those aspects of him faded because his most memorable feature was a big smile and kind eyes. Rahim Gul was skilled enough to give me three stitches, however he did not believe in any numbing agents. For the longest eight minutes of my life, I felt the stitching needle and catgut thread in my fresh wound.

Not only did I get to experience the tugging sensation of his stitching, but also the pain of having stitches without any anesthesia. By the beginning of the third stich, I was clenching my teeth and holding my breath. At one point I gasped for air, and my grandmother shoved her hand in my mouth. I got my final stich, biting my grandmother's hand. I was lost in the pain and the fear, but as I bit down on her hand, I thought, She must love me!

Rahim Gul was washing his hands when my uncle asked him about money. Rahim refused and said he just took care of a daughter. He then inquired if the dog, Dabu, had had any shots. Of course not; no one gives a dog shots. Even leashes and collars are rare in this part of the world. Rahim Gul then mentioned rabies, and recommended having a fourteen-day vaccination treatment. He wanted the best for me, so he recommended getting the vaccines flown in from Switzerland since these vaccines were not manufactured locally. According to Rahim Gul, the Swiss rabies vaccines were the best.

After a thirty-minute visit, I was stitched up and headed home to Dabu's house. Because no one puts collars on dogs in Pakistan, there was no way to tie him up. Most houses had walls, and the people and their pets are protected by the walls. I came home with gauze and stiches, no painkillers. After an exhausting day, I fell asleep.

Three days later, the rabies vaccines arrived from Switzerland. Usually, my favorite part of the day was when school ended so I could go home and play with my friends. But for the next two weeks, as soon as school ended, my grandma picked me up and we drove straight to the hospital. Rahim Gul would be there every time with the greeting, "May peace be upon you." He would then lower his gaze, to show respect for my grandmother and treat us as guests in his hospital ward. He would address me as ma'am. Yes, me, the twelve-year-old child, he addressed with honor and respect. As he was filling the syringe, he would ask, "Ma'am, when this is over, how are you going to celebrate?" And then I would see the needle. Rabies shots are awful; as the vaccine entered my body it felt like someone was taking a knife and cutting out my belly button. No matter—one done and thirteen shots to go. We offered to pay, but again Rahim Gul refused any money.

The next day I wished that school could last forever. I watched the clock and it seemed to move so fast. The first class sped by and then the second class, then recess and lunch. School was almost over, and I would soon be heading to the hospital. I wanted to go anywhere but there. I hated the rabies shots.

One day blended into another. The same routine—get up, get dressed, go to school, watch the clock, go to the hospital. Get a shot from Rahim Gul and have him ask, "Ma'am, when all the shots are over, how will you celebrate? Will you buy sweets or have a party, or go out to Chinese food with your friends?" Then we would offer money and again and again Rahim Gul refused.

On the fourteenth day I was excited. It was the end. No more hospital, no more watching the clock the entire school day, and no more shots after today, but I would miss Rahim Gul. We stopped at the sweets store to get some traditional Pakistani *methai* for Rahim and his family. The pretty cubes of sweet ricotta cheese and fried orange rinds dripping in sugar are found on every street corner and market. We went to a shop and bought three boxes of the best sweets for our kind friend. The fancy foil boxes in red and gold were wrapped up in strings that also served as handles. I walked into the hospital ward for the last time. I was so happy the end was near. I got my final rabies shot and gave Rahim the *methai*.

Even after stiches and fourteen days of sterilizing syringes, giving shots and cleaning up, Rahim would not accept any money. Rahim had fulfilled his commitment and shown me respect, and I was forever grateful. He explained to my grandmother, how could he take money from a child? He did accept the sweets after I explained that today I was celebrating and the treats were for his children.

The story of Luqman ends with the question of who is the best among all people. Luqman said it was the wealthy. And his peers replied, "Oh the ones with property and riches?" Luqman said "No, the wealthy person is the one that always does good but does not need anything back from others." Rahim Gul was a really poor man, but by Luqman's definition, I realized Rahim Gul was wealthier than me.

What if just being human were more than enough?

Summer 2016 is one I would like to forget. It started with open-heart surgery for my dad. I prefer to avoid hospitals at all costs, and that policy was violated. I was sitting at my desk on an average Wednesday in June with the day going as planned. My four kids were still in school, so I was completing my phone calls before they came home. I received an urgent call from my mom saying that my dad had an irregular EKG and that he was admitted him to the hospital. A short eleven hours later I was talking to my mom as she was following an ambulance from the hospital near her home to one in Silver Spring, Maryland, where my dad was being admitted. He needed open-heart surgery Thursday morning. We had no time to think or process the decision. Life was moving fast, and at midnight on Wednesday, I drove across the Washington Metro Beltway thirty miles to visit my father before surgery.

I spent the night on a hospital chair bed, watching my dad sleep. At six in the morning, all the pre-surgery staff came in and started the preparations. We were lucky. My dad did really well and was resting in the intensive care unit by the evening. I was now focused on my dad and his recovery, going to the hospital for a week and then the rehabilitation center for another two weeks. My attention had shifted, and since I was distracted, I forgot that my grandmother was also in hospice care.

Six weeks later, I buried my grandmother Sajeela, my role model and one of the loves of my life. It was only August third and I had forgotten to count my blessings. For the previous fifty years, I had avoided death and hospitals. I watched funerals only on the television set. I had seen several on my previous trips to Saudi Arabia, Turkey, and Pakistan but never really participated in one. After all, I did not know the deceased and the funeral prayer was just an exercise for me.

My grandmother's funeral prayer was different. It really impacted me, and I was highly conscious of each section. The funeral prayer in Islam is prayed standing up. Muslims are only allowed to bow to God but in this prayer the body is in front of the congregation and no bowing is allowed. This prayer is short. I would say a long prayer lasts about two minutes, so if we are late, we miss it easily. I was grateful for all the family and friends that just stopped their lives to show up early to pray for my grandma and for us.

While I grieved for my grandmother, I did not know that in two-and-a-half weeks I would be saying the funeral prayer for my husband's Uncle Nazir. The day before my grandmother died, Uncle Nazir had a heart attack and was placed on life support. To add to our family stress, we learned that his eleven-year-old granddaughter Eman was also in the hospital for some blood tests. We left my grandmother's funeral to visit Uncle Nazir in the hospital. And then we went back to my mother's place to be with family. After seventeen days, the doctors saw no progress with Nazir and recommended removing the ventilator. Uncle Nazir was able to breathe on his own for another thirty hours and then left us.

Still sad about my grandmother, I attended my second funeral that month. In Islam, we are always taught to count our blessings. I did not feel blessed and certainly was not counting any blessings. We learned Nazir's granddaughter Eman, was admitted for routine blood work. The test results indicated leukemia. Eman smiled when I visited her. She was in great spirits and excited about her new toys. She talked about her lack of hemoglobin and platelets with the incredible enthusiasm that only an eleven year old can have. As the month progressed, we visited her after visiting Uncle Nazir while she received induction therapy. Both were in the same hospital, and both needed our prayers.

My final blow came on August 29th when I received yet another unexpected call. Eman's infection had spread, she had a heart attack, and she was on life support. I went immediately to the hospital with my husband to see if we could help out. Forty-five minutes after I left, Eman passed away too. Her room still had her backpack with the school supplies she wanted for fifth grade. Her young death shattered me. She was younger than my children. I have total faith in God and God's plan, but I can tell you in those moments I was wondering, What is the plan? One month in the hospital and her light was extinguished forever. As with my grandmother, I participated in the bathing ritual of preparing the body for burial. For the final time, we did the *wadoo,* or preparation for prayers, by washing the right hand three times, followed by her left hand, and then her face, arms, and feet. We wrapped her in the white linen cloth for her final journey to her Lord. I had never performed funeral preparation on a child. Attending my third funeral that month seemed even harder. I had acclimated to the funeral prayer and the lump in my throat. Once again, we cancelled the kids' activities that filled our calendar.

I received cards and condolences. They were all helpful, especially when we realized that so many people were out there supporting us in their thoughts and prayers. We called our son's soccer coach, saying my son would miss the game to attend his cousin's funeral. The next week, the team had another game. Good people come in all shapes and sizes. An all-American man that only knew us for a short soccer season made an impact on our grieving family. Every week we received an email from him on the location and uniform selection for the soccer game, along with the time the team needed to be there to practice pre-game. This week, the email was different, and here is what he said:

Hello Parents,

Hani from our team recently lost his eleven-year-old cousin to cancer.

As a mark of respect and in memory of Hani's cousin, we will be making the following changes for tomorrow's game.

1. *All the players are requested to wear white T-shirts and white shorts, with black socks.*

2. *Our team and the McLean team (who we are playing against) will form a circle in the middle of the field before the start of the game to observe a minute of silence in memory of Hani's cousin.*

3. *We are requesting a parent on our team to photograph this moment of silence. Our team will be signing the photograph and presenting it to Hani's family to hand over to his cousin's family at an appropriate time, as a formal tribute from our team.*

Please let me know if you have any questions.

Thanks

We were so touched by the gesture. We then received a second email saying that the opposing team was also supporting the moment of silence and the uniform change.

Game day Sunday was a beautiful fall day with sunshine and a cool breeze. Perfect weather to watch a soccer game between two teams of thirteen year olds. The girls' team was playing on the field, and our boys were warming up on the side. I was so touched that every single kid on the team had worn the black socks for Eman. Our humanity, our souls, and sharing our hearts make a beautiful gesture. The kids were waiting for the other game to end to have their moment of silence. Before the ceremony, the coach from the McLean team brought us beautiful flowers and offered his condolences. The parents from our team gave us cards. The moment of silence was beautiful.

Later that day we went to Eman's house and gave her mom the flowers. Every time I re-read the emails, I still tear up. I realized that we all want to be remembered and know that we made an impact. That is exactly what my son's coach did for Eman, my son, and our community.

I was reminded how amazing most individuals are in this world and how kind our world really is. We need to have these behaviors highlighted and shared since such acts are more frequent than the negative acts shown in our media. I started to remember all the times I had been helped by a stranger to whom I could give nothing in return. Although I am still not sure what God's plan is, I know that I am blessed to be surrounded by a community of humanity filled with generous loving hearts.

Life has come full circle from me trying to learn how to be an immigrant in the US to now teaching my American-born kids how to be Muslim Americans in post-9/11 America. When I came to the US in 1971, the individuals I interacted with had not heard about Islam or the Quran. I went from life where an Afghan is a crocheted blanket to my community knowing the names of cities in the country of Afghanistan. Now, my kids live in a world where the terms Islam, Muslim, and Quran have a negative connotation.

I wanted to give them the basics of the faith but also empower them to choose the path of Islam on their own. I had seen too many kids with strict parents that enforced a rigid moral code. Regardless of religion, when these children went to college, they often developed reactive habits of drinking and partying. I wanted Islam to be an internal choice for my kids. I had to hold myself to a higher standard. I had to be a good example.

I am not sure that kids like to listen to their moms, especially on matters of faith. But I got a tutor to teach my four kids the beautiful and complex Arabic language and script. I wanted them to be able to read the Quran and come up with their own conclusions on life. My kids are part of an electronic era where religion is ridiculed and self-control is labeled as old-fashioned. I knew that I could not police my kids. They needed to police themselves by knowing in their hearts that God was with them and watching their actions.

Ironically, even after forty years and living in four different states, I see that my children face the same challenges as I did. I had thought that with all the easy access to information about other religions, my kids would not have to deal with the same discrimination that I did. There was a time I blamed myself. I am Muslim and I love my faith, so I felt that is why my sons and daughter were different and were singled out. But they have the same challenges I did, like teachers making snippy remarks or random kids walking up to them and telling them that they are not welcome here. I asked my kids how they felt about all the derogatory comments and some of the hurtful actions. Their answers impressed me. My son said, "Mom, but my friends are cool and they understand. I just find people that like me for me and don't worry about the others." Great advice from a twelve year old in junior high; we all need to find the group in which we belong and are accepted. I realized that it did not matter where I lived or what religion we practiced, we all have to find our own community that supports us instead of tears us down.

With email, Facetime, and social media, I thought I would be raising my kids in a more educated, inviting, and connected world. For example, they are able to take religious lessons from scholars that are across the country and the world. I found several great religious videos on developing strong character. When my kids ask for a treat or more money than their allowance, I have them earn the treat by watching religious education. We are electronically connected but still individually isolated for being different than our community and peers.

We had a family discussion on my view of discrimination. Most people start by discriminating on race, and then if we are all the same skin color, they discriminate based on religion. I continued to explain that if we are the same race and religion, they then discriminate on nationality. In places I've lived where all three of those are the same (race, religion, and nationality), we then move on to discrimination according to wealth. And if we are the same race, religion, nationality, and income level, we will discriminate based on education. After education, we discriminate on other factors such as the neighborhood we lived in or if we had a great job. I told my son that people are always looking for a way to make themselves appear better than someone else. I encouraged him to be the kid that looks at character and not at the surface.

My son got the message. He noticed in high school that kids were trying to differentiate themselves, such as the athletes versus the academics, or by a status symbol, such as what type of phone they possessed. I asked him about his real friends and if he ever thought of their status. For most of his close friends, he had no idea what faith they were or if the parents had great jobs. So I asked my son, "Why do you consider these people as your friends?" His answer was simply, "I like spending time with them."

I also didn't ever think my kids' "type" of people would come under attack. But I am proud of my kids because they have defended their friends that are discriminated against or bullied. My daughter went and talked to the principal about the importance of Black History Month on behalf of her more reticent African American friend. Being an outsider at times has helped us identify with the struggle of other races that have endured discrimination. I want my kids to be proud of their country and their faith. I know that the United States and common human religious values go hand-in-hand, even if their religion's name is not Islam. I sometimes feel like an outsider in my own country. But I am grateful for the journey through which my beliefs were tested. I became a better Muslim.

I am aiming for full enlightenment. I was told a story as a child, which I taught to my children, on how to handle challenging situations. This famous Islamic story tells of an old woman who was a neighbor of Prophet Muhammad (pbuh). Her home was on the path to the mosque where the Prophet (pbuh) prayed. Every day when he left his home, she would throw her trash on him. He never reprimanded her, nor did he choose to complain about this mistreatment to anyone. Month after month, she continued her daily practice of throwing out her garbage on her neighbor.

One day, Prophet Muhammad (pbuh) went outside and no garbage was thrown on him. He became concerned and asked a man standing on the street, "Where is the woman that throws her trash on me?" The man responded that she was ill. So Prophet Muhammad (pbuh) went to her home and knocked on the door. The woman saw him and was frightened. She had thrown trash on this man for months and now she lay weak and ill in her bed. Her eyes filled with fear as she thought that she would be avenged for her actions. Instead of taking revenge, the Prophet (pbuh) came to her bedside and asked how she was feeling. He helped clean her home and make her a meal. She was filled with gratitude. She said, "Your way is a way of taking care of the weak and those in need. I was wrong to misbehave, and now I choose to follow your faith."

This tale teaches that we can never solve a problem with hate. Violence can get us some hollow, short-lived attention but no support or understanding. We change hearts with our character. Love and kindness are our soul's gift to our creator and this world.

"A BELIEVER IS SOMEONE WHO AVOIDS HARMING OTHERS WITH THEIR TONGUES AND HANDS"

PROPHET MUHAMMAD

CPSIA information can be obtained
at www.ICGtesting.com
Printed in the USA
BVHW041159260620
582430BV00011B/189